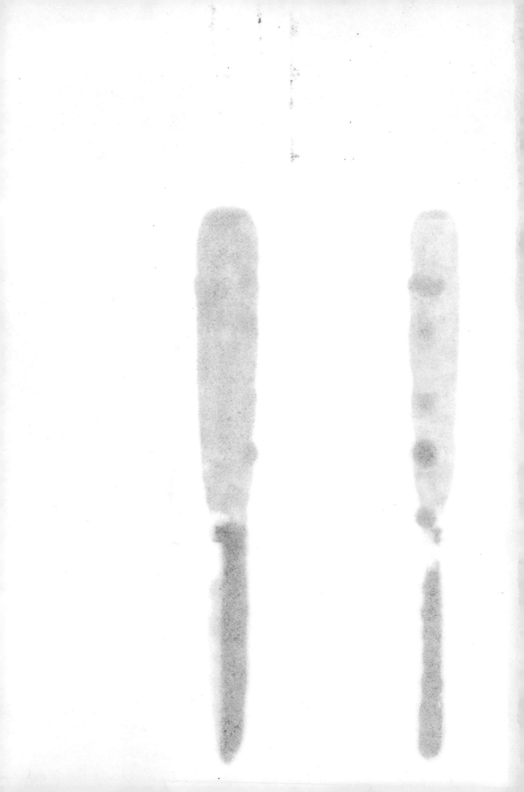

SURVIVAL
IN THE OFFICE

ALSO BY ANDREW J. DuBRIN

The New Husbands and How to Become One
Managerial Deviance
Fundamentals of Organizational Behavior
Survival in the Sexist Jungle
The Singles Game
Women in Transition
The Practice of Managerial Psychology

SURVIVAL IN THE OFFICE

How to Move Ahead or Hang On

ANDREW J. DuBRIN

MASON/CHARTER

NEW YORK 1977

Acknowledgment is given to Books For Better Living for permission to reprint excerpts from Survival in the Sexist Jungle.

Library of Congress Cataloging in Publication Data

DuBrin, Andrew J
  Survival in the office.

  Includes index.
  1. Success. 2. Industrial sociology. 3.Psychology, Industrial. I. Title.
HF5386.D77   650'.14   76–54768
ISBN 0–88405–448–9

TO DREW

Contents

PART V.   MANAGING YOUR FUTURE

PREFACE

Few people move ahead or even hang on in their careers by chance alone. A fortunate minority effortlessly move from one career triumph to another and resolve squabbles with the aplomb of a tournament tennis player rallying during a warm-up session. For all but a small minority of people who work for a living, succeeding or surviving involves considerable planning, maneuvering, sidestepping, game playing, and determined effort. Climbing the organizational ladder or staying perched on the rung that suits your preference is not a chance phenomenon.

A dizzying amount of information has been written around the theme of "how to succeed in business," but most of it is directed toward the male middle manager struggling to become an executive in a male-dominated business hierarchy. The executive success manuals—including a few written in the mid-1970s—often incorporate some ideas about the ways in which a wife should adapt her life style to fit the demands of the corporation. As part of the thrust of the women's movement, a few helpful success manuals for career-minded women have been published.

What the world seems to need next is a unisex, up-to-date collection of ideas about gaining advantage in the complicated world of work. Any modern guide to career acceleration or survival must consider three facts about the present world. Fact one is that prosperous times never last for very long, which means that you cannot become complacent, hoping to be dragged along in your career by a boom phase of the economic cycle. Fact two is that the large difference in status between males and females in an office environment has been shrinking. A modern career person thus must become capable of handling sexist attitudes on his or her part that could be acting as a career retardant. Fact three is that the relationship between career and family success has become increasingly intricate. A modern career man or woman who wants to maintain a tranquil relationship at home simultaneously must become a skillful juggler.

Survival in the Office is an attempt to offer useful and candid advice about a myriad of problems and situations that confront anybody who takes working for a living seriously. Readers curious about the behavioral science research underlying my suggestions will have to read some reference literature. My book is intended for those who are looking for advice and suggestions about career survival (or even how to find a job) but who have no immediate interest in lengthy explanations, underlying theory, or research substantiation. To use an analogy from another popular human concern, my book is more like a sex manual than a research treatise on the anatomy, physiology, and psychology of sexual behavior. Read ahead if you are looking for more job-related thrills, higher income, and less aggravation in the office.

ACKNOWLEDGMENTS

A number of people made important contributions to this project. Tom Curley, Public Affairs Editor for the Rochester Times Union, suggested that I submit a feature series to his paper. Labelled "Survival in the Office" by an anonymous copy editor, the series became syndicated by Gannett News Service. Nancy Davis, my editor at Mason/Charter, and Olie Petrocelli encouraged me to expand my series into a book. Mary Ann Vezzosi and Production Manager Dan Allman guided the manuscript through its copy editing and production phases.

K. Lois Smith turned in another fine performance as my manuscript typist. Deborah Cole, my research assistant on the project, helped keep me abreast of articles about career management. Dottie Miller and Kathy Kulp promptly and efficiently duplicated materials for me.

Marcia DuBrin, my wife, helped to create a home life conducive to productive work. She also served as a contributor of many case examples for my concepts and served as an informal, positive critic. Drew and Douglas, my sons, receive my thanks for their continuing interest in my writing. Melanie, my prenursery school daughter, gave me something to laugh and smile about as a counterbalance to my concentration on the manuscript.

ROCHESTER, NEW YORK   *Andrew J. DuBrin*

MARCH 3, 1977

PART I

HANDLING ORGANIZATIONAL POLITICS

Winning
at Office Politics

1 Job competence remains the most vital ingredient for moving ahead or staying on the payroll. The combination of hard work and a few breaks along the way will probably enable a competent person at any job level to earn his or her share of salary increases and promotions. Despite the validity of this observation, many hardworking talented people, to whom fate has not been unreasonable, still go nowhere in their careers. Without the extra ingredient of political savvy—playing sensible office politics—an ambitious person could remain trapped in an unfavorable job situation.

Political strategies for garnering your fair share of organizational plums can be roughly sorted into two types—those related to office politics in your immediate surroundings and those related to going for bigger stakes in the overall firm. For the present, we will concentrate on office politics concerning your relationship with your boss, getting a salary increase and a bigger job for yourself, and dispensing praise in the most effective manner. A beginner's guide to power grabbing comprises the next chapter.

HELP YOUR BOSS SUCCEED

When you are caught up in the pressures of pursuing your own ambitions, it is easy to forget the primary reason you were hired. Your boss or the manager who hired you originally thought you could make a positive contribution to helping him or her accomplish his or her job. Even if you were hired into the company on the basis of nepotism, the person who accepted you into his or her department believed that you would contribute directly or indirectly to his or her success. Recognizing this fact of organizational life provides you a vital success strategy—help your boss succeed.

Remember Your Boss Has Problems, Too. Neal called his boss's secretary, Joan, on the intercom, demanding to speak to his boss, Jerry. Recognizing that her boss was tightly scheduled for the day, Jerry's secretary suggested that perhaps Neal could accept an appointment for the next day. Joan buzzed Jerry to explain the situation to him. "Well, if it's a true emergency, I guess I can see him at 4:30 this afternoon," responded Jerry.

At the afternoon meeting, Neal laid bare all the problems he was experiencing in his department. He pleaded, "Jerry, you've got to help me out. We can no longer wade our way through our incredible load of paper work without additional clerical support. The budget you have set for personnel is unrealistically tight. You have got to give our unit more support in your meeting with top management. My people are getting weary. I'm afraid we're going to lose Virginia, my best worker. She claims she won't put up with these intolerable conditions much longer. Can't you see how critical this situation has become?"

Neal's mistake. Perhaps Neal deserves credit for his openness in discussing departmental problems with his boss, but he is being politically unwise. His sense of timing is wretched. Neal's conversation with Joan should have made him realize that Jerry had his share of emergencies for the day. Laying into Jerry with another load of problems is tantamount to a doctor's telling a patient that, in addition to having venereal disease, he appears also to have prostate gland trouble and an ingrown toenail. There is a limit to how much bad news somebody can absorb in one sitting.

A sounder strategy would have been for Neal to have scheduled an appointment with his boss a day or two later. At that time, Neal would have been wise to present Jerry with an objective analysis of his problem, accompanied by a *proposed solution*. For instance, he might have brought information to his boss about the cost advantage of hiring temporary office help to ease his department over the present emergency situation.

Keep Your Boss Happy. Midge could not help noticing that her boss, Jean, was emotionally down in the dumps. At staff meetings, Jean seemed unusually sullen, rarely smiling. Even when she purchased a line of inexpensive handbags manufactured in Taiwan that proved immensely profitable for the store, Jean still seemed emotionally down. Midge also noticed that Jean stopped talking so enthusiastically at lunch about the store as a place with good opportunities for ambitious people. Even worse from Midge's standpoint, Jean had not paid her a compliment about her work performance in several months.

Midge's successful strategy. Assistant Buyer Midge put her analytical mind to work. She began to inquire through unofficial channels about what might be bugging Jean. Could the problem be job-related? Could it be a personal problem? Or could the problem be Midge?

A contact of Midge in the Personnel Department, Don, had a good pipeline to the store president through his relationship with his girlfriend, the president's administrative assistant. Midge pleaded with Don: "Could you find out for me if anything bad has happened to Jean lately? I'm trying to figure out if my perception is correct that she is experiencing some kind of problem related to her work. See if you can find out anything that could be adversely affecting Jean. But don't jeopardize your position in the process."

Don dutifully came back with some potent inside information. Apparently, Jean was being considered for a suburban branch manager position but was turned down in favor of another capable person in the store. Ambitious Jean could not control taking this news badly. Don's morsel of information was that the company was in the process of buying another downtown store. Should the negotiations be carried out to completion, Jean would be the number one contender for the store manager position. The manager of the store in the process of being acquired was due for retirement.

At lunch, Midge took a few risks to brighten Jean's spirits. She confided to Jean, "What I'm about to say could get me fired as a corporate spy or a big mouth. I'm willing to take this risk for a boss I admire. A very informed source has told me that Ms. Wonder Woman herself, Jean, is in line for a very big job at our store providing a new acquisition goes through as planned. I would bet a lobster dinner for two that within three months from now, my boss will have moved onto bigger and better things. Identify me as the source of this tidbit, and I'll write a letter of resignation on the wall outside your office."

The inside information conveyed by Midge to her boss was enough encouragement to return Jean to her usual mood tone. As her boss became less discouraged about her own situation, she was once again receptive to listening to Midge's job-related suggestions. Had the inside information proved to be false (which it was not), Midge's strategy would have aborted. Also of significance, if Jean had remained sullen, she might not have been able to evaluate Midge's good work performance objectively.

Discover Your Boss's Objectives. Larry intuitively recognized that unless his boss could reach his own objectives, nobody working for him could be considered a truly effective subordinate. In many modern business and nonprofit organizations, every department's performance is measured against its ability to reach certain goals. Such was the case in Larry's sales order department.

Larry's deft strategy. Larry asked his boss, Ken, what improvement in department functioning was called for in the upcoming year. Ken informed him that the primary concern was to get sales orders shipped out faster—a personal project he was undertaking.

Larry's response was, "I'm glad you told me about your interest in minimizing delays in shipping orders. I recognize this is your project, but I happened to come across a mechanical system that might prove very beneficial to our situation. My brother-in-law works for an industrial supply house in Jersey City. They have a mechanical conveyor system running through the office. It looks almost like an elaborate network of electric trains, but it is relatively inexpensive. If it sounds promising to you, I will investigate further. Perhaps we can get the manufacturer out here for a demonstration. I'm willing to do all the leg work."

Larry's recommendation proved instrumental in enabling the department to reduce shipping time on orders an average of 36 hours. The savings proved to be substantial both in terms of being able to bill customers sooner and decrease customer complaints.

Kurt's blooper. In contrast, Kurt had a run-in with his boss because he made some assumptions about his boss's objectives that proved to be inaccurate. His boss, Mel, had worked as a bank branch manager five years. At age 52, Mel was quite comfortable in his position. He regarded himself as an outstanding citizen of the community and reveled in the prestige of being a bank manager. Intent on climbing the organizational ladder himself, Kurt assumed that Mel had similar goals.

Thus, at lunch one day, Kurt leveled with Mel: "I know as well as you do, Mel, that you've been in one spot too long in this bank. Undoubtedly, you want to move on to bigger and better things, don't you? Well, the only way you can move forward is to identify a willing and able successor. Excuse me for being immodest, but I think I'm that person. I want your job, and I'm willing to take on the responsibility as soon as you see a promotion in the offing for yourself."

Within one week after that luncheon conversation, Kurt's relationship with his boss took a turn for the worse. Mel began to find fault with aspects of Kurt's work that he previously praised or did not comment about. During a performance appraisal conducted two month's later, Mel criticized Kurt for being "impatient for promotion" and "personally ambitious."

Had Kurt practiced the common sense political strategy of discovering his boss's personal objectives (perhaps even by asking him about his plans for the future), he would not have erred by making the assumption that Mel wanted a promotion. An alternative strategy for Kurt would have been to ask about promotion possibilities in *other branches*.

Display Loyalty.   A loyal subordinate can express his or her loyalty in many ways other than by being a sycophant. One characteristic of a loyal subordinate is that he or she makes an extra effort to insure that his or her boss does not make avoidable mistakes. Mike, a systems analyst, was adept at practicing this "help your boss be right" strategy.

Seth, the manager of systems and procedures (Mike's boss), divulged to Mike his recommendation that the company purchase some computer-related equipment. The justification for purchasing this particular brand of equipment was that it would perform the same functions as competitive equipment but at cost savings of 25 percent.

Mike, with a concerned look on his face, said to Seth: "Watch out Seth, you could be in for trouble going with that manufacturer. I recently learned from my stockbroker that they are going out of the business equipment business. Should they be able to sell off their business equipment line to a reputable manufacturer, we would be okay. Service on the machines would continue uninterrupted. But should they be unable to sell the line or should it be taken over by an unreliable company, we would be left with very poor repair and maintenance service."

Accepting Mike's cautionary information, Seth put the equipment purchase proposal on a pending status, awaiting further development. Four months later, a public announcement was made that the manufacturer in question was divesting itself of its line of business equipment. Mike had thus enhanced his position with his boss, further improving his chances for growth in the company.

Avoid Disloyalty.   Brian illustrates how disloyal comments made about your boss in a big company can backfire. Seated in the company cafeteria, Brian was chatting with the project leader of a cost reduction team, Wendy, about the progress of her project. She commented, "You might say, Brian, that our work has just begun. What we are trying to do is trim some of the fat from the organization without cutting into muscle. We are finding a goodly number of departments with an excess of personnel. We have got to get our headcount down by at least 15 percent."

"You're speaking to the right person," replied Brian. "Our department has more than its share of blubber. My boss, Vance, is the empire builder par excellence. Right now we have 20 people doing the work of nine or ten. I think you could save the company $200,000 per year just by bringing an ax down on part of Vance's empire."

Two weeks later, Vance confronted loquacious Brian. "I have some good and bad news for you, Brian. The good news is that we are beginning the personnel cuts that you have so generously informed the cost-cutting team are needed. The bad news is that we are beginning with you. Apparently, there is no other job opening in the company that matches your qualifications. So please consider yourself terminated as of 30 days from now."

Disloyal Brian was left speechless and jobless.

Become a Crucial Subordinate.   An eminently sound bit of political advice is to accomplish tasks for your boss upon which his or her performance is to be judged. Save your boss's hide, and he or she will put you in the faithful servant category. Tony, aside from being a competent go-getter, was also a politically astute college administrator. His immediate superior, the dean of the College of Business, was under pressure from the college Board of Directors to do some good for culturally disadvantaged people. Offering free tuition to poor people was one possibility, but the college could only afford to admit people who had tuition money.

Tony to the rescue.   As associate dean, Tony decided to flex some of his administrative muscle on his boss's behalf. He spent most of his discretionary time over a three-week period exploring all possibilities for helping his boss out with his most vexing problem. Pouring over government periodicals, Tony discovered that the Department of Health, Education and Welfare had some funds available for "Operation Headstart" programs for culturally disadvantaged young adults.

The program worked quite simply. Any business school located near or in a metropolitan area was eligible to design a program that would prepare disadvantaged people for college level courses. Schools that qualified for a grant would receive a generous funding from HEW—enough to support the program fully. Spearheaded by Tony, his College of Business did win a handsome grant from the government. The Board of Directors was pleased that the dean performed such a social good, and the dean was pleased that his biggest problem was now safely resolved. At salary negotiation time, Tony's contribution was well remembered.

HOW TO GET A SALARY INCREASE

A salary increase is not simply a cost-of-living adjustment for inflation. A real salary merit increase (or merit raise) begins where the cost-of-living adjustment leaves off. Myra, a marriage counselor in a community agency, needed a real salary increase. She presented it to her boss in this way: "Roz, I desparately need more money for next year, and I know there is money in the budget for salary increases. My husband and I have legally separated. The amount of child support and alimony he is paying, even combined with my salary, is simply not big enough to make ends meet. Can you understand my position?"

Roz replied, "I certainly can see your point, Myra. You need more money because of your personal situation. You're getting divorced; so it's going to cost you more to live. I hear needy cases all day, but that doesn't mean I give every needy case some bonus money. Your argument is almost without merit."

A Better Strategy for Myra. Documenting your accomplishments and making a clear presentation of them to your boss are the most effective ways of demonstrating that you deserve a raise. In asking for a salary increase, Myra focused on a poor reason for being given a salary increase—economic need. In most work organizations, those people with the most money —and, therefore, presumably least in the need of more money —typically get the biggest raises.

Recognizing that salary increases need to be justified, Myra might have tried this thrust: "Roz, I have some interesting statistics to show you. During the last year I have been 35 percent more productive than during the previous years. I have been able to see 35 percent more couples than last year because I have shifted to more group marriage counseling than individual counseling. In the past, I was handling a work load suited for one and a half marriage counselors. Now I'm almost carrying the work load of two marriage counselors. If you agree that my analysis is correct, I would say that my job performance deserves at least a 12 percent salary increase."

In this situation, Roz would be hard-pressed to deny a substantial increase for Myra. Myra could conceivably have avoided the need for this confrontation if she had sent a report to Roz about her increased work load several months before salary review time. Conceivably, under those circumstances, Roz would have taken the initiative to have offered Myra a generous salary increase.

What about Getting a Raise during Hard Times?   When business conditions are very poor (either for your firm or the economy in general), getting a salary increase is often, but not always, almost impossible. An important principle to remember here is that during hard times the requirements for getting a raise become more stringent. In practice, this means that you are standing on weak ground when you expect to receive a salary increase for having simply carried out the routine requirements of your position.

Astute Stan.   Recognizing that he would not get a salary increase for merely emptying his in-basket on a daily basis, Tax

Adviser Stan thoroughly documented his case for more money. The tax consulting service for which he worked began to tighten up drastically on expenditures of all kinds. A problem they faced was an uneven work load due to the seasonal nature of the income tax advising business. Basically satisfied with the work and the company, Stan looked for a way to make more money without having to leave the firm.

Around November, Stan presented his case with an argument of this nature:

> I think I'm well compensated for the basic reason I was hired. As tax clients come to us with their problems, I take care of all the cases assigned to me. I knew when I took this job that there would be lots of night and weekend work during the months of February, March, and April. The records will show that I handle as many or more cases than anybody else in the office.
>
> But I'm not asking for a salary increase because of my ordinary work load. The aspect of my performance that does require a careful salary review is my discovering new business for the firm at almost no additional cost. During the off season I've been busily scurrying through the files of our present and old clients to see if we can be of additional service to them. Using this technique, I've come up with $3,000 worth of client fees paid for income averaging. Almost everybody I talked to was willing to pay us a fee if it meant that he or she could get some money back from the government because of having one good year in comparison to his or her usual income.
>
> Besides that direct business from doing income averaging during the off-season—when we obviously need some business the most —I suspect I've established some additional good will for the firm.

Stan's documentation of his out-of-the-ordinary perform- ance helped him get the 8 percent salary increase he deserved, whereas others in the office were fortunate to receive a 3 percent increase.

POSITIONING YOURSELF FOR PROMOTION

Most people who work for somebody else would happily accept a promotion if it carried a more impressive job title and more money. Nevertheless, most people employ only one strategy for getting promoted—Keep on sawing wood. By working hard and carrying out assignments, the wood sawers hope that they will be recognized and promoted. According to the Protestant ethic, this is a sound strategy, but you may not be working for a firm that really follows that ethic. A more reliable approach than simply working hard and hoping to be recognized is to capitalize upon a few sound career advancement strategies.

Stay on the Move.   Gloria is a job-frustrated woman today at age 42. She has accumulated 15 years of experience in the public relations field; yet she still holds the title of public relations associate despite her lengthy experience and college degree. As Gloria describes her dilemma,

> When I graduated from college, I had to go the route of most career women. I began as a secretary in a public relations office of a large company. I stayed in that job for four years. Next, I held down an editorial assistant's position five years in the communications section of the P.R. Department.
>
> Following that, I was promoted to an administrative assistant's position reporting to the manager of community relations. I became more and more curious about working things from the other side of the street; so I finally found myself a position in a public relations firm. But because I lacked experience with an actual public relations firm, I began as a public relations associate. That's where I am today practically at the midpoint of my career.

Gloria had poor footwork.   Hardworking, dedicated Gloria made the mistake so many loyal employees make. She waited passively for promotions to come to her without taking the initiative to alter her career path. Following the dictates of *mobilography* (Management Psychologist Eugene Jenning's term for the science of managing your career by judicious job hopping), Gloria should have displayed much fancier footwork earlier in her career. She should not have allowed more than two or three years to go by without searching around for broadening experiences. Lacking breadth of experiences early in her career, she was limiting her chances for big promotions later on in her career.

Although Gloria is still chronologically young, she needed a couple of varied experiences early in her career to prove to management that she was ready for a big job later on (such as publicity director).

What Should You Do If You Cannot Find Another Job?
The first place to look for another job is within your own company. Next find a job in another company. In moderation, experience in a variety of companies can be quite helpful to your career. A third approach is to look for broadening experiences within the confines of your own job. Gloria might have looked for significant special committee or task force assignments while working for the large company. Her vantage point in the Public Relations Department should have been valuable in making contacts for such temporary assignments.

Find a Patron. Somebody up there in your organization must like you if you are to be catapulted along in your career. Preferably your sponsor or patron should be somebody of high rank in the organization, but even an ambitious and competent boss can serve as a sponsor. Gary felt boxed in as a manager of payroll in his company. His immediate boss, the manager of administrative services, appeared to have reached his final placement in the company. Gary didn't think his relationship with his boss's boss was developed enough to pull an end sweep (running round his boss). Yet he needed to find somebody else whose recognition of his talents would lead to an eventual promotion.

Gary gets assessed. Fortunately for Gary, he did his homework about modern techniques of management selection and development. His company periodically ran an assessment center whereby lower ranking managers would have their management potential assessed through such means as depth interviewing, simulated work exercises, and psychological testing. Gary spoke to a friend in personnel, who recommended to Gary's boss that he (Gary) be granted permission to attend the upcoming assignment center.

Gary's confidence in his own potential was vindicated. At the assessment center, Gary stood out as a person of management potential. His name went into a file of "promotable individuals." When this achievement was combined with good performance ratings from his boss, Gary was now in a much better position to extricate himself from his present spot. One of the assessors, a plant manager of a small division, offered Gary an assistant controller slot in his organization. If he had not volunteered for the exposure of the assessment center, Gary would not have been noticed by the plant manager.

Watch Out for Backfire. A hidden danger of the "find a patron" technique is that if you are too closely identified with the sponsor, you may fall when he or she falls. Politically minded Jamie did everything to ingratiate himself with his boss, Ralph. At staff meetings Jamie would nod in agreement and approval at Ralph's key points. Ralph was invited to his home to share the delicacies of his wife's home cooking and the velvet cushions of his pocket billiard table.

Jamie's loyalty seemed to pay enormous dividends. An executive search firm enticed Ralph into accepting a vice-presidential position in another company. Four months after Ralph joined the new firm (in a city 300 miles away), he extended Jamie a job offer as his assistant. Three months after that, Ralph was canned for lack of results. Simultaneously, Jamie was asked to resign. Jamie was perceived as strictly a right-hand man to Ralph and not as a manager in his own right.

Strategic Self-positioning. Ideally, an aspirant to career growth should find himself a job environment with considerable potential payoff for growth. It is not unlike playing the stock market, for you have to invest in the right situation to experience growth. A strong element of guesswork and risk taking, therefore, goes into strategic self-positioning, but time spent in digging for facts can be beneficial.

Lorraine does her spadework. On her way toward obtaining a master's degree in business administration with a major in accounting, Lorraine sought to work for a growth industry. The fact that she was job-hunting during the recession of 1971 did not disturb forward-thinking Lorraine. She and her stock analyst friend, Tim, deduced that replacement part businesses would show good growth during the 1970s. Ergo, Lorraine applied for a position as an accountant with a wholesale supplier of automotive replacement parts. Within three years, Lorraine became manager of office services at this rapidly expanding company. Had Lorraine entered a large bank (as many of her classmates did), she might now have been one troop among a small army of bank accountants.

Swim against the Tide.   Quite similar in approach to Lorraine's gambit is "swimming against the tide" or "Go where the action isn't" (at least in other people's perceptions). Personable Kevin had a bachlor's degree in physics and three years of military service in America's most unpopular war. Kevin reasoned, "I'm hardly a physicist anymore and being a 'Nam vet won't even get me a sympathetic ear from a personnel interviewer. So far the only job openings I've found have been as a junior computer programmer or a low level lab technician. Maybe I should take a flier and do something different with my career from the usual approach taken by physics majors."

Kevin's artful maneuver.   Fortunately for Kevin, his sense of logic in physics was carried over to his sense of logic in career planning. Kevin decided upon a career in sales. He took a job as sales representative for a line of imported women's shoes. To his relatives and friends who asked directly and indirectly, "What's a nice Irish boy with a degree in physics like you doing peddling shoes on the streets of New York?" Kevin replied: "Trying to get ahead by doing something different. That's what."

Kevin is now a marketing manager in the firm he entered as a shoe salesman. His steadfastness and charm coupled with his sharp intellect helped him stand out among the other shoe sales representatives. Singled out by his company, Kevin was immediately put on a fast track to the top. Who knows where Kevin would have been today if he had taken the first job offered to him—junior computer programmer in the Motor Vehicle Bureau.

USING PRAISE TO GET AHEAD

Praise is classified as an "evaluative reinforcer" by behaviorists. In giving praise to others, you are essentially telling them that in your evaluation what they are doing or have done is worthwhile and meaningful. It is precisely the kind of reinforcement that most people need to keep functioning at a high level. Few people at work feel they get enough praise. Thus the individual who uses praise effectively in the office can gain an advantage in many situations without being accused of doing anything underhanded or immoral. With practice and by following some easy-to-follow suggestions, most people can learn to praise effectively. By judicious use of praise, you can influence many people in the direction you want.

Praise Can Save a Situation. "Thank you, ladies and gentlemen, for having invited me here tonight," concluded Ross in his after-dinner speech. "I am convinced that if you follow my action plan, we will be able to launch a victorious fund-raising campaign in 1977." The audience reacted with a blank stare. Dean, a manager who worked for Ross, seized upon the situation and reacted in the one way that would save Ross the anguish of an audience gone dead. Dean began to clap, simultaneously uttering, "fine talk." Within seconds, almost everybody else in attendance joined forces in clapping for Ross.

Dean's strategy. Dean's situation-saving praise was hardly a random event. As an individual intent upon climbing the organizational ladder, he had mastered the art of knowing when and how to praise people. Of crucial importance, Dean uses praise in a natural manner that can only stem from practice.

Praise Actions, Not Persons. In general, it is more effective to praise the actions of another person than to praise him or her as an individual. Praise seems to take hold better when somebody compliments something you have done. Under these circumstances, you can make the deduction that if your work is praiseworthy, so are you—a subtle but important distinction.

Roy, a design engineer, developed a car door lock that would not freeze up in subzero temperature. With good intentions, his boss, Pete, lavished praise on him: "Roy, you are something else. When your former boss told me you were a tough guy on the design board, I thought he might be just handing me a line so I would welcome you into my department. Now I know what he was talking about. You've got a lot of talent between your ears." Roy reacted with embarrassment.

A better approach to Roy. A talented person generally prefers to receive credit for the artistic, inventive, or craftsmanship quality of his or her work, rather than to receive a compliment as a person. Roy's boss might have praised him by commenting upon the functional value of his freezeproof door lock as follows: "Roy, that's an incredibly fine piece of craftmanship. I'm sure our customers who have to leave their cars outside in subzero temperatures will welcome your design."

Individualize Praise.   To be used as a means of influencing people, praise must be individualized. One person should not use the same praise for everybody. Jay, a friendly, but insincere department head, complimented all the people in his department on their appearance. On a daily basis, despite his good intentions, most of Jay's praise is wasted. At least half the men in his department are told, "You sure are a good dresser. You set a model for the rest of us that is hard to match." About one half the women in the department receive the question and comment, "How are you today, beautiful? You're the prettiest girl in the company." Only newcomers to the department feel flattered by Jay's indiscriminate use of praise.

What Jay should do.   Although many people seem to share Jay's mistake of indiscriminate praise, he is still getting very little mileage from his praise. A more effective approach would be for Jay to praise the people in his department only for praise-worthy things. In this way, everybody would not be receiving the same praise. Thus one woman might be praised for a new set of eyeglass frames she wore for the first time, or one man might be praised for his youthful appearance (a euphemism for saying, "I like your new wig.")

Better yet, Jay might intersperse praise about people's clothing and appearance with praise about their work results. A simple statement to a subordinate such as "Your report was very useful," is likely to be more effective than "You're the most beautiful woman in this department."

Effective in What Way?   Effectiveness in using praise refers to influencing people. If you want people to do more of the same (such as write a good report), positive statements about that report will be more influential than statements of general praise. People need to know specifically what good deeds to repeat.

Everybody Has Something Praiseworthy.   A major task facing you if you are dealing with a substandard performer is to find some behavior worthy of praise. As an individual receives praise for one action, he or she gradually grows in self-confidence, performs better, and soon produces more action worthy of praise. Ideally, the process continues in a spirallike fashion. However, it must begin with legitimate praise for some specific behavior. Assume you have a secretary reporting to you who is chronically disorganized. Assume also that you are dependent upon her because, if she is fired, you will not be authorized to hire a replacement.

What you might praise.   Complimenting Sarah about her appearance or hobbies makes no sense in this situation because you are concerned primarily about improving her job performance. A search for something to praise might lead to a comment of substance: "Sarah, I'm delighted to see that you have moved the letters for filing from the middle of your desk to the 'to be filed basket' on top of the file cabinet. It certainly is a step in the right direction."

Praise People at All Levels.   An often overlooked strategy in gaining advantage for yourself in the office is to praise people above you, at your level, as well as below you on the organizational ladder. (This strategy can be utilized both for office politics or in power grabbing.) Your reputation among your peers, as well as among superiors not directly in your chain of command, is very important. As frequently happens in a large organization, the person at your level or below you today may be your boss of the future. It is easiest to remember those individuals who praised you (in a sense, exhibited loyalty) when it comes time to choose a new team. Thus the executive outside of your department whose performance you praised in March may be looking for a new department head in December. Executives, like most people, work best with people they believe are impressed by their results.

Ray's executive love letters. Politically minded Ray worked in the Personnel Department of a big company. When an executive received a substantial promotion, Ray would usually send him a note of praise about two months after the effective date of the promotion. (Ray recognized that within the first two weeks after receiving a significant promotion an executive is usually bombarded with propositions of one kind or another.)

Ray dutifully sent a note of praise to a 34-year-old man just promoted to the exalted post of division president. It read quite simply:

DEAR BILL,

Allow me to express my admiration for your meteoric rise to the top. Rarely in American industry has an individual moved so swiftly in a forward direction.

Best of luck in your new assignment. I'm sure you will be an outstanding success.

Sincerely yours,
RAY ALBANESE

Two months later, Ray was selected by Bill to be the manager of management development in Bill's division. During the negotiation interviews, Bill did not even mention the congratulatory note. Praise worked quietly and effectively for Ray, the ethical office politician. It could work for you.

A Guide
to Power Grabbing

2 Power is like money. Not everybody is obsessed with power or money, but few people would refuse more of either if it were offered to them. Without attaining power, you run the risk of early dismissal in times of a business recession or when political infighting becomes intensified. It is not uncommon for a person in a high position (formal power) to make an early exit from the organization because he or she was unable to acquire a solid power base. You also need a modicum of power at lower levels in the organization in order to qualify for additional responsibility and money.

Techniques of acquiring power are essentially another variation of the art of office politics. As with any other suggestions offered in this book, it is best to choose those techniques or approaches that seem to fit best your personal style. For instance, if you are a low risk taker, you might not want to "swim against the tide," but acquiring seniority or expertise (all three techniques to be described shortly) might be well suited to your personal inclinations.

BE DISTINCTIVE AND FORMIDABLE

Many people acquire power on the basis of their distinctiveness as individuals—a relatively natural way of accumulating power. *Personal power* is the technical term given to this notion, which is equivalent to the ubiquitous term *charisma*. Although it is difficult to mold a bland personality into one of distinction and uniqueness, sometimes an ordinary characteristic suddenly becomes unique. Being Puerto Rican per se will not make you a person of distinction in a San Juan company, but it can make you distinctive in a management training program at Bank of America.

Chester's Minipower Play.   Chester, an Englishman working in a Jersey City steel fabricating plant, commented to me, "In my native land, English mannerisms and speech certainly give you no added edge. In Jersey City, people think I'm refined and sophisticated. In no time at all I was promoted to manager of telephone order sales. Undoubtedly, management believed that an English voice responding to telephone inquiries added some distinction to our office. I am not implying that I do not deserve my position. I'm simply pointing out that being English gave me an edge over here."

MAINTAIN ALLIANCES WITH POWERFUL PEOPLE

For centuries, organization power seekers have recognized maintaining alliances with powerful people as a basic strategy of power grabbing. Knowing the right (powerful) people is undoubtedly important. Being known by the right people for the right reasons is even more crucial. If powerful people keep you imbedded in their mind as an individual who was personally helpful to them, your alliance may pay handsome dividends.

Mitchell Stays in the Air.   A vice-president in a large company confided to me,

> "I'm not sure if I'm doing the right thing with Mitchell. His current assignment is as our international marketing representative at an unusually good salary. My true feelings are that we really don't have a critical need for anybody in that assignment. He's more of a goodwill ambassador than somebody who actually closes orders.
>
> I put Mitch in that job for a peculiar reason. As the story goes around here, he is a very close friend of Max, the president. It seems

as if he got the president started in this line of business and was kind of a father figure to him. Max has felt indebted to him for many years. Because of his feeling of indebtedness, he has promoted Mitch into some very good jobs.

When I arrived on the scene, the president told me I had complete control of the marketing end of the business and that I could hire and fire as I saw fit. Mitch was holding down the manager of market research slot. My opinion was that Mitch was miscast in that job. I really didn't have an assignment into which I thought Mitch could profitably fit. He's much more of a talker than a doer. Perhaps Mitch has some hidden talents of which I'm unaware, but I just couldn't see him heading up one of the key departments reporting to me.

My first inclination was to give Mitch his walking papers. After all, Max gave me carte blanche to hire and fire as I saw fit. But then I reasoned that firing an old friend of the president would be a very unwise thing to do. Instead I put Mitch in a job where he might be able to do some good. But most of all, he won't be interfering with my plans for an overhaul of our marketing effort.

Mitch is quite happy in his new assignment. I figure while he's up in the air, he can't do us any harm. At times I wonder to myself if Mitch knows the real reason he's our international marketing representative.

CHOOSE THE RIGHT PATH TO THE TOP

Corporate superstars—those who make it to general manager or presidential positions—rise to the top from a number of paths. Many top corporate officials were formerly marketing, financial, manufacturing, or engineering managers. Other company presidents are former corporate legal advisors. The key point is that for different industries and different companies within those industries the most likely path to the top is not the same. If we assume that a person is a highly talented executive (still the number one reason somebody becomes a president of most public firms), he or she is best advised to seek out a company that seems favorably disposed toward his or her discipline.

Chet's Lament. Chet, engineering manager in an industrial company, lamented to me, "Here I am 50 years old, with 25 years of experience in this company. In all our 13 divisions, not one general manager is a former engineering manager. It looks as if I'll never get to be a general manager staying in this corporation."

After bringing his problem to the attention of top company officials, Chet received no encouragement from them. He was told that he was not out of consideration for a division general management assignment, but that no openings fitting his background were contemplated in the near future.

Chet's Last Resort.   Impulsively, Chet resigned from the company and began his arduous search for a company presidency or general management job. After one year he was still looking but was only offered jobs at lower pay and with less responsibility than the one he left. In desperation, Chet finally bought a car wash franchise. He was finally a president (the local "Mr. Washateria") but presiding over a much smaller operation than he envisioned earlier in his career.

Chet is not disgruntled today, but he perhaps should have begun his job search ten years earlier. Although he may not have found a company presidency for himself, he might have found a position as an engineering manager in a company that did not discriminate against engineers for top corporate assignments.

Marlene's Artful Maneuver.   Working as a department secretary in a high school, Marlene felt a growing sense of frustration. She aspired toward administrative work, yet realized that in high schools secretaries were rarely promoted into administrative jobs. Virtually all administrative positions went to former classroom teachers. Her solution to her dilemma was straightforward and logical. Marlene sought a high level secretarial job in a business firm. Upon applying for the job, Marlene made her intentions known—that she was looking toward a position as an administrative assistant or toward a supervisory position.

Marlene's talents were quickly recognized in the competitive business environment she chose. Within two years she had been promoted to a position as an administrative assistant, reporting to the director of procurement. She had chosen the right path to the goal she was seeking.

DEVELOP MAZE BRIGHTNESS

Just as the food-hungry rat learns his (or her) way around the experimental psychologist's maze, the power-hungry person learns his or her way around the organizational maze. The "maze bright" individual learns who makes the big decisions and who influences the big decision makers. A discrepancy usually exists between the way decisions are supposed to be made and the way they are actually made (the formal versus the informal organization).

Perry, an ambitious bureaucrat, had a legitimate plan for becoming a more powerful person in his company. He recognized that his talents were not being fully utilized in his present post of manager of quality control. He believed he was capable of handling much more responsibility. His empire-building plan was to acquire control over purchasing and manufacturing engineering. The new job title he hoped to vote himself was that of materials control manager—an idea gaining popularity in industry.

After carefully doing his homework, Perry brought his scheme into the vice-president of manufacturing, who quickly rejected Perry's plan as "needless empire building." Perry was defeated and deflated.

Perry Should Have Checked Out the Company Maze. Despite the logic of Perry's approach and the fact that he did some homework, he could have done more homework. A careful assessment of how decisions about organizational reshufflings are made in his company would have revealed that Ned, the director of personnel, carried considerable weight. The president defers most decisions about organizational restructuring to Ned, the local expert in these matters. Equally important, he believes that Ned is objective in these matters and that people directly involved in the changes lack objectivity. Had Perry discovered these facts, he would have first taken his case for becoming the manager of material control to Ned. Had Ned agreed with the plan (which was logical), he would have brought it to the attention of the president with a favorable recommendation.

ANALYZE THE COMPETITION

Paul wanted very much to play on a college basketball team, but he was hardly a high school all-American, all-state, or even all-conference. Instead of confining himself to intramural basketball at a big or medium-sized college, Paul chose to enter a small private school that competed in the weakest conference in New England. His plan was a spectacular success in terms of reaching his goal. Paul won a starting berth on the team in his freshman year. The school had not had a winning season in ten years, but Paul was a personal winner. Instead of entering a school with a powerful basketball team and getting all his basketball thrills vicariously, he achieved the real thrill of being an active participant.

In the quest for power in organizational life, the competition has to be similarly analyzed. An effective power tactician figures out what the competition has to offer and whether or not the league in which he is competing is too stiff. Why voluntarily compete in a league in which you will finish last? Instead compete in a league in which you have a chance of finishing near the top.

Paul Keeps on Dribbling. The basketball player just described kept his power acquisition tactics sharpened when he entered law practice several years later. Paul noted that the highest-paying job offers came from the biggest law firms. He, therefore, was tempted to accept a position as law clerk with one of the major firms in Boston, his hometown. A flash of insight occurred to Paul. Law firms that paid the highest were recruiting the aggressive young lawyers who finished close to the top of their respective classes. Thus Paul would be competing for promotion with the toughest competition.

Paul's solution to the problem of unreasonable competition was to seek employment in a small, but not miniscule firm. The ten-lawyer firm of McKnabe and Cohen welcomed Paul into its employ.

When asked the inevitable question, "Why do you want to work for McKnabe and Cohen?" Paul replied:

> For the same reasons that I chose to enter the college I did. I want a chance to become a powerful and influential lawyer. You are the size and type of firm that gives a young lawyer a chance to prove what he can do. While interviewing for a beginning law position, I visited a couple of those giant-sized firms. Each one had a large number of brilliant young men doing virtual clerical work.
>
> I think I have good potential, but I question whether I would ever get a chance to display my potential under such an arrangement. With all that competition in one place, how would I ever be noticed?

At this juncture, Paul's analysis of his competition seems to be paying large dividends. Three years after joining McKnabe and Cohen, he is doing interesting, diversified work. In his opinion, he is much closer to becoming a partner in a law firm than are his counterparts in some of Boston's better-known firms.

Another approach to analyzing your competition is to analyze what characteristic or experience of yours would give you a competitive edge—and, therefore, an improved chance of acquiring the power that you desire. Sometimes the answer can be fairly obvious.

Eric Cashes In on His Background. A power-oriented person, Eric was becoming increasingly frustrated as a middle manager in a corporate behemoth. His sound managerial skills combined with his flair for financial analysis were not enough to catapult him into a powerful position—at least not at this time. Eric pondered the problem as he approached his fortieth birthday. He arrived at a conclusion in conference with his career counselor:

> Patriotism is not my biggest virtue. I've given 15 years of my business career to my company. As manager of pricing, I'm not relegated to unimportant tasks, but I know I can handle more responsibility than I'm currently assigned. The best way for me to cash in on my experience is to find a job with a fledgling firm in our line of work—I have at least two in mind.
>
> A small firm in our field needs somebody with big company expertise. Usually, the people in these successful businesses are darn good entrepreneurs, but they are sorely lacking in the skills needed to help them manage their success. If I join one of our small competitors, I can show them how pricing is done in big business. It was their talent that launched the business, but now they need my talent to make it viable.

Eric's analysis of the skills of his presumed competition (those people in the small competitive firms) proved to be eminently correct. Carefully documenting his case, he was able to join one of the two companies he had in mind as a vice-president and controller.

COLLECT AND CASH IOUs

People of higher rank than you in your office need your cooperation, and this phenomenon can be used as a source of power for yourself. After you have done somebody of higher rank than yourself an important favor, he or she then owes you a favor (the equivalent of gaining some power for yourself). This type of power can be used to bargain for favors, favorable assignments, and even raises and promotions.

A Little Sunshine Enters Barney's Life.   Barney worked as a dispatcher in a national moving and storage company. After spending most of his life in Minneapolis, Barney and his wife longed for the chance to live in a southern climate. One day a unique opportunity presented itself, and Barney had enough foresight to recognize it's value. An executive in Barney's company wanted a friend's personal belongings shipped in a hurry.

A telephone call to Barney (whom the executive knew only slightly) was all the executive needed to make the necessary arrangements for his friend. Thanking Barney for his quick action, the executive stated, "Let me know if I can ever help you out of a jam."

Six months later Barney telephoned the executive with a request. "Mr. Higgins, do you remember me? I'm Barney Wetherbee, the dispatcher in charge of routing the moving vans. My wife and I have a little problem that requires your help. Her arteries are beginning to harden a little, making cold weather in Minneapolis unsufferable to her. We're wondering if I could be given favorable consideration for a transfer to our Miami or Tampa office. We both would be grateful to you for the rest of our lives if the transfer did come through."

The executive replied, "I'll see what I can do." Within one year Barney, who had extended himself for the executive (slightly bending company regulations in the process), was transferred to a comparable level position in Tampa. His IOU had been reimbursed.

Flora Forgets to Cash Her IOU. Guidance Counselor Flora, received a frantic phone call from a parent of one of her senior students: "Mrs. Benjamin, is there any way you can help my son get into college? He's been rejected by four colleges so far. He's so discouraged that he believes he can never go to college. Right now he's talking about just bumming around for a year. Can you please help Marty get into college?"

Feeling reluctant to turn away a worthy cause, Flora spent extra time and energy trying to help Marty get placed in a college that fitted his talents (or the lack thereof). Finally, a small private college in New Hampshire was located whose admission officer felt Marty had a good deal of untapped potential. Considering that Marty did not require financial assistance, the college in question was eager to help Marty develop his potential.

The following year Flora wanted a three-month leave of absence to go on a dig with her archaeologist husband. She told her husband, "I couldn't possibly ask for a three-month leave of absence during our busy season. It would be unreasonable to ask for a special favor."

Flora was being too much a martyr. If she had carefully reviewed the chain of command in her school system, she would have recalled that one of the key administrators (in fact, the superintendent) owed her a favor. Hadn't Flora helped place his son, Marty, in college when he and the son were too emotional to face the situation in a logical manner? Her professional scruples (or her naïveté) prevented her from cashing a legitimate IOU.

DEVELOP EXPERTISE

A person who controls the significant resource of important information automatically becomes a more powerful individual. (Blackmail, of course, is an unethical variation of this strategy.) As described by Alan S. Schoonmaker in his book, *Executive Career Strategy*, "Hundreds of former assistants have succeeded their bosses (sometimes pushing them out) because they were the only people who knew what was going on."

In the recent past, computer experts were catapulted into high-paying and responsible jobs because of their esoteric knowledge. As more people have acquired knowledge about computer science (and some programmers have been replaced by computers!), computer expertise has lost some of its power-giving status.

Mannie Hangs On.   Fifteen years ago, Mannie was instrumental in developing an over-the-counter drug that proved to be one of the most profitable items in the history of the pharmaceutical firm for which he worked. Mannie spent himself intellectually on that product (or he was lucky once). Since then he has developed no new idea that has resulted in a marketable drug. Nevertheless his position as senior scientist has enabled him to work directly with many of the company's best-guarded trade secrets.

During a major downturn in the company's profitability,

each vice-president was ordered to reduce his work force by 25 percent. In turn, each vice-president conferred with his department head to discuss specific people who were to be given the ax. The vice-president in charge of research said to Mannie's boss, "Why not give Mannie his walking papers? He hasn't had a new idea in ten years."

Mannie's boss vigorously defended his remaining on the payroll: "If Mannie goes, so go many of our trade secrets. Mannie may not have created anything new in a while, but he has been associated with all our pending developments of significance. Any one of our competitors would be willing to hire Mannie, even if just to pick his brains. Our company is better off if Mannie just sticks around doing odd jobs for us. He knows too much to be let loose."

ACQUIRE SENIORITY

However elementary advice to acquire seniority may be, it is of practical significance. In our society, longevity in a work organization still garners respect and privilege. Labor unions have long emphasized the rights of seniority. Although seniority alone will not prevent you from being ousted from your company or guarantee you more power, it helps. The compulsive job hopper is forever working against the implicit threat of "last in, first out"—even at the executive level.

The Perils of Peripatetic Pete. One manager in the food business, Pete, accepted a position with a Boston company as the manager of new product development. Three months after he arrived on the scene, he was informed that the company had no funds left to invest in new products. He was given one month's severance pay and faced with the embarrassment and awkwardness of finding a position at a comparable level. As last reported, he is still searching for a new job.

OUTMANIPULATE THE HUSTLERS

Hustlers of many different varieties can be found in large organizations. Dr. Robert F. Pearse, writing in *Personnel*, has identified most of them. According to his analysis, one particular form of hustling is prevalent in a seniority-oriented bureaucracy. The hustler in this situation plays it safe by not deviating from policy, procedure, and custom. In the process he or she placates superiors and avoids all controversial situations, thus establishing an "unblemished" record.

Melanie's Manipulation. A young management consultant was able to land a position with a well-established, albeit old-fashioned, management consulting firm. One of the first women assigned to the professional staff of the firm, Melanie was eager to make a quick showing. After six months of training and participating in miscellaneous minor assignments, Melanie was ready for more action. She offered her boss, Fred, this proposition:

> It's about time our firm did something constructive in the women's rights area. As consultants to leading companies, we must be pacesetters. We could perform a valuable service by helping our clients become more sensitive to the necessity for upgrading women in their companies. A company should get moving in the area of women's rights before they are forced to by government decree.
>
> My suggestion is that we offer management awareness training to our clients. This would involve setting up some workshops to help both the male and female managers in the client companies become more sensitive to the many ways in which they are consciously or unconsciously holding women back.
>
> My digging into the area reveals that about 100 companies already have some form of management awareness training. I hereby volunteer to head up a task force group to develop an awareness training program that we can offer clients.

Fred responded, "Not a terribly bad idea, Melanie, but I would want to move very slowly before we do much about women's liberation. It is still a very controversial topic, and the whole thing might blow over before we had the training program under way. Why don't you think this problem through a little more? A firm like ours should not be jumping too fast in these areas."

"Okay, have it your way," responded Melanie, but she did some manipulating of her own. She wrote up her proposal and sent one copy to Fred and one to Fred's boss, the senior partner. Receiving a note of praise from the senior partner, Melanie requested an interview with him. During the interview she explained how Fred was obviously resisting the management awareness training idea.

Without castigating Fred, the senior partner gave Melanie a special assignment. She was appointed project leader of a newly established management awareness training group, reporting directly to the senior partner. Fred did not appreciate being outmanipulated, but he was relieved not to have a wave-making project under his jurisdiction.

PLAY CAMEL'S HEAD IN THE TENT

A gradual approach is sometimes the most effective means of acquiring power. Just as the camel works his way into the tent inch by inch (beginning with his nose), you might grab power in a step-by-step manner until you emerge victorious.

Elmer Was More of a Hog Than a Camel. Ambitious and power-hungry, Elmer was hired as controller of a medium-sized chain of supermarkets. After two months on the job, he began conducting inquiries into neighboring departments in the home office about what functions they were performing. His pattern was consistent. Elmer would request a luncheon appointment with the department head. At lunch he would request the opportunity to visit the luncheon companion's department to "learn more about what's going on in the company."

During his visit to the department, Elmer would conduct interrogations with supervisors about what activities they performed. His approach was regarded by the other department heads as harmless prying. However, when Elmer reported to several department heads that he believed that most of their work was considered a "treasury function" in his previous company, they no longer regarded Elmer's prying as harmless.

Elmer next presented his master plan of reorganization to the president. In summary, he told the president, "I think I could save you a good deal of headaches by having the controller, data processing, and the Systems and Procedure Departments all report to me. I am accustomed to running those types of operation. With me in charge of these activities plus the treasurer's department, you would have a lot more time getting involved with planning the future of the company."

Somewhat shocked by Elmer's quest for power, the president asked the head of the three departments Elmer wanted to acquire, "How are things working out between you and Elmer?" All three had the same opinion. Elmer was too power-hungry for his own good.

Today Elmer is functioning satisfactorily as company treasurer with two clerks and one secretary in his direct command. Should he someday join another company, he will probably try a more subtle means of building an empire for himself.

Matt Eases His Way into the Tent.   A patient person, Matt was willing to take one bite at a time. His maintenance crew had the responsibility of doing repair work and preventive maintenance in one plant of a multiplant operation. One day Matt commented to his boss that because his crew were doing most of their preventive maintenance work at night, they would be happy to supervise the night janitorial work. His boss happily agreed at least to try out the arrangement.

Night cleanup crew efficiency picked up under Matt's direction. As a consequence, when Matt suggested that perhaps daytime janitorial functions could comfortably be handled by his group, he found a sympathetic ear from the plant manager. Several months later, Matt suggested that because his supervisors were accustomed to working at night, perhaps they could supervise the security force.

Matt was now doing a competent job of managing equipment maintenance, janitorial services, and the security force—all in one plant. He then casually suggested that he now supervise an additional plant on a trial basis. Three months later the vice-president of manufacturing sent out a memo to management, countersigned by the president:

Effective March 1, Matt Johnson is appointed Manager, Manufacturing Support Services, in all four plants. Reporting to him directly will be all equipment maintenance, janitorial, and security forces. I am sure you will join me in congratulating Matt and will give him your full support in his new function.

Matt's path to quadrupling his power was so gradual and logical that no objections to his appointment were heard. Matt enjoys his new tent and has no plans for increasing his sphere of influence.

WIN BIG AND YOU'LL BE ACCEPTED

"I've been made department head, but nobody listens to me," exclaimed Arnie. "For two years I fought it out in minor skirmishes, trying to impress management that I should be the head of the department. Now that I'm here, I feel like a eunuch. It was more fun being an engineering supervisor in the department. I was never loved, but at least people listened to me and gave me their cooperation. If conditions don't change soon, I may ask to be reassigned to my old job."

Arnie's Strategic Error. What Arnie didn't realize is that it is difficult for peers to accept your success when you outdistance them by a small amount. A sports analogy helps to explain this phenomenon. When a tennis club member ekes out a win in the finals of a club tournament, his fellow players will not readily give him the accolade of "champ." Several of his regular partners will boast that they play even with him in most of their encounters. Many will say, "When I'm at the top of my game, I beat him easily."

Should the club champ be a ranking tennis player—somebody who has performed exceptionally outside of the club environment—he or she will readily be accepted as the club champ. People find little threat in acknowledging skill in others who have an undeniable superiority over them. It is much more threatening to admit that someone close to us in skill is superior.

Douglas Outdistances the Pack. A social scientist, Douglas had his sights focused upon becoming a small college president. His knowledge of human behavior taught him to look for such a job when the timing was right. He recognized that one of the many reasons life is so difficult as a college administrator is that most department heads and faculty members do not necessarily hold college administrators in high esteem. Only when an administrator has proved himself as an outstanding scientist or scholar will he gain total acceptance from most of the lower-ranking key people in the college.

Doug moved along well in his career, combining a small amount of administrative work (university department head) with an active interest in original research. He and his graduate students conducted some highly original research about how some people seem to "hear" colors. One year Doug won a National Science Foundation award for being a distinguished scientist.

With this accolade in his back pocket, Douglas submitted his credentials to an academic employment agency. When the search committee of one small college reviewed Doug's credentials and interviewed him, they recommended that he be chosen as their new president. Ensconced in the job, Doug met a minimum of resistance from faculty members and lower-ranking administrators. His reputation as a National Science Foundation award-winning scientist spread across campus to facilitate his acceptance.

REMOVE THE OPPOSITION (NICELY!)

A pure Machiavellian, if pressed, would resort to devious tactics to remove the opposition. Les is a case in point. He and another department head, Tim, were of comparable age, experience, and capability; therefore, Tim represented a rival for any promotions that might occur in the next several years. Les felt that only by discrediting Tim or at least by arousing suspicions about his loyalty would Tim become less formidable opposition.

Les tried this gambit. In casual conversation with their common boss, Les commented, "I'm beginning to wonder if Tim is facing some kind of crisis in his career. At first I noticed he was reading the *Wall Street Journal* employment pages at lunch. I didn't make much of it because this practice is so widespread. But just the other day when I was speaking to an executive employment agency to fill a vacancy in my department, in walked Tim. He seemed somewhat embarrassed."

A Less Devious Approach. Les might have tried a variation of the "goodmouthing" technique to have eased Tim out of the picture. Saying something nice about a rival in the right places can be very helpful in removing the opposition. As described in my book *Fundamentals of Organizational Behavior:*

> Bernie Stapelton, a personnel manager, learned that his boss, the corporate director of personnel, would be accepting early retirement within one year. Stapelton and one other personnel manager were logical contenders to replace the corporate director of personnel. Bernie felt his chances for obtaining the promotion were slightly less than those of his rival. In order to eliminate his competition, Bernie submitted the former's name to an executive search firm as a good candidate for any executive search assignments the firm might have for a personnel manager. The strategy worked. Bernie's rival was placed in another company and Bernie received the promotion he wanted.

Cutting Your Way through Red Tape

3 "Aggravation, aggravation," said Pedro. "You would think that our $20,000,000 company was General Motors. All I want is some simple information about how many parts my customer in Toledo received. Instead of facts I get some apologies about the company shifting from one system of accounting to another. Nobody can give me a direct answer on whether or not my customer's order has been filled. I ask myself, 'What are we in business for?' "

Pedro is not alone in his lament. As organizations grow in size, they develop elaborate sets of rules and regulations for conducting their affairs. What the frustrated individual calls "red tape," the policy maker calls "formal policies and procedures"—elements necessary to keep an organization running smoothly.

Bigness alone does not create red tape. An organization under state or federal government regulation must also conform to a multitude of rules, regulations, and procedures. The small village bank is just as bureaucratic as its giant-sized counterpart in Manhattan.

Considering the inevitability of bureaucracy, a career-minded person must develop strategies for cutting through red tape while still remaining part of the system. The alternative is perpetual frustration. Knowing how to circumvent red tape is an essential part of winning at office politics.

THE COMPETENT PERSON TRICK

However disorganized and ineffective an organization may appear, there is usually a dedicated cadre of people at the lower levels who keep the place glued together. It is these people who keep track of the important transactions of the organization and who can furnish the information you might need to get your job accomplished. It usually takes a few phone calls—and perhaps a few visits—to identify that competent person who can come to your aid when things really need to get done. Once you discover that lower-ranking competent individual, write down his or her name and phone number.

Pedro, the frustrated salesman, should be advised to find somebody in the warehouse who keeps an accurate recording of shipments. The next time Pedro has a need to know about customer shipments, he can contact that person.

John, the Benevolent Slumlord. A city landlord, John uses the competent person trick with considerable effectiveness. He never has a vacancy despite average tenant turnover in his buildings. Whenever he needs a new tenant, the housing department of Social Service provides him about 20 applicants for each vacancy.

John simply puts in a call to a mysterious Mrs. F——, whom he has never met in person. She posts the information with the right caseworkers, and the tenant applicants come forth. John's reputation for providing decent housing for welfare recipients facilitates his getting preferential treatment. (In truth, John is a landlord with property in the slums, but he is far from being a "slumlord.") Yet he believes that knowing a knowledgeable, hardworking person buried a few levels down in the complicated social service bureaucracy is his success strategy.

EXCHANGE FAVORS

It is common practice in profit and nonprofit organizations to exchange favors, which has given rise to the aphorism, "There is no such thing as a free lunch." Exchanging favors is another method commonly used by people who successfully cut their way through red tape. Usually, this technique is a follow-up step to having identified a competent person. After he or she provides you the information you need to get your job accomplished, you reciprocate at some later date (a variation of the IOU technique described in the chapter about power grabbing).

Phyllis Exchanges Favors with Scott. Phyllis, a mortgage application officer at a bank, interviews a couple of modest income about their request for a house mortgage of substantial size. Going through the entire application process for a mortgage is a time-consuming—and therefore expensive—procedure. To save both the couple and the bank time, Phyllis pays a quick visit to her "contact"—a high-ranking loan officer.

Scott, the loan officer, gives her a quick reply about the probable decision of the mortgage committee: "It's worth a chance" or "It looks very doubtful. Suggest they apply to another savings bank first." Assuming the couple accepts these suggestions, Phyllis has short-circuited the need for another extensive episode of paper work.

What kind of favor can Scott expect in return? Assume that the savings bank is in the enviable position of having ample money to invest in home mortgages. Phyllis might gently encourage her next affluent mortgage applicant to take a larger mortgage than originally requested. Most applicants would be happy to consummate a home purchase with a smaller down payment than they originally planned.

DO NOT PUT EVERYTHING IN WRITING

In a bureaucracy, once something goes into writing, it becomes a permanent record and could be subject to misinterpretation by anyone of the several people who receive the original or a copy. The person who did you a favor that required bending of a policy is, therefore, liable for reprimand. Of more severe consequence, acceding to your request might be in violation of company policy. Thus the bureaucrat who says yes to your written request for him or her to violate policy has simultaneously collected documented evidence that he or she has stepped out of line.

Bernie Gets His Day in Court. In the midst of negotiations about legal separation, Bernie needed a good deal of time during normal working hours to manage his legal affairs. Meeting with lawyers, transferring accounts at the bank, and a house closing were gobbling up Bernie's quota of company allotted time-off for personal reasons. According to company regulations, an individual was allowed a maximum of three days of paid leave per year to take care of personal business.

The complexity of Bernie's separation had already consumed three days' leave. A court appearance was scheduled to settle the hassle in which Bernie, his wife, and the opposing lawyers had become embroiled.

Bernie thought to himself, "My boss is a little rigid but not unreasonable. If I put in a request in writing for time-off without pay, I know I could have it. But, unfortunately, I can't afford to lose a day's pay. If I asked for a day off with pay to borrow against next year's allowable absences, I'd be asking Larry [his boss] to put one foot in a bucket. His boss would be all over him for starting a precedent."

Bernie formulated a simple plan with which to approach his boss: "Larry, I'm going to be sick and in no shape to come to work on June 10; so please don't count on me for anything that day. I can predict now that I'll come bouncing back from my sick day with twice the energy I normally have. I'll be so energetic that within three days I will have made up for my lost day of work. I can also assure you that I won't be needing any days off to conduct personal business in the foreseeable future."

Larry responded sympathetically and bureaucratically: "I see no violation in company policy if a valuable employee reports in sick. But remember a sick person can inform the company about his sickness no earlier than the day on which he is actually sick."

DON'T POUR YOUR HEART OUT TO A BUFFER

A curious aspect about most bureaucratic organizations is that many of the people who listen to your complaints are not empowered to do anything about them. Even if these *organiza-*

tional buffers are sympathetic to your problem, the best they can do is represent your point of view to a higher-ranking official. At colleges, irate students frequently divulge all their course scheduling problems to friendly secretaries, who listen to the students but who lack the administrative clout to make the desired changes. Thus the student has to repeat his or her story at least twice.

Bonnie Gets Buffered. Bonnie, a product manager in charge of Androgen (a new male cologne), found that her advertising budget for the upcoming year had been slashed by 40 percent. Infuriated, she telephoned the vice-president of marketing, Sid Boswell. His secretary replied, "Mr. Boswell will be out of town for a week. What is it you wish to talk about?"

Bonnie replied, "I'm simply infuriated about the budget cut information that came to me in the mails this morning. It's imperative that this issue be resolved within 24 hours."

Reflectively, the secretary responded, "Well in that case, why not speak to Hal, Mr. Boswell's assistant?" Bonnie replied affirmatively, and a meeting was set up between her and Hal. Bonnie poured her heart out to Hal: "Hal, this is ridiculous. Androgen is as good as dead with the paltry advertising budget I've been allotted. With cologne it's the advertising hype that does the job. There are no bad colognes, only poorly advertised ones. Without the budget I've begged for, Androgen is ruined, and we've poured all our development dollars down the drain."

"Bonnie, you might have a point," Hal replied, "but a budget is a budget. I'll look into the matter real soon. Expect to be hearing from me in the near future."

Predictably, Bonnie did not hear from Hal real soon. When Sid returned to the office, Hal mentioned to him that Bonnie was a little perturbed about her budget cut, but "because she's a mature person, I'm sure Bonnie will be able to take some disappointment."

A Better Approach for Bonnie. Aside from wasting time, Bonnie decreased her chances of getting the advertising budget decision reversed or modified. Sid, the marketing vice-president, listened to a buffer (Hal) interpret the legitimacy of her request. By now, Sid has already accepted Hal's interpretation of Bonnie's problem (it is not very serious). Bonnie has decreased her chances of even receiving a fair hearing.

When the secretary suggested to Bonnie that she meet with Hal, Bonnie should have declined and asked to be one of Sid's first appointments shortly after his return. (Note: A good office politician never hits an executive with a thorny problem immediately upon his return from a business trip. An executive has to review important mail, return important phone calls, and get refocused on the office environment in the first couple of hours back from a trip.)

If it appeared that Hal insisted on getting involved in the budget review session, Bonnie might have requested that she, Hal, and Sid thrash the problem out in a threesome. The stakes are large: if Androgen fails, Bonnie's reputation may falter.

SYMPATHIZE WITH THE BUREAUCRAT

Julio, a research physicist working for an optical equipment manufacturer, hit upon what he thought was an important scientific discovery. He developed a heating process that would diminish the chances of an optical lens cracking in subzero temperatures. His method showed promise of helping other optical physicists enlarge their understanding of optics. Julio enthusiastically prepared a paper he intended to submit for publication in a scientific journal.

Wise to the world of the industrially employed scientist, Julio proceeded with caution. He approached the person in charge of scientific administration, Ted, with his plans for publication.

Ted's immediate reaction was predictable from the company point of view: "Julio, we will have to proceed with caution about publishing your results. I don't doubt that your experiment is scientifically sound, but might we be giving away trade secrets with this publication? Are you sure we want to admit that we even had lenses in stock that had cracked in subzero temperatures? Do we want the world to think that we had the problem of some of our lenses cracking in field conditions?"

Recognizing that Ted was paid to be cautious, Julio sympathized with his position:

> You're right. A company of our reputation must try to put our best foot forward. I'll write an introduction to this study for company purposes only, which will help explain how our publishing in this sensitive area will contribute to our standing in the scientific community.
>
> I also recognize that the values of science may not always be the values of business. I think at least four senior executives should approve the submission of this article to a journal before I proceed ahead. Perhaps they will have some constructive suggestions about improving my paper.

Surprised by Julio's appreciation of his role in guarding against the publication's unfavorable information, Ted eagerly went about obtaining authorization for the scientist's paper. Six months later, the manuscript came back with five concordances for submission outside the company. Each executive had a minor suggestion that Julio was able to incorporate into the paper without sacrificing his scientific scruples.

A ramrod approach on Julio's part would probably have resulted in nonapproval.

EXPLAIN HOW YOUR PROPOSITION FITS INTO THE SYSTEM

Jeanne, an associate professor in a conservative community college, decided it was time that her school (Bryant Community College) offered a course in human sexuality. Even high schools in the locale offered some instruction in human sexuality, whereas Bryant offered no courses of this type. Jeanne asked her dean if she might offer such a course for the following year. He replied that a new course could be authorized only after a committee had studied its feasibility—a process that usually took six months.

"Another thing we have to be sure of," pondered the dean, "is that human sexuality is not just a passing fad. Today people are interested in studying sex on a serious level. But in two years from now the interest may have shifted to outer space exploration. I suspect you realize that many of the Black Studies programs initiated in the early seventies collapsed for lack of interest several years later. Sex may not be a fad, but taking sexuality courses for credit may fall into this category. If you want, go ahead and file the necessary forms. Make sure that you prepare a thorough prospectus for the course. Include exactly what benefits you think students will derive from taking this course. Equally important, please include a detailed statement of how you intend to measure these benefits."

Jeanne Grooves with the System.   What Jeanne heard her boss really saying was, "We defy you to get a new course into our curriculum. If you want to try and get past our complicated procedures for getting a new course approved, we can't stop you. Furthermore, are you sure we should have a course in human sexuality at Bryant?"

Receiving these messages with clarity, Jeanne came back to the dean one week later with a proposition he approved on the spot. Said Jeanne, "Maybe we don't need a whole new course on sexuality. The Counseling Center offers a seminar in personal growth that students can take for one credit. Next year we can emphasize human sexuality in that seminar and see what happens. If it catches on, I may propose a formal course. For now I think we can do quite nicely without having to make any changes in the catalog or making any big production out of college students rapping about sex in an organized way."

EXPLAIN WHAT THE BUREAUCRAT IS DOING TO YOU

One logical approach to disintegrating red tape is to confront the responsible official with the problems created by an unreasonable rule or regulation. In defense of the bureaucrat it may be pointed out that he or she may not have a firsthand report of the way in which a particular directive is creating a malfunction.

Darryl's Dilemma.   Darryl was elevated to the challenging post of national service manager for a company that made and sold minicomputers. He and his field forces were supposed to keep company equipment running smoothly in the field. Customers bought a service contract along with the computer. Should a customer's computer stop working, he or she would expect prompt repair work. Without good service when needed, most customers would want to return a computer already purchased.

Darryl began with a field force of 15 men and two women, called "field engineers." Basically, their job consisted of repairing broken computers under tight time constraints. Promptness of repairs was a crucial factor. Field engineers were well compensated for their high-pressure work and heavy travel. Despite these favorable aspects of the job, turnover was unusually high. Nine field engineers had to be replaced by the end of the first year; the second year ten out of the 15 left voluntarily.

Darryl Does His Homework.   Realizing that his field operation was sinking, Darryl conducted an investigation of why turnover was so high. He telephoned present and former field engineers from his firm to inquire about the nature of their discontent that was leading to such a high quit rate.

A veteran field engineer gave Darryl a consensus opinion: "As you may already know, a field engineer is not a good job for a college graduate. Every college graduate who took a field engineering job did so mostly because he or she thought that it would lead to a management job in the near future. The troops are not quitting because of the company, the management, or the pay. It's because they don't think repairing computers is a proper job for somebody with a college degree."

Armed with careful notes from a variety of comments such as these along with turnover statistics, Darryl requested an appointment with the president and founder of the company, Sy. Darryl presented an impassioned case:

> We're getting wrecked by turnover in the field engineering force. Right now our turnover is running about 85 percent, which is unreal

for a professionally run business. It's wasting over $100,000 per year. Worse than that, it's creating customer ill will. A few customers have poked fun about our inability to keep service reps on the payroll.

The nub of the problem, Sy, is that a few years ago you mandated that all field engineers must be college graduates. The world has changed. Technicians from two-year schools would be best suited for this type of work. We need people who love machinery, not ambitious people angling for a berth in the executive suite. Our regulations about hiring only college graduates for field positions need to be discarded.

Confronted with the negative implications of what he thought was a constructive regulation, Sy reversed his decision: "It looks as if we goofed on that one, Darryl. You're the national service manager. Make up your own qualification list for field engineers. But don't overcompensate in the process by giving anybody who likes to tinker with mechanical equipment a job as a field engineer with my company."

DEVELOP STAYING POWER

When the bureaucratic system realizes you will not go away with your demands—that you are willing to invest the time to sweat out having your demands met—the systems *sometimes* bends. Developing staying power is a technique that is often necessary when you are an outsider to the system. For instance, you might have to turn a bureaucracy around to your way of thinking in order to advance your career.

Bette, the Bookseller. Entrepreneurially minded Bette decided what her suburban town needed was a used bookstore. Having worked as the manager of the book department of the suburban branch of a major department store, Bette was familiar with the tastes of the suburban book buyer. She was also familiar with the sources of supply for used books of good quality. Three months of careful digging led Bette to the conclusion that the best location for her contemplated store would be an old house on a busy avenue. She discovered four such old houses as possibilities, three of which were for sale.

Bette figured that she would need to borrow about $12,000 for buying inventory and remodeling an old building to make it suitable for a store. In addition, she would need a building mortgage of about $25,000. All she needed now was a cooperative bank. The "all" proved to be quite formidable. Three consecutive banks refused Bette a loan, each providing an euphemism for the fact that they didn't think Bette's used bookstore was a financially sound idea.

Bette Burrows In. Dismayed but still determined, Bette would not accept no for an answer. She revamped her loan application by offering her house as collateral. In addition, she assembled some facts about the return on investment of other used bookstores in suburban areas. She even casually dropped the comment that she hoped her gender had nothing to do with being turned down for a commercial loan. Bette reapplied to the same three banks plus two more. Again rejection on all the applications. But this time one loan officer suggested that her level of personal indebtedness was high in comparison to her income.

Bette pressed her aging mother for $2,000 in family money. Her mother complied, and Bette used the $2,000 for reducing her personal debts. Next she reapplied to the bank that seemed sympathetic toward her loan application but was concerned about her level of personal indebtness. Success at last. Bette had conquered the bank bureaucracy and is now proprietor of an ongoing business called "Bette's Book Boutique."

ACCEPT BLAME IF SOMETHING GOES WRONG

A calcified bureaucrat is fearful of making mistakes. The *bureaupathic personality* (a person who pathologically follows rules and regulations) often behaves that way because he or she is fearful of being wrong. As long as organizational policies are literally interpreted, the interpreter cannot be accused of making a mistake.

Helmut Borrows Some Nuts and Bolts. Twenty-eight-year-old Helmut was proud of his position as foreman in a large, multilayered manufacturing plant. The biggest problem he faced was dealing with the tightly drawn budgets imposed by the power figures in his company. Next to stealing company tools, the worst offense any member of management (including foremen) could commit was to exceed budget. In this respect, the company was absolutely rigid.

Twenty days before the new budget cycle began, Helmut realized that his department's supply of nuts and bolts was just about depleted. Helmut saw three options open for himself. One was to plea with top management to let him exceed budget for the quarter. Another was to purchase the nuts and bolts himself and sneak them into the plant. A third was to scrounge up some nuts and bolts without publicizing what he was doing. Helmut thought the first two alternatives would inevitably lead him into trouble with the company.

Helmut chose option three. He approached Jeb, an old-timer running a neighboring department, with this proposition: "Jeb, you've got to help me out of a bind. I need about 150 pounds of nuts and bolts to do me until the first of the month. I can't help but noticing that your bins are amply supplied. If you'll give me 150 pounds of your surplus nuts and bolts, I'll be forever grateful."

Jeb answered bluntly, "What and get my nose in the company wringer? That's a violation of company policy. Each department budgets separately for its own supplies."

Helmut wrangled his nuts and bolts from Jeb with a final plea: "I promise, Jeb, that if the plant superintendent or anybody else ever finds out about this, I will tell them that the whole plot was mine and that my men were worming their way into your department and taking out nuts and bolts by the fistful. If you are in any way ever blamed for this teeny little stretching of budget policy, I'll keep you supplied with Coors beer for ten years."

"Well, just this once," replied Jeb, "if you are willing to take all the blame if something goes wrong."

MAKE WAVES: THE ORGANIZATION MAN IS DYING

Organizations of today are increasingly cost-conscious and profit-minded. Consequently, there is less emphasis upon conformity for its own sake, as implied by the notion of the organization man. If a person can achieve the kind of results the firm needs, he or she often escapes the pressure of needless conformity. Your wave making will be tolerated if your splashes stir up profits or result in cost savings.

Giles Circumvents an Old Regulation. Patent Lawyer Giles and his wife, Darlene, had long wanted to take a six-week journey to Russia. Having saved money for many years, the couple was financially able to afford the trip. Before plans could be formalized, Giles had to figure out a way to arrange the necessary vacation time. (Darlene's position as a high school history teacher allowed her ample time for the trip.)

Giles's company had very specific provisions about vacation time. No employee could take more than two consecutive weeks of vacation, and the maximum vacation for any employee (no matter how long employed) in one year was four weeks. Giles's boss sympathetically listened to his request for a six-week vacation but cited the company's policy manual as the final arbiter of these matters. Giles thanked his boss for listening to his case but noted in parting, "I'll be back to talk about this later."

Two weeks later, Giles returned with a precedent-shattering argument, which he presented in a three-way meeting between himself, his boss, and the latter's boss:

> My wife and I have planned for a six-week trip to Russia for many years. My inability to get the time-off from work is the only remaining barrier to our taking the trip. You tell me that company policy would not allow me to schedule a vacation of this duration. Well, I see a gross contradiction between company policy and company philosophy.
>
> According to our philosophy, what counts in this corporation and in our department is results. We are supposed to be measured by

the results we attain, not by the work schedule that we use to obtain them. I know from my performance reviews that I'm about the highest-producing patent attorney in our department. Therefore, what I say about producing results has some merit.

This upcoming year I will produce in 46 weeks what I would ordinarily produce in 48 weeks—the amount of time an employee with four weeks of vacation actually works per year. How I achieve these results is my business. By working an occasional Saturday morning or Monday night I'll be able to produce two extra weeks of work in about 15 weeks.

If some nit picker in the department wonders why Giles has been away from his desk so long this summer, just tell him, "Giles has produced so much in the past few years that he is on a medical leave of absence."

Wave-making Giles kept his promise to himself, Darlene, and the organization. The year he went on his six-week junket to Russia he was still the number one producer in his department.

PART II

HANDLING
JOB PROBLEMS

Coping
with Job Stress

4 The president of a worldwide corporation used his attaché case to chop his way through a permanently sealed window of an office building. After smashing out a large enough hole, he jumped over 40 stories to his death.

A quiet, good-natured mathematics professor closed his garage door and raced the engine in his station wagon. His body lying in the front seat of his station wagon was discovered three hours later by his teen-age daughter.

A pediatric nurse working in a leukemia ward gradually increased her intake of amphetamines to the point that her employer was forced to grant her a medical discharge. Her ward supervisor deemed her unfit to practice nursing until rehabilitated.

Each person just mentioned was facing unusual job stress. The executive had been making illegal payments to foreign officials; the professor had been refused promotion from assistant to associate professor; the nurse became morose about dealing with so many dying children. Although each represents an extreme case, many other people fail to survive in the office because they have not acquired effective ways of coping with job stress.

HOW MUCH STRESS IS HARMFUL?

Evidence has been accumulating for over 30 years that people in a variety of occupations perform best when they are faced with the *right* amount of stress or pressure. People vary in the amount of stress they find optimal. Dr. William R. Cunnick, Jr., deputy medical director at Metropolitan Life Insurance Company, cogently expresses the findings about job performance and stress in his comments to *Dun's Review:*

> We all need stress. The goal is not a state of nirvana where the executive (or any other worker) is suspended in emotional nothingness. But we have to distinguish between satisfying the unsatisfying stress. It is satisfying when you are running around achieving goals. It is unsatisfying when everything gets out of control. That's when people develop symptoms such as headaches, diarrhea and heart palpitations.

Harry Absorbs Too Much Stress.   Harry worked in a specialized end of the stock brokerage business called the options market. Based in Chicago, Harry's business consisted basically of helping clients predict whether the market would go up or down for one particular issue at a time. He dealt with very sophisticated investors who could not afford to make too many wrong decisions. Harry told his story to a career counselor:

> My career as an options broker has got to come to an end. It is the weirdest kind of business imaginable. People are trying to make precise bets about the movement of a stock in a very volatile market. My commission per transaction is pitifully small; so I have to attract a large volume of business. By the second hour of the day I can begin to feel the phone buzzing in my ear.
>
> If you leave your desk for more than 15 minutes, you could miss out on your biggest transaction of the day. Almost everybody who buys or sells an option is under a good deal of pressure. You absorb a lot of the pressure yourself. I've developed the feeling that if my client makes the wrong decision, he thinks I've failed him. If he makes the right decision, it's his investment genius. My advice counted for nothing.

My profession is ruining my personal life. On weekends I try to read my daughter a story before she goes to bed. The other night I was reading her "The Three Little Pigs," and it made me think of a few thousand dollars a client of mine had lost betting that a food stock would go down in price. When I've been dreaming about my job, I wake up at night with pains in my chest.

I've got to find some other way to make a living.

Lyndon Wants More Job Pressures.   Lyndon, a supervisor in the accounts payable section of a well-known corporation, finds his occupational life too serene. Nothing exciting ever seems to happen to Lyndon. As he described it to his friend in another company,

I envy your working for your uncle in that chaotic little family business. At my company nothing ever goes wrong. I could just as well be a P.O. box number as a supervisor. The five women and three men in my department are old-timers who are satisfied with their pay and working conditions. Because we are a wealthy and well-managed company, all our suppliers get paid on time. I doubt that most of the people we send money even know we exist. They think our department is some machine that automatically dispenses checks.

I can honestly say that we have not had an emergency in my department in three years. I welcome an occasional snowstorm because that means I might be a few minutes late for work owing to road conditions. Other than that, there is almost no deviation from the normal schedule.

My boss says I'm doing a fine job and that in five years I might be eligible for promotion. My secret dream is that the company will fire me and that I would be forced to do something exciting for a living.

TAKE CONSTRUCTIVE ACTION ABOUT YOUR PROBLEM

My number one recommendation about coping with job-related stress (or stress of any kind) is to take constructive action. Your problem will never be resolved until you take the first step of doing something positive about the problem. Your first step in a positive direction can be likened to the first table-spoon of warm soup to a disaster victim; it won't cure your problem, but it's a welcome start.

Shana Gets Rubbed the Wrong Way. Fresh out of community college with a liberal arts major, good-looking Shana took an interim job until she could someday find a position with a magazine. Shana entered the stewardess training program of a major domestic airline. One year later she was experiencing an intense case of job stress. Recognizing that jobs were in scarce supply for a woman of her educational background and experience, Shana was apprehensive about telling the company about her problem. Nevertheless, she felt that something had to be done about her problem. Shana's important first step was to confer with her supervisor:

I have a somewhat embarrassing problem to discuss. When I was accepted into the stewardess training program, I was fully confident that I would want to do this kind of work for at least three years. I still think this is invaluable experience for a woman who wants to someday become a magazine editor. You come into contact with so many people. I like the airline personnel just fine. You folks have kept every promise you have made. No complaints on that score.

Despite all the good things I've said so far, this job is getting me sick. I can no longer take being rubbed and felt by strangers. I gently kneel down to pick up a plastic cup, and wham! Some unseen hand rubs against my rear end. At least once a flight some wise guy glides his elbow across my breasts.

I can almost spot the type who thinks a stewardess is there for his rubbing pleasure. The type I hate the most is the one who comes stalking down the aisle toward the lavatory. He weaves back and forth with the pitch of the airplane. When he nears you, he mistak-enly falls against you, rubbing his body against yours. Then he apologizes, saying that it's a rough flight. You feel so defenseless. It would look terrible for the airline if a stewardess shouted and screamed. It would look even worse if you punched the guy in the face—a punishment he deserves.

What I'm saying is that the pinching and rubbing part of my job nauseates me. I'm beginning to dread coming to work; yet I really like the airline. Is there any way I can get a job in the flight reservation department?

Shana found a sympathetic ear. Her supervisor arranged for Shana's transfer to an assignment as a reservation clerk. Today Shana is an editorial assistant with an airline magazine. Her airline experience and her college major education were the right combination for such a job. Had Shana not taken constructive action about her discontent (asking for a transfer), she might have quit in disgust. In quitting, she would have missed out on some valuable airline experience acquired behind the reservation desk.

Reggie Writhes in Pain. Working as a computer operator, Reggie was developing headaches and stomach pains. He would occasionally mention to his wife that the worst thing about being a computer operator was the fact that computer rooms almost never had windows. Windows—even if they were hermetically sealed—made temperature control difficult. Because computer rooms need careful temperature control, none of them had windows that opened and few had any windows.

Reggie decided that his concerns about windows might be causing his headaches and stomach cramps, but through self-discipline he would overcome his affliction. But self-discipline was not enough for conquering Reggie's job stress. One day he became an emergency patient in a local hospital. With half his stomach removed, Reggie sits staring out the window of his hospital room. He finally found a room with a window, but now he has another problem: How to lead a comfortable life with half a stomach.

If Reggie had sought medical treatment sooner for his headaches and cramps, maybe he might have received tranquilizing medication to arrest his symptoms of tension.

ATTACK THE CAUSE, NOT THE SYMPTOMS

Your job stress will continue to gnaw at you unless you modify the conditions that underly your problem. Hank, a production supervisor for a commercial printer, noticed that his smoking and drinking were approaching the danger level. With the encouragement of his wife, Hank enrolled in separate clinics for smokers and drinkers. He was able to stop smoking and control his drinking, but he still felt that too much stress existed in his job.

Hank's Underlying Problem.   Hank was responsible for one of the largest commercial printing operations in his city. Top management told him to cut operating costs by 25 percent in order to improve the firm's profitability. Hank decided it was necessary to introduce two new pieces of labor-saving machinery to meet his cost-cutting objectives. The labor union objected to this machinery and expressed its dissatisfaction to top management. Hank was chastised by management for not keeping peace with the union; yet they insisted on costs being reduced.

Hank's management had placed him in the untenable position of not having sufficient power to carry out his responsibility. Many other instances had occurred in the past of Hank's being limited in the authority he needed to carry out his mission. One time he was told to accomplish a major printing job in one week less time than it ordinarily took, but he was not authorized to use overtime help.

What Should Hank Have Done?   The root cause of Hank's dilemma is a common one in organizations. People are often given responsibility for a project but are not given commensurate authority or power to accomplish the responsibility. Hank should have discussed this problem in depth with his management, explaining how much and what kind of authority he would need to accomplish his objectives. For instance, in the 25 percent cost reduction episode, Hank should have explained that the only way he could achieve that goal was to bring in labor-saving machinery. He might have admonished management that if they were not willing to accept some complaining from the union, the cost reduction goal would be unachievable.

STRENGTHEN YOUR PERSONAL QUALIFICATIONS

Many of the stresses a person experiences in his or her career stem from the fact he or she can readily be replaced. A statement familiar to many people at all job levels is, "If you dislike things around here, move on. There are many people with qualifications as good as yours who would be willing to do your job for less money than you are making." The more unique (in a positive sense) you are, the less your concern about job security. Personal qualifications can be strengthened in a formal way (credentials such as education and specialized training) or in an informal way (for example, good reputation or valuable job experiences).

Priscilla Leaves Her Peon Status Behind. Career-minded Priscilla was an electrical engineer in the days when a female electrical engineer was a rarity. Proceeding along usual career path lines, Priscilla found employment with an areospace contractor. She helped design some instrumentation for the cockpit of a commercial aircraft. After three years on the job, Priscilla felt acutely underutilized:

> I'm an electrical engineer by education but not by job activity. What I do for a living could easily be done by an eager high school student of above average intelligence. At best, I would classify my job as a medium-level technician's work. My job classification and pay grade reflect professional status, but my job is well below those levels.
>
> Aside from the frustration of doing technician's work, I'm treated like a peon. One of the fellows I work with thinks that secretaries have more status than engineers in our company. My feelings are that we are treated with the individuality and dignity of a copying machine. When somebody needs some electronic engineering done, the typical request is, "Run this through an electrical engineer."

Priscilla followed the lead of many people facing her problems. She spent three years working part-time on a master's degree in business administration. No promotion was immediately forthcoming, but the personnel department made careful note of her elevated formal credentials. A requisition came through shortly thereafter seeking an electrical engineer with a background in administration to serve as the head of a small project. Priscilla was awarded the assignment and found it much more satisfying (and, therefore, less stressful) than her cockpit chores.

Chad Makes Himself a More Valuable Salesman. "I'm as good as my last order," lamented Chad to his wife. "If the company decides that I'm drawing too much salary they might easily replace me with a salesman half my age and pay him half my salary."

"But you're worth much more to the company than an inexperienced salesman," replied his wife.

"That's not true enough to suit me," pondered Chad, "but I think I know how I'm going to make it true from now on."

His thinking sparked by his conversation with his wife, Chad developed a logical plan for improving his worth as a salesman —not only to his present company, but to others in the area. Chad joined both the Rotary and Elks clubs. Soon he became luncheon companions of many of the small business owners in the area. Not only did his sales volume increase, but Chad was seen by his company as an influential businessman in the community. Chad now had one less source of stress in his life—the worry that he could readily be replaced. His informal qualifications were now enhanced on the strength of his personal acquaintance with key customers.

TALK OUT YOUR PROBLEMS

Strain (the effects of stress) is reduced somewhat by the mere process of talking about the problem bothering you. Almost everybody familiar with human behavior recognizes this adage, but few people put it to use. Talking about your problems with a sympathetic listener is a good start toward dissipating stress. An important by-product of talking about your problems is that it may lead to constructive action that contributes to their resolution.

Roger Pours Out His Feelings to the Group. Roger skeptically participated in a personal development group of people from different occupations. A friend of his had urged Roger to give this rap group a try. The first group exercise was for each person to give his or her first impression of every other group member. Eight of the ten other group members used terms such as "tough guy," "hardened," or "supermasculine" to describe Roger. Asked to react to the feedback he was receiving, Roger replied, "Not much to say. I'm not afraid of the truth. I've always been seen as a tough guy."

Later that evening each group member was asked to share with the group the most pressing personal problem he or she felt comfortable in sharing with the group. When Roger's turn came, he responded, "I wish I earned a few more thousand dollars per year."

One of the group interaction exercises at the next meeting was for any member to ask any other member any question he or she wished. The person asking the question had the option of answering or not answering. A young man turned to Roger and said, "Last time we met, you said your biggest problem was making a few more thousand dollars. I don't believe it. You must have a more important problem than that. Could you please tell us what is *really* your biggest problem?"

Roger blurted out,

> Okay, I'll spill my guts to you people. You look honest to me so far. I'm 43 years old, and I'm frightened. I worked all these years to get into the executive suite, and I'm almost there. But all of a sudden it's these young people who are a threat to my getting a promotion. A friend of mine has a woman for a boss who is ten years younger than himself.
>
> In my field, computer expertise is important, and I'm kind of weak in that area. It could easily happen that a man much younger than myself could pass me by on the strength of his computer knowledge.
>
> To tell you the real truth, so long as I've gone this far, it's not only computer knowledge that worries me. I think our company is be-

ginning to phase younger and younger men into higher-level jobs. I thought that I would land my executive post by age 45. Now I'm worried that my hoped for position will go to a 35-year-old man. Maybe even a woman.

Another person in the group challenged Roger: "Do you think you might be overreacting to a minor trend? Is it really true that a manager with something to offer the company will be bypassed by a younger person? Or is giving a few younger people a chance for good jobs just a way of the company's telling people that you cannot get promoted on the basis of seniority alone?"

After that evening Roger began to take a more realistic view of threats from below. He felt less under stress as he began to realize that the best way to guard against the competition was to perform well himself. He also carefully reviewed recent promotions in his mind and came to the conclusion that most of the managers bypassed for promotion were not particularly effective individuals.

REDESIGN YOUR JOB

Organizational sociologists have recognized for a long time that many of the stresses that take place in organizations are caused more by situations than by people. In other words, some jobs are inherently stressful. An accurate clue to this phenomenon is when several consecutive people fail in a given position. One example of such a job is being a collection agent in a high-crime area. All examples of poorly designed jobs, however, are not so obvious.

Barry, the Psychosomatic Credit Manager. "Barry you miserable character, you've done it again. I had a big sale all lined up, and you called for a cancellation. The company I sold that drill press to would have to pay for it promptly. Without a new drill press, they could never make their production schedule. They couldn't afford *not* to pay us for the equipment. And you go and cancel the sale. You made me look like a fool.

The customer said they would never do business with us again."

Unfortunate Barry, in his role as credit manager, would absorb stress like this whenever he was forced to cancel a sale when his research showed that the new customer had a substandard credit rating. Each time Barry canceled an order or refused a customer the terms the salesman had promised him, Barry would be in for another hassle. Each hassle left Barry handicapped with a severe headache, often combined with an intestinal disturbance.

Barry disliked both the stress in his job and the symptoms he was experiencing. He also disliked being seen as an adversary to sales personnel. Barry needed relief, but quitting his job or gradually searching for a new one were not feasible alternatives. Barry realized that, as a machine tool credit manager, he would inevitably face the same kind of conflict in any company he worked for.

Barry Gets His Job Redesigned. An article Barry read in a trade magazine discussed decreasing conflict by changing around reporting relationships. It sparked Barry's thinking to make a formal proposal to top management about the proper sequence of handling sales orders. In conference with the sales manager, the controller, and the president, Barry made this suggestion:

> Sales people often blast us for throwing cold water on their hot customers. The problem, as I see it, is that the sales people are committing the company to shipping new customer equipment before we have cleared their credit ratings. We are sent sales contracts to approve. It would be much wiser for us to get involved before a new customer actually signs a contract. It would make sense for the salesman to say that he needs two signatures to approve a capital purchase of the magnitude of our drill presses.
>
> I don't see where this procedure would lose us more than one order a century. Anybody can wait three days for final approval on the purchase of major equipment. With repeat business, the sales-

men can do whatever they want, but I still think that checking with the credit department first is a financially sound idea.

Top management agreed to try the new credit approval arrangements. It worked, and Barry gets into fewer hassles with sales representatives. Of equal significance, Barry's head and intestines are feeling much better on a consistent basis.

TELL YOUR BOSS TO PRACTICE GOOD MANAGEMENT

Many of the stresses you face in your job are caused by your boss or by your company. For example, if you are told to increase production and simultaneously decrease errors, you will probably experience stress. The stress comes from being caught in the middle of competing demands. So-called management principles are usually an extension of common sense, but not every member of management is long on common sense.

How Can You Put This Idea into Practice?   It takes self-confidence and tact, but after a few rehearsals with friends you should be able to point out to your boss that his or her violation of management principles is stressful. Lance, a salesman in the industrial laundry business, attended a regional conference in a downtown hotel. During the conference each salesman was to meet with his manager to discuss sales quotas for the upcoming year. Lance's manager informed him that his quota would be raised 25 percent for the following year. The "no holds barred" atmosphere of the sales conference provided the right setting for Lance to retort, "Hold on, Bud. I thought National Laundry had become a sophisticated company. In modern management, everybody who has to make a quota come true is supposed to participate in setting that quota. I wasn't even consulted about how much my sales should be increased."

Bud saw the logic of Lance's thinking and advised Lance to make an analysis of how much sales could be increased during the upcoming year. In the interim, Bud discussed the problem with his boss, who agreed that an effort should be made to have more people participate in goal setting.

By the end of the day, Lance returned with his analysis:

> Bud, I've arrived at a projected increase of 15 percent. The reason for the discrepancy between my quota and the one you established is that I have some inside information about three of my largest customers. Two are hotels and one is a factory, and all three are shrinking in business volume. With less business activity, there is a slow erosion of demand for laundry service.
>
> Instead of beating upon old customers for more business, I would like to establish a quota of opening up five new accounts next year. This should more than make up for the 5 percent difference in our quotas.

Bud and his manager bought the logic of Lance's position and respected him for his appeal to the practice of sound management.

CHANGE JOBS OR CAREERS

For many people, the only way out of a stressful situation is to flee to another job or career. (Switching jobs or careers is an important enough topic to be allocated a separate chapter each, later in this book.) Clancy's situation will suffice for now as an illustration.

Clancy Hates Working in a Delicatessen. Clancy, a personnel manager, was conferring with me about some management problems in his plant. Suddenly, the door burst open, and the manufacturing vice-president shouted, "Clancy get these goddamn labor reports out by tonight."

Clancy smiled at the vice-president, then turned to me with an anguished look on his face: "You see what I mean? I hate this delicatessen store approach to management. When somebody wants something done, they don't use the intercom or write a memo. They must shout. It's management by panic. I hate this place. I intend to quit as soon as I can find a new job. I've heard that our biggest competitor is looking for a new personnel manager."

I commented, "But, Clancy, if you hate working for a 'delicatessen,' why go work for another one? What you seem to be objecting to is the style of management that is prevalent in small firms in this field. Maybe you need to work in a large efficient company where things run smoothly and people are well mannered."

Today Clancy is working as a personnel specialist in the headquarters of a multinational business. He deals mostly with reports and never has to interact with ill-mannered or gruff-operating people. The only noise in his office is the chatter of electric typewriters and the tinkle of the coffee wagon bell in the morning and afternoon.

HOW CAN CLEANING YOUR DESK AND OFFICE REDUCE STRESS?

"I know I have your mortgage application somewhere. I was just working on it because we need some more information. It must be somewhere. The cleaning woman never throws out a bank form. What day was it that you filed the application? It must be somewhere. I never lose an important bank paper."

Fumbling Tracy will remain under stress until she revamps her filing system and clears out the clutter from her office. The mortgage papers she sought were finally found lying horizontally under a batch of vertical file folders (one month after Tracy involuntarily left the bank).

It's not unheard of to find a successful person working out of a cluttered, disheveled office, but most successful people are in control of their immediate work area. Being out of control—not knowing where to find things and not knowing which assigned tasks are completed—is a needless source of stress for many people. When you are placed under the pressure of completing a major assignment, a good starting point is to invest two hours in tidying up your work area. In the process, you might locate information that will assist you in getting the project accomplished.

WHAT ABOUT PHYSICAL EXERCISE TO REDUCE STRESS?

It is well known by industrial physicians and other health specialists that being in good physical shape helps you to cope with the job-related stress. A person with a cardiac system beautifully toned by constant exercise is less likely to have a heart attack when overworked than a person whose heart is already weak from lack of exercise. It is also well accepted by many people that physical exercise helps prepare your sensorium for taking on tough mental tasks. Finally, being in good physical shape makes you more resistant to fatigue; thus you can handle a bigger mental or physical work load.

Another issue is whether a person under stress can dissipate some of the accompanying tension by physical exercise. For many people the answer is yes.

Billy Takes to the Slopes. At age 49, Billy is a beautiful physical specimen. At work he is known as a demanding, somewhat insensitive executive. He keeps himself and his people under unremitting pressure to increase profits and cut costs. Asked how he relieves some of the pressure from work, he answers: "I hit the ski slopes and I hit them hard. I'm getting on in years to jump, but I bang down hard on the moguls. By the end of a few hard runs down the slopes, I feel recharged. I feel calmer and better able to tackle whatever monster of a problem is facing me next."

Suppose You Are Not a Good Athlete? Billy is a skier; so he has an enjoyable method of physical exercise to help him reduce stress. Other people who are not so athletically inclined can still capitalize on the same principle. As the physical exercise cult has spread, many office workers are now doing push-ups on their office floor (with the door closed), trotting up and down stairs, running to the mailbox, jogging during nonworking hours, running back and forth from lunch, and walking part or all of the way to work.

Evidence has accumulated that *natural* exercises such as walking, running, or dancing are as good for you as some of the routines offered in a formal exercise class. My hunch is that one of the real tension-reducing benefits of many formal sport or exercise routines is the shower activity that follows.

TRY MEDITATION

An extraordinary benefit of all forms of mediation is that they help reduce the kind of tensions accumulated in a work environment. Transcendental Meditation (TM) is the most widely publicized tension-reducing technique, but the available evidence suggests that it is no more or no less effective than other forms of meditation. Meditation, in general, acts as a natural tranquilizer, reducing stress and stimulating the mind. Many stress symptoms such as spastic colitis, high blood pressure, and migraine headaches can be reduced by proper meditation.

How Can Meditation Reduce the Source of Career-Related Stress?   Many stresses people face in their careers are induced by their own attitudes toward work. A relevant example is the person who succumbs to the stress of frustrated ambitions. Should you establish a goal of becoming a vice-president by age 40 and you don't become vice-president, the result could be frustration-induced stress. Your company did not say, "If you do not reach the rank of vice-president by age 40, you will be considered unworthy and, therefore, fired." It's a form of self-induced stress helped along by cultural expectations.

Meditation can help in this situation by making you less concerned with moving upward in the organization. Dr. David R. Frew of Gannon College discovered in his research that meditators are more content to perform well at their current positions than to invest energy in climbing the organizational ladder.

Leslie Takes It Easy.   Leslie is a convert to meditation. Before TM he was a hard-driving, slightly obnoxious, organizational climber. One year of meditation has helped him become a more relaxed, more contented person. As he describes his attitude,

Now I can stop at lunch hour to talk to the frankfurter man or look in a store window at some children's toys. I can laugh at the little mistakes made by my coworkers. When a friend rushed into my office with the news of his promotion, all I could respond was, "You feel good because you were promoted."

In the past I was into climbing the ladder and acquiring material things. Now I'm serene and having fun diddling around with the interesting parts of my job. If I don't have a report out on time, it's no big concern of mine. Work is now fun for me, and why should it be anything else?

Handling Job Conflict

5 "I just about cannot take it anymore," complained Marv to his sympathetic wife. "For 13 years I've been selling insurance for the company, and they've let me down again. I had one of the biggest premium packages put together that our branch has seen in a good many years. Underwriting fouls me up. I ask them for quick service, and they tell me not to be so pushy. I told the restaurant chain I had on the hook that our company would love to have their business. Underwriting next tells me that they may not want to take this line of insurance. It's a helluva lot easier doing battle with my customers than with the people inside our company."

Marv's conflicts are not unusual. People in responsible jobs often find themselves locked into disputes with people inside their own organization. Conflict is an inevitable part of life when your job involves contact with a variety of people, whether they be people directly in your chain of command, people from other parts of the organization, or outsiders.

The ability to handle conflict deftly thus becomes an important factor for your growth and survival in most organizations. (As a rule of thumb, the more competitive the organization, the more pronounced the conflict.) Few people can get very far in their careers without being able to manage conflict effectively. Particularly important is the ability to handle conflict as it manifests itself on a day-by-day basis.

Elaborate techniques have been developed by industrial psychologists for resolving conflict between two individuals or groups of people. Here we are concerned with seven strategies for dealing with person-to-person conflict—the kind most of us become involved in as we try to forge ahead in our careers.

PRACTICE GENTLE CONFRONTATION

The art of gentle confrontation leads all contenders as the best way of dealing with person-to-person conflict—particularly when the person with whom you are in conflict has a power advantage. In this technique you make a candid statement of the problem facing you without hinting at any form of violence or retaliation. Here is how it works.

Pam is hired into a company as a senior programmer with the understanding that after six months of orientation she will be promoted to a systems analyst position. After five months of good service, Pam is ready to claim her system analyst title. At this point her boss departs from the company, and a new manager, Alex, takes over. Alex issues the edict that, because of a retrenchment in the company, there will be no promotions in his department (where Pam is working) for another six months.

Pam is deservedly upset by this change of events. It appears that she will not get the promotion she was promised at the end of the six months' orientation period.

What Actions Should Pam Avoid or Take? A poor strategy for Pam to use would be to file a complaint with the vice-president of personnel or the company president that she has been treated unjustly. Even if she wins her point (and her deserved promotion), she will have alienated herself from her new boss, Alex.

According to the art of gentle confrontation, Pam should request a conference with Alex and patiently explain to him that his edict has canceled out a prior commitment—one that may not have been in writing. It would also seem important for Pam to indicate that she feels victimized by a change in policy and ask if Alex could help her with the situation. Assuming that Alex is a rational person, he may likely bend his new edict. To save face, he will probably agree that his policy was not meant to be retroactive.

Gus Gets Ridiculed.   Throughout his teen-age years, Gus aspired toward becoming a radio engineer. As an adult, he took a job as an electronics technician while pursuing his study of radio engineering as a hobby. Finally, his big break came. He applied for and was accepted for a position as an engineer for a local radio station. Gus's first major assignment at the studio was to serve as the engineer for a popular local disc jockey, Freddie the Frog.

One night Freddie mentioned to his listeners that a new engineer had arrived and that "although he doesn't look too bright, my boss tells me he's really a genius." Gus winced at Freddie's insulting humor but felt that such humor was perhaps harmless.

Gus soon found out that Freddie's ill-conceived humor persisted. Freddie mentioned to his listeners one night that Gus was hired into the studio with the provision that he would never leave his booth when visitors were on the premises of the studio. Another night he told the audience that Gus was 5'9" when wearing shoes, but 5'3" in bare feet.

Gus Gets His Gripe Resolved.   Fearful of being fired if he complained to Freddie the Frog, but acutely uncomfortable with the frequent ridicule, Gus was in conflict. Finally, his concern for his dignity exceeded his concern for losing his treasured radio engineer slot; so Gus confronted Freddie over coffee: "Freddie, I enjoy being an engineer on your show, and I admire your following and many of the things you do as a dee jay. But it's getting to the point that it hurts whenever you poke fun at me to the audience. Could you possibly see your way clear to find another running joke? My friends are beginning to ask me why I take all the abuse on the air."

"See what I can do, kid. Don't take life so seriously," replied Freddie. The next night Freddie told his audience that he had a confession to make. "You out there in radioland, I must admit a fault of mine. I'm jealous of a man who is better-looking than

I. And, of course, that means I'm not jealous very often. But my engineer, Gus, is one great-looking guy. That's why I've been insulting him right along. You don't think that old Freddie the Frog himself would insult somebody who is defenseless, do you?"

DISARM THE OPPOSITION

When engaged in conflict at the office, the armament you take away from your opposition is his or her negative criticism of you. You can capitalize upon the same principle that children often use in handling conflict with their parents: "I broke a lamp by mistake. Go ahead and beat me. I deserve it."

The technique of "Disarm the opposition" is highly recommended for solving an interpersonal conflict because of its widespread application. Here is how it works in an office situation.

Jason, a sales manager in a home improvement company, has been in conflict with the home office because of declining sales in his area. Irritated, his boss, Barney, schedules a trip to Jason's office in which he plans to administer to him some verbal blasts about declining sales. Barney would not be acting out of character to give Jason an ultimatum—improve sales or leave the company.

Jason's worst strategy would be to marshal an immediate counterattack during the meeting—to dazzle Barney with a long list of reasons why sales have been below forecast.

Jason Disarms Barney.   A preferred strategy is for Jason to disarm Barney by agreeing that sales are poor. He is advised to say, "Barney, you are probably upset because our sales are 25 percent below target. I agree that we should not be proud of our performance. Now that you are here, maybe you can help me develop a plan of attack to improve our sales situation."

To this Barney will probably reply, "Jason, why else do you think I came here?"

How Can this Strategy Help You Overcome the Cause of the Conflict?   An essential part of the "disarm the opposition"

74 HANDLING JOB PROBLEMS

strategy is to place the issues on a problem-solving basis once
the opposition has been disarmed. It is almost as if the opposition has some punishment they want to clobber you with. Once
you have clobbered yourself, the opposition is satisfied, and
the two of you can get to the serious task of conflict resolution.

Similarly, if you have been in conflict with a lending institution (or even a loan shark) about seriously overdue payments,
don't hide from them. Take the initiative in this manner: "Your
records and mine agree. I am sorely delinquent on my payback
schedule. Do you have any program of refinancing old debts
that could help me get back on my feet financially?" Such an
approach is psychologically sound and beats getting your car
repossessed.

EXCHANGE IMAGES WITH YOUR ANTAGONIST

An oft repeated scenario in the office of a marriage counselor
goes something like this:

MARRIAGE
COUNSELOR: Okay, Bill and Jan, I want you to tell each other how
you feel about this issue. Also tell each other how you
think the other person feels on the same issue. Jan, why
don't you go first?

JAN: I'm a mature person, and I think I should be able to have
friends of both sexes. Therefore, if I want to have an
occasional lunch or play bridge with a male friend, I
don't think you should object. From your viewpoint,
that is terrible, almost immoral behavior. You think a
married woman shouldn't have male friends.

BILL: The way I see it, marriage is sacred. If a woman is
married, she gives up the right to date men, even if sex
isn't involved. I see no compromise on this issue. Of
course, from your standpoint I'm being somewhat old-
fashioned. You think that if I thought you were mature,
I wouldn't try to stop you from lunching or playing
cards with a member of the opposite sex.

Following the lead of the widespread application of this technique in resolving marital disputes, exchanging images or viewpoints can be used in the office. The essential point is that you and your antagonist make it clear that you understand the other person's point of view. Empathy of this kind may then lead to a useful and productive compromise.

Ted and Luke Exchange Viewpoints in order to Improve Patient Care. Ted, a psychiatrist, and Luke, an internist, are both army majors in charge of busy wards. The surgical department routinely referred all patients with no observable medical problems to the psychiatry department. Psychiatry, in turn, would refer to internal medicine only those patients suffering from obvious contagious diseases or open sores. Ted and Luke both did not appreciate the quality or quantity of patient referrals from each other's ward.

As their mutual disenchantment grew, patient welfare sometimes suffered. Some referrals were sent back to internal medicine from psychiatry (or vice versa) with cryptic notes such as "Patient cannot be admitted without more complete information." A psychology officer serving as a training consultant to the hospital offered to intervene in the conflict. With his assistance, the two medical officers were able to resolve some of their differences. Not until core issues were penetrated, did Ted and Luke begin to remedy the situation. Some of the more meaningful dialogue included this commentary:

TED: Consciously or unconsciously, your pattern is clear. The kind of people you send over to us are those you think have no physical problems. Therefore, their problems are imaginary in your eyes. You see us as kind of a dumping ground for the patients you choose not to treat. I think you object to psychiatry on philosophical grounds.

As you see us, Luke, you think we don't give enough credence to the importance of physically based problems. You believe that we think that unless somebody is bleeding externally or coughing up blood, he is suffering an emotional disorder.

LUKE: I am concerned that you folks in psychiatry dismiss too
readily the possibility that some of the people coming to your
ward with vague complaints may be in need of medical attention. I also think that you attach too little importance to the
physical and chemical side of illness.

You think that we send you a lot of "crocks" and that we
don't really understand what your proper function is. You
think we in internal medicine take psychiatry too lightly.

What Finally Happened?   Ted and Luke did not exactly
live happily ever after, but they did develop a more rounded,
less subjective view of each other's contribution to total patient
welfare. Out of their image-exchanging sessions came one immensely constructive suggestion. A representative from psychiatry attends internal medicine staff meetings. As part of the
same bargain, an internist is found at every staff meeting held
by psychiatry.

INTERPRET THE OTHER PERSON'S GAME

A good deal of game playing goes on in organizations. Many
of the conflicts you face on the job stem from the fact that
somebody is playing games with you whether or not your adversary realizes he or she is playing a game. A *game* (in the
framework of transactional analysis) can be described as a human interaction that takes place repeatedly which on the surface seems to be of genuine intent, but contains a concealed
motivation. Games have been given labels such as "Now I've
Got You, You SOB." Here is how "SOB" works in practice:

One afternoon, in lieu of attending a committee meeting you
have been assigned to by your company, you spend two hours
at lunch with an old friend. The next day the committee head
drops by your desk to comment, "We missed you at the meeting yesterday. How come you weren't there?

You reply, "I gave priority to some other activity I had
planned for yesterday. I'll be able to make the next meeting."

He replies, "Isn't that peculiar? I took a late lunch hour after
the meeting broke up. As I was looking for a luncheonette, I saw

you coming out of a restaurant with somebody not from our office. Is that your excuse?"

A logical way to squelch this kind of game recurring in other contacts with the committee head is to interpret his game directly: "It's obvious you were trying to trap me into saying a falsehood, which I didn't. If you knew I was at a restaurant during your meeting, why did you ask me where I was?" With a little practice you can be skillful at interpreting much game-playing activity, even if the game being played against you has not yet been labeled by transactional analysts.

Rich Counterzaps His Boss. As a product manager in a food company, Rich is paid to be an idea man. Unless he comes up with ideas for food products that sell, he is doing only two-thirds of his job—tending to the successful products already in-house. Rich began working for his new boss, Lola (the vice-president of Wholesale Foods), over one year ago. During that time Rich has presented plans to Lola for five different products. Lola rejected each of Rich's suggested new products either on-the-spot or after careful deliberation. At Rich's first performance review under her jurisdiction, Lola commented, "Rich, I'm afraid you're falling down somewhat on your responsibilities. So far no workable idea for a new product came out of your department."

Perceptive Rich came back with a rejoinder:

Lola, are you sure I haven't given you any creative suggestions, or is it that you haven't *accepted* any suggestions? No idea is workable until you try it out in practice. Let's look at the record. You told me my suggestion for pastel colored instant potatoes was unesthetic. You rejected my mint flavored coffee as too radical. You said that my instant stew was so much like *Gravy Train* that people would only feed it to their dogs. You claimed that instant apple pudding was impractical. The grand rejection was my idea for a mineral enriched beverage for warm weather sports enthusiasts. A competitive company has grossed $20 million on that product idea so far.

You're playing a game with me. You reject all my ideas for one reason or another, and then you zap me for not having good ideas. You won't let me carry out my job, and then you punish me for not having carried it out.

The review session lasted another hour. By then Lola was apologetic for having been too critical of Rich's suggestions. Close to the end of the meeting, she asked her product manager, "Rich, do you think it's too late for us to get into the ball game with your mineral enriched sports drink? Competition is natural and healthy in the food business."

Nelson Gets Set Up for a Letdown. A junior person in the financial analysis department of his company, Nelson was busily at work gathering together information to prepare the annual report. A fellow management trainee, Wayne, one day asked Nelson how he liked his assignment.

"Fine," replied Nelson. "But right now I'm submerged in work. My boss has given me the chance to pull together the company's year-end figures that will go into the annual report. But before the figures are actually used, I will have to present them to top management. I'm designing some visual displays right now."

"Hold on," said Wayne, "As you know, I'm in the public relations department. We have the talent to help you with that project. Why be a do-it-yourselfer when you can get professional help? Drop by for help when you are ready."

One week later Nelson called Wayne and said, "I'm taking you up on your offer. My presentation is due in one week. Do you think this will give you enough time to make up a few charts for me?

Wayne answered, "Nelson, I'd like to help out, but we're pretty busy right now. We have to establish priorities. We can't be helping everybody who needs a chart drawn for a routine presentation."

How Nelson Should Have Handled Wayne. A good approach for Nelson in this situation would have been to interpret to Wayne the type of pointless game he was playing as follows: "Hold on, Wayne. Do you see what you're doing here? You volunteered to help me get some charts drawn. I didn't ask for your help. Now you tell me you can't help me when it's close to my presentation day. If you are trying to help somebody else on the management training program fail, tell me directly. I won't be party to another one of your setups."

MOCK THE OPPOSITION IN A NICE WAY

A conflict is difficult to win until your adversary recognizes that perhaps he or she may be in the wrong (or at least partially wrong). Telling somebody else, "You're absolutely wrong. Why can't you see it my way?" is a consistently ineffective strategy. Much more can be gained by sharpening your ability to mock gently—or point out good-naturedly the inconsistencies in—your adversary's logic.

Gene, a sales manager in a small chemical company, is facing a win-lose situation with Baxter, the head of manufacturing. If Baxter loses, Gene wins, and vice versa. Gene wants a 100-pound sample of a chemical compound made to the specifications of one customer. To complicate matters further, he wants the material delivered in 30 days. Baxter, upset by Gene's request, tells him: "Gene, it just won't work. Our production facilities are set up for the large batch customer. We need business in large volume. The small occasional order just gets in our hair. It's a losing proposition for us to stop the production line just to run your order for 100 pounds of gunk."

Gene intensifies the conflict by angrily responding, "Do you think we're in business to please our customers or to please your people? Ram this order through for me, or I'll be talking to the president about your lack of cooperation."

A Preferred Approach for Gene. To lessen the tension and win his point, Gene might have said, "Okay, we marketing people have been bad boys again. We're out soliciting new business without accepting only customers who'll order 100,-000 barrels and who won't need it for a year. I'll try harder next time, but I think this 100-pound sample could lead to substantial orders next time."

Misunderstood Ivan, the Corporate Planner. Five years

out of college, Ivan found himself an avant-garde position as the assistant to the vice-president of corporate planning. Included in his job was helping his boss figure out the true worth of companies that the corporation planned to acquire. Although Ivan recognized the importance of his position, he realized that not everybody understood the true function of his department. Keith, the head of an overhead reduction task force, requested an interview with Ivan.

Keith's basic question was, "What do you people do in corporate planning?" Realizing that Keith was really asking him to rationalize why his department should be carried by the corporation, he replied, "Why absolutely nothing of value. I think the corporation set up this department to serve as needless overhead. That way when an overhead reduction committee is appointed, it will have something to do. How else can I help you?"

Keith laughed, and an atmosphere was established whereby Ivan could carefully explain the activities of the Corporate Planning Department without Keith's preconcluding that the department must be reduced in size or eliminated.

HOW TO HANDLE A SQUEEZE PLAY

One facet of life in complicated organizations is that you are sometimes caught between two opposing pulls. In one situation your profession and your company may have different expectations of what you should do in a given situation. For instance, the accounting profession may have devised certain rules for depreciating equipment whereas your company may want a different approach in order to look better to stockholders or to decrease taxes. In another situation your functional manager (the top person in your speciality employed by your company) may have different expectations of your performance than does your immediate boss. The former may want you to use elegant and expensive techniques whereas the latter may demand a "quick and dirty" solution.

Eldon Gets Squeezed. A management development specialist, Eldon was asked by Art, the corporate director of management development, to conduct a series of training programs for factory foremen. The subject matter was to deal with motivating the youth culture toward higher levels of performance and less absenteeism—a formidable task. Eldon dutifully gathered together information he could find about such programs conducted in other companies. He also contracted a consultant to conduct several of the training sessions.

Eldon was complimented by Art for the apparent soundness of the program. The remaining task for Eldon was to schedule the training sessions properly. He scheduled a meeting with his immediate boss, Ben (the plant superintendent), to establish dates for the training programs. Following the dictates of the director of management development, Eldon suggested that the sessions be scheduled during normal operating hours.

Ben protested: "An absolutely unworkable idea. I believe in foremen being trained, but not on my time. Having ten foremen at a time attend a training program will play havoc with our production schedule. Run your program on Saturdays and Sundays. Many executive programs are run that way. Why treat the foremen differently? They are supposed to be part of management. I just won't go along with your proposed schedule."

Eldon Confronts the Problem. Recognizing that he was caught in a situation of divided loyalties (the technical term is *role conflict*), Eldon asked the consultant's advice about how he should proceed. Acting on the advice he received, Eldon asked Art and Ben to meet with him for 45 minutes to discuss his dilemma. At the meeting he articulated the problem:

> Both my bosses have a different view of when to schedule the training sessions. Fortunately, you both agree that they *should* be scheduled. Art thinks these programs are so job-related that they should be scheduled during normal operating hours. You, Ben, think that such scheduling would be disruptive to production.
>
> My opinion is that we have to find a way to show that the program is important, yet not play havoc with the production schedule. I might add that I also want to protect my hide. I en-

joy working with both you guys. Right now I'm unlucky Pierre.

If we run the program on Saturdays and Sundays we'll hear grumbling from the foremen that too much is expected from them. We may think foremen are part of management, but they are paid more like skilled workers. Yet Ben won't go along with a program that will disrupt production.

What I suggest is that we run the programs for two two-hour sessions, catching the foremen right before they begin their normal shifts. But most important, we pay each man or woman for the two hours with premium pay. I think the cost will be minor in comparison to shipping people off to a resortlike setting for an entire weekend."

Ben and Art bought the idea without further negotiation. The foremen enjoyed the program and seemed to benefit from it, and Eldon developed skill in working himself out of a squeeze play.

APPEAL TO A POWERFUL THIRD PARTY

At times you may be placed in a conflict situation where the other party holds the major share of the power. Perhaps you have tried techniques such as "Practice gentle confrontation," "Disarm the opposition," or "Intrepret the other person's game"; yet he or she still won't budge. In these situations you may have to enlist the help of a third party with power—more power than you or your adversary have.

In some situations, just implying that you will bring in that powerful third party to help resolve the conflict situation is sufficient for you to gain advantage.

Ezra Exercises His Familial Muscles. A bank teller, Ezra, was ready for a new position in a large downtown location of his bank. His Puritan ethic boss, Wilbur, felt that Ezra's work was satisfactory but that he was not yet deserving of a promotion to another department in the bank.

Ezra and Wilbur exchanged ideas on this topic for at least once a week for four weeks. As a last resort, Ezra (who is now an assistant trust officer) said, "Perhaps Alstair Bentonworth (the bank chairman) can help us with this issue. He is much concerned about the proper utilization of bank personnel. Asked by Wilbur why Mr. Bentonworth would help him, Ezra replied, "He's my wife's father."

CAPITALIZE UPON YOUR ANGER

One by-product of office conflict is that people get angry, including you. Your anger could lead to your demise if you physically assault your opposition or you tell your boss that he or she is a "stupid bastard." In contrast, you can make constructive use of your anger if properly managed. Anger is an energizer, and this increased energy can be used to goad you on toward higher levels of achievement. Anger can also be used for dramatic effect—to illustrate by action that you are a person who does not care to be trampled on.

Alma Becomes Energized.   Working as an executive secretary in a casualty insurance company, Alma was unexpectedly given the opportunity to apply for a position as a personnel manager in her company. A pending threat of white-collar unionization made it mandatory for the company to begin promoting people from within (perhaps something they should have done more of in years past). After he reviewed her personnel file, Alma was told by the vice-president of personnel, "I'm sorry, but your lack of any formal education beyond college makes you unqualified for a professional level job."

Alma became enraged (in a controlled manner). She insisted, "I'm sure you'll find no person in the company better qualified than I for this position. I know the people, and I can do the job. I insist on being given the job."

After three weeks of reviewing the credentials of other company employees for this position, the vice-president asked to see Alma. He sheepishly admitted that Alma did seem like the best candidate available, but he added, "Because your formal credentials are so weak, I'm putting you into this job on probation. If, after six months, your performance is not satisfactory, you will be transferred back to your old job."

Alma's first inclination was to say, "Up yours, buddy," but logic prevailed. She decided that instead of directing her anger toward her new boss, she would channel her anger into her job. Alma carefully studied her job description and company policy manuals and took a home study course in personnel management. She met with other personnel specialists in the area to exchange information about personnel strategies. In general, Alma did everything within reason to improve her performance as a personnel manager.

At the six month's review, Alma was told by her boss, "Welcome to my department as a full-time, permanent personnel manager. Not only are you off probation, but I rate you as an outstanding employee."

Malcolm Thumps the Table. On the basis of physical appearance alone, Malcolm hardly fitted the image of a confident and competent elementary school principal. His pink complexion and his fine features connoted an image of a mild-mannered, almost passive individual. Unfortunately for Malcolm, his image was limiting his effectiveness in his newly acquired position as principal of the John Glenn School. The administrators and some of the teachers in his school did not take many of his directives seriously.

Particularly irksome to Malcolm was his staff's nonchalant attitude toward his campaign for school cleanliness. One day in staff meeting, the group seemed bored by his complaint that "the building looks as sloppy as it did the day I took over." One teacher commented, "Really, Malcolm, are we trying to develop young minds here, or are we breeding tidy little housekeepers?"

Malcolm jumped up from his chair, leaned over, and began pounding the table with both fists: "I don't give a damn if you think cleanliness is important or not. So long as I'm principal this place isn't going to look like a campsite for a bunch of slobs. The days of the pigpen at John Glenn are over. Clean up or ship out."

These days even the brass doorknobs at the John Glenn school sparkle. Quiet looking Malcolm is now listened to a lot more carefully by teachers and administrators alike.

DISSIPATE THE OTHER PERSON'S VIOLENCE

Watching a professional hockey game, I noticed that the referee and other players did not intervene until a fight between two players had lasted about three minutes. Seated next to me was an avid hockey fan and former player. I asked the gentleman about the delay before hockey combatants were separated. He replied, "If you break them up too soon, they'll get right back to fighting. You have to let them blow off most of their steam before you try to separate them."

Similarly, if your conflict with another person in the organization is so intense that he or she is verbally violent, play it cool. Let most of the violence dissipate before you return with a salvo. Until the other party has expressed most of his or her angry feelings, he or she won't listen to your side of the story.

Lou Blasts the Opposition.   Lou, an account supervisor in an advertising agency, pirated one of Warren's strongest account executives (Sheila) to serve as the account executive on the former's biggest account. After Sheila told Warren of her intention to join Lou's team, Warren ran down the hall to Lou's office. Barging past the secretary, he entered Lou's office and began shouting, "What the hell do you think is going on here? You can't take the best talent out of my department just to build up your own empire. You think you can get away with that shoddy maneuver? We'll see."

Lou counterattacked, "Who do you think you are blasting into my office like this. I'll take anybody from your group I damn well please. The way you manage people, the other supervisors have to turn down requests for transfers almost every week. If you're looking for trouble, I'll show you what trouble is."

Mutual hostilities became so intense that Lou and Warren developed a destructive working relationship. As charge was met with countercharge, the two advertising executives said things to each other that created permanent communication barriers between them.

A Better Way for Lou.   Recognizing that Warren's mood

was as violent as one might find in an office environment, Lou should have allowed him to vent his anger all at once. He might have tried to remain cool and let Warren shout until he ran out of angry words. Then Lou should have asked, "Surely, there must be something else about me you would like to criticize?" Perhaps then Warren would have one or two more negative points to make.

As Warren cooled down, Lou might have countered, "What you say is true. I did ask Sheila if she would like to work in my department without first consulting you, her boss. I may have violated the chain of command, but I was only trying to give Sheila a chance for advancement. Are you opposed to that?"

Outwitting
an Ineffective Boss

6 An engineer enrolled in a career development seminar became visibly irritated during a discussion of strategies for getting ahead in business. "There is something fundamentally wrong with what we are talking about," he stridently commented. "Everything we have talked about so far implies that your boss is a rational human being, a decent citizen, and a person who knows what he's doing. What do you do when your boss is a loser, a misfit, a person out of the Stone Age? As in my case, I'm simply beating my head against a brick wall. I'm end played. What do you recommend for me?"

The dramatic statements uttered by this engineer have been repeated (however silently) by many ambitious people in all types of organizations. A conservative estimate would be that one out of ten people who work for somebody else are faced with this problem. Outwitting or coping with an ineffective boss is one of the biggest challenges any person faces in his or her career. Unless you skillfully deal with an ineffective, obsolete, or deviant boss, your career could be set back. I offer you seven suggestions for handling this delicate situation.

LEARN FROM YOUR BOSS'S MISTAKES

The most generally useful way to exploit the hidden value in having an ineffective boss is to learn from his or her mistakes.

Although it is preferable to learn what to do rather than what *not* to do, some learning does take place from observing negative models. Many children become responsible adults or compulsive savers in adulthood because one or both of their parents was irresponsible or a spendthrift. Many competent college professors claim they learned their effective teaching techniques from observing how poorly one or two of their worst professors conducted a course. People have long been urged to profit from their own mistakes. Why not learn from the mistakes of your boss?

Tina Learns about Procrastination.   Tina worked for a boss who responded to pressure with procrastination. To cite an example, once Tina approached her boss with an urgent problem: "We stand in danger of not getting this contract proposal out on time unless you authorize some clerical overtime."

Tina's boss responded: "Let's table that idea until tomorrow. I need time to think it over. We have to look at every decision from the total company point of view. If we rush into authorizing overtime for you, we could be weakening ourselves in another area at the same time."

Rather than become infuriated and resign or insult her boss, Tina patiently waited for a transfer. The transfer was forthcoming, and Tina became an office supervisor. She is noted for her willingness and ability to give a rapid reply to any request made of her by a superior or subordinate. Tina expresses her decision-making philosophy this way:

> If anybody asks me a routine question such as "Am I eligible to take out a home improvement loan through the company credit union?" I try to get an answer within one day. When I'm asked a major question from above, such as "Can your department handle this project this quarter?" I respond in one week.
>
> Some questions cannot be answered off the cuff, because a lot of factors have to be weighed. But even then I try to give the person requesting the information a status report of how I'm progressing in terms of answering his or her question.

Karl's Absentee Boss. Intent upon making it big as a hotel manager, Karl landed himself a challenging position as the manager of a downtown hotel. His hotel was one of a small chain of hotels and restaurants. Karl enjoyed the autonomy he had in his new position. His boss, Ludwig, rarely ever visited him. At first, Karl believed that Ludwig was leaving him unattended because he was an able delegator who had complete confidence in his subordinates.

As time passed, Karl began to suspect that Ludwig rarely ever conferred with him or visited his hotel more out of disinterest than thoughtful management strategy. Ludwig's absentee management approach created some problems for Karl. When major decisions were to be made, Ludwig was difficult to reach. In one instance, Ludwig's unavailability created a serious delay in the initiation of renovation work that was necessary because of a fire.

What Karl Learned from the Situation. Gradually it dawned on Karl that instead of merely complaining about his boss's absentee tactics, he might be able to learn from them. He began to review his own performance, asking himself questions like "Do I have enough contact with my people? Am I available enough? Do I know what's actually going on in the areas I'm responsible for?"

Karl's candid answer to these questions was, "I could be doing a better job on all counts." As an antidote to his not getting close enough to the troops, Karl now made unscheduled trips to the hotel kitchen and made a point of chatting with the chambermaids. He also was frequently seen walking through the hotel lobby.

Karl was now profiting from the mistakes made by Ludwig in two important ways. He noticed that hotel cleanliness picked up markedly and that the help experienced a boost in morale. As Henri, the head chef, commented, "It's nice to have a manager who knows that a hotel can't run without a kitchen."

ASK FOR A TRANSFER (TACTFULLY)

Requesting a transfer is the most straightforward approach to coping with an ineffective boss. Although straightforward, this strategy can be difficult to implement. Obtaining a transfer assumes (1) there is another job fitting your qualifications available in the company, (2) the people in the other department want you, and (3) your boss will let you go. Before requesting a transfer, you need to do some digging for facts about the first two questions.

Marty Feels Oppressed.   Working as a senior accountant for the county, Marty believed he had a personality clash with his boss, Felix. Marty did what he could to develop a better working relationship with Felix, but his approaches failed. When they lunched together, both men felt restless and ill at ease. When Marty asked Felix a friendly question such as "Did you have a nice weekend?" Felix would answer "Why do you want to know?"

Recognizing that they could not get along socially, Marty then shifted all the conversations he initiated to work topics exclusively. One day Marty mentioned to Felix that he had spent most of the weekend working on a quarterly report. Felix replied, "So what? A professional person is supposed to work whenever the job calls for it."

Marty Does Some Fancy Footwork.   It became apparent that he would no longer work for Felix, despite his general satisfaction with working for the county. Marty believed that the county offered ample advancement opportunities for accountants, leading to managerial positions with excellent benefits including a hard-to-match pension.

Marty telephoned for an appointment with the personnel director in his division. Deciding that something had to be done to get out from under Felix, Marty made these comments to Carol (the personnel director):

"I haven't requested an appointment with you for the simple purpose of asking for a job transfer. I know enough about agency regulations not to do anything that's naïve. The first step should be a conference with your boss explaining why you want the transfer. If I made a formal request for a transfer to Felix, he would turn me down or think of every legitimate stalling tactic at his disposal. I can say that with certainty because when I talked to him in the past about the possibility of a transfer, he just became evasive and defensive.

"Before I ask for a transfer, I want to have a job almost lined up. You have my credentials on file. All I ask from you, Carol, is to cue me in when and if an opening for a senior accountant occurs in another department of this agency."

Carol pondered the situation and indicated that what Marty was requesting did not seem to be in violation of personnel policy. Two weeks later Carol contacted Marty to inform him of a senior accountant opening in the Income Maintenance Department. Marty followed up by requesting an interview with Phil—the department head with the open requisition.

Marty explained how he was looking for broadening and that he would very much like to fill the open position. "However," he noted, "It would be much cleaner administratively if you would contact Felix and say that my background exactly fits the requirements of your job opening. In that way, he will have a difficult time turning you down. It is much easier to ignore a subordinate than a department head. And I know Felix is a very busy man."

Later Felix asked Marty if he would be interested in transferring to Income Maintenance. Marty replied, "I guess we both know that we have had some differences of opinion about minor things. But I've learned a lot from working for you Felix. I would feel much better about the transfer if I knew that I would be welcomed back into the department if things didn't work out well for me in my new job."

Marty's deft maneuvering paid off handsomely. He received his transfer without any animosity between himself and Felix —the man with whom he had a long-standing personality clash.

FORTIFY YOUR BOSS'S WEAKNESS

You may secretly delight in seeing your ineffective boss fail, but his or her failure could hurt your career. If your department fails (even though it might be your boss's fault), it will not help (and will probably adversely impact on) your reputation to be associated with a losing effort. If there is something that your boss is doing wrong that could ultimately shroud you in failure, intervene before the situation gets out of control.

Esther Is Horrified at Her Boss's Actions. School Psychologist Esther was part of a mental health team charged with the task of reducing drug abuse at the high school where she worked. Vanessa, her boss, spent two months working on a program to achieve such ends before she consulted Esther about its content. Vanessa's program was called "Drugs Only Paralyze Everybody" (DOPE). It included a number of filmstrips showing automobile accidents, fires, drownings, muggings, and mutilations—all allegedly the by-product of drug addiction.

Vanessa's plan was to show these filmstrips at high school auditorium meetings. Guest lecturers at these meetings were to include prison wardens, policemen, and members of the clergy. Esther recognized from her knowledge about teen-agers and drugs that such scare tactics only tended to make young drug users more defensive. Previous studies had shown that drug abuse actually increases with such negative approaches.

Esther analyzed Vanessa's potential mistake as an error in judgment rather than as a serious attempt to fail in her mission. Five years ago Esther had watched Vanessa unwittingly precipitate a small epidemic of daredevil driving by showing an old James Dean movie in which somebody gets killed playing "chicken." She did not want to be associated with a similar professionally embarrassing situation.

How Did Esther Save the Situation? She reasoned that Vanessa, the filmstrip aficionada, might like a private filmstrip presentation. Esther made up some simple transparencies that summarized the relative effectiveness of several different approaches to changing the attitudes and behavior of teen-agers about drug or alcohol use. One of the conclusions she reached was that Vanessa's filmstrip and lectures might be quite effective in alerting parents to the magnitude of the drug problem. In contrast, these presentations would be of negative value in discouraging drug and alcohol abuse with younger people.

Vanessa told Esther that she liked the "slight modification" of her ideas and encouraged Esther to come up with the portion of the program aimed directly at the teen-agers. Esther proceeded to develop a drug information program that was more factual than emotional. Members of the school, the principals in the school she served, and many parents were quite pleased with the outcome of the new drug abuse program. Reported instances of teen-age drug abuse showed a slight decline after implementation of the program.

Alfred Speaks for his Boss.   Another variation of "Fortify your boss's weakness" is to help your boss with his or her most befuddling assignment. Alfred worked on a product team responsible for the introduction of a lightweight motorcycle that would compete directly with two fast-selling Japanese models. Alfred and his boss, Chris, knew that their product was fighting for its life. The company was becoming increasingly cautious about investing much money in products that were highly competitive.

Alfred had compiled an impressive dossier of facts and figures about the market for motorcycles in this price range in the United States and Canada. Although Chris was the product manager for the "LP-690," Alfred had acquired more knowledge about this motorcycle. Of greater significance, Alfred recognized that Chris was relatively ineffective in making verbal presentations under pressure. He reasoned that, with Chris making the presentation, the LP-690 was headed toward an early grave.

Confident of his own ability to make a verbal presentation to top management, Alfred approached his boss in this manner: "Chris I'm willing to put my head on the block over the LP-690.

I'd welcome the opportunity to make the presentation to top management about our need for more funding on this hot little bike. With you in the meeting room to fortify me with any additional facts I might need, I know we can do a job swinging management around to our way of thinking."

Chris replied, "Good idea, Alfred. I have a few commitments coming up in the next two weeks that would make it difficult for me to make the presentation. I'm sure you'll do a first-rate job. I doubt if I could do a better job myself."

TAKE OVER PART OF YOUR BOSS'S JOB

A pernicious form of ineffective boss is one who jealously guards exciting portions of his job and delegates only its routine aspects to subordinates. As one frustrated middle manager expressed it during a management discussion group, "Nobody has a worse boss than I do as far as making life interesting for his people. He wouldn't delegate a decent assignment if he were in an iron lung."

To the lazy person, the nondelegating variety of ineffective boss is ideal. He or she gets paid a full salary and benefits and doesn't have to tax himself or herself with demanding work. But to the organizational climber, the nondelegator is a curse. Until you get meaningful assignments, you can't improve your competence. Worse, until you perform well on meaningful assignments, you will be unable to establish a solid reputation.

How Do You Get a Nondelegator to Let Go of Interesting Work? The way to begin is to look for a task currently performed by your boss that you are confident you can handle well. One fundamental reason many nondelegators hold on to important work in their department is that they have an underlying fear that anybody else who attempts to perform such work will fail. If the subordinate fails to perform satisfactorily, the boss will suffer because he or she is accountable for all work performed in his or her department. For starters, don't ask to take over an assignment unless you believe you can handle it effectively.

Once you have identified tasks your boss is performing that you know you can perform well, select an appropriate time to ask for the take-over. An ideal time is when your boss is overloaded with work and beginning to falter because of his or her burdensome work load.

Milt Grabs a Nice Chunk of Work. Working as a psychiatric social worker in the neuropsychiatric ward of a general hospital, Milt was miffed at his psychiatrist boss, Dave. Milt was interested in developing himself professionally by taking on interesting therapy cases of his own. But before Milt (or any other professional on the ward) could be assigned a case, Dave would have to approve. As time wore on, it became apparent to Milt that Dave would only refer the most hopeless cases to him—precisely those people who had a negligible chance of benefiting from psychotherapy. In contrast, Dave would hoard the intriguing and healthiest patients for his personal case load.

An open person both by training and personal inclination, Milt broached this topic with Dave on several occasions. Each time Dave responded that great selectivity had to be exercised in assigning patients to psychiatric social workers and that most therapy patients were better suited for therapy with a psychiatrist than with a social worker.

Milt, nevertheless, persisted. He realized that Dave's pronouncement was basically a rationalization. Research had long since proved that the competence of the therapist was more important than his or her field of speciality in influencing whether or not a patient was helped.

A situation finally developed that gave Milt a valid opportunity to handle a wider variety of cases. Due to a cutback in federal and state funding, the hospital mandated a freeze on hiring. Simultaneously, the same economic phenomenon—hard times—created an increased supply of patients on the ward. With the increased stresses of inflation, unemployment, and the threat of unemployment, the inpatient population rose 25 percent.

As Dave became increasingly harassed, Milt moved into action. One day, on ward rounds, he casually mentioned to his boss, "Dave, things are looking more hectic than ever on our ward. My individual patient case load is low despite how busy you are. Perhaps I can take over some of your work load."

Dave responded, "Good enough. Tell Nurse Higgins you'll be taking the next four patients requiring individual therapy." The precedent set a pattern. Dave became permanently less selective about which clients were referred to Milt. Now Milt gets his share of both the curables and the uncurables even though Dave still works with only the curables.

PAY YOUR BOSS AN HONEST COMPLIMENT

Why would anyone want to compliment an ineffective boss? One important reason is that ineffective people tend to become more defensive and more ineffective when they receive no praise for what they are doing. Never receiving compliments from anybody can be a nagging source of stress in a job environment. Aside from being altruistic, you could be improving your own chances for success in your company.

Even if your boss is ineffective, his or her evaluation of you is given some weight by the organization. An ineffective boss rating your performance "superior" still beats an ineffective boss rating your performance with "fails to meet company expectations."

To implement this strategy, look for something that your boss has done well, however minor, and pay an appropriate compliment. Even a generally ineffective boss does a few things that help the organization. Here are a few examples to give you the proper mental set:

Subordinate to boss of overworked department: "Clyde, I must say you give us enough work to keep us busy in this department. Some departments in our company are overstaffed, and job monotony is the result. Everybody in our department has enough work to keep busy."

Subordinate to boss who never works overtime: "Sara, I do appreciate the way you have set the tone for people leaving promptly at quitting time. I have heard several positive statements from my coworkers about the fact that we are not expected to work late. You don't find anybody in our department doing busywork after hours just to look good."

Subordinate to boss who approved salary increase for him: "Mark, my latest payroll slip showed a $100 per month raise. I really appreciated it. I recognize that it's not easy for a manager to get an increase approved these days. Money isn't the only reason I'm working, but it puts my mind at ease to know how I'm going to pay for my daughter's orthodontia bill."

BECOME YOUR BOSS'S SIDEWALK THERAPIST

A sidewalk therapist is a person who in casual settings helps people with personal problems. A bad sidewalk therapist offers a lot of advice and makes many suggestions such as "If your boss is really that bad, just tell him to go to hell and walk out the door." Even worse: "You didn't ask me, but I think the problem with your career is that inconsiderate husband of yours. Chuck him, and you'll be better off."

Direct advice like the two foregoing examples is rarely listened to unless the person is mentally set to accept such advice. Therefore, your advice won't do much harm. At the other extreme, if your unsolicited advice is accepted, it could be damaging to the person you are attempting to help. Quitting your job or leaving your spouse are shocking life changes that should be carefully planned, with viable alternatives chosen.

A good sidewalk therapist simply listens sympathetically to his or her distressed friend or boss. Frequently, that is all the distressed person is seeking—somebody to act as a sympathetic listener. Ineffective bosses often have many problems they would like to talk about with the right person. If you're the right person, the result could be an easier boss to live with and a bolstering of his or her perception of you.

How Do You Get Your Boss to Discuss His or Her Personal Problems with You? My strategy for getting your ineffective boss (or even an effective one) to divulge his or her personal concerns to you is so simple that you might wonder why more people aren't using this technique.

First, you need a sympathetic-looking face and a relaxed manner. Practice by looking into the mirror at your "listening expression." If you need a few tips, watch almost any television actor or actress playing the role of a sympathetic listener. Eye contact is very important. If you keep your eyes focused on a person without a glaring stare, he or she will interpret your actions as being a listener. Remove sun or dark prescription glasses. Eye contact is difficult to maintain through a filter.

Second, you need a good setting for listening. A natural time to begin your sidewalk therapy would be after discussing a work-related matter in your boss's office. Lunch or an after-work drink are okay if your boss initiates the occasion. Inviting your boss out to lunch or for an after-work drink for the purpose of listening to his or her problems is awkward.

Third, you need a few good conversation openers. Remember that they have to be low-key because an unwritten law in almost all organizations is that the person with higher rank has the right to ask prying questions. You might want to try one or more of the following nonthreatening approaches.

You, speaking at the end of a conversation about a routine work problem: "I've got a question for you. As department head, what's the biggest problem you face on your job?"

You, standing in the hallway: Your boss approaches, looking as if he or she were in terrible emotional shape: "It looks like you're facing a lot of biggies today. Why don't you come on into my office for a cup of coffee and get out of the rain for awhile." (*Caution:* Use only when your boss is particularly in need of help. Otherwise, he or she might resent your volunteering shelter.) Once your boss does come in out of the rain, you might ask, "What are you faced with today?"

You, seated in a restaurant with your boss (he or she suggested the luncheon): "You must get a lot of pressure in your job. What is it like facing those pressures day after day?"

You, seated next to your boss in a bar (he or she suggested you two drop in for a drink after work): "I know you must have something pretty big on your mind to take time out for a drink. Would you like to share it with me?"

You, seated in your boss's office after a discussion about a problem you are having with another department: "Thanks for listening to me about my problem. It must get tiresome doing all the listening. If we could switch chairs, what would you like to tell me about?"

CONFER WITH YOUR BOSS'S BOSS

When the situation is serious and other strategies have failed, you may have to confer with your boss's boss about the former's deviant behavior. In extreme cases of managerial ineffectiveness, upper management usually has some inclination that a problem exists, but they may need corroborative evidence. Alcoholism, drug addiction, and sometimes compulsive gambling fit into this category.

Oscar's Department Was Drowning in the Boss's Alcoholism. Oscar was a project leader in the Chemistry Department of the Research and Development Division of a large company. All the people in his department were aware that their boss, Jason, had a serious drinking problem. As Jason's absenteeism and tardiness mounted, people in the department (including Oscar) waited eagerly for Jason's boss to take action about the situation.

Questions went unanswered, and decisions were left pending as Jason's situation steadily deteriorated. Oscar and another project leader were running the department the best they could, but their alcoholic boss served as a final roadblock on many important matters. Oscar felt that unless Jason were rehabilitated or removed, the reputation of the entire department would suffer.

Oscar Takes Action. Encouraged by a friend to be open about the problem, Oscar requested a conference with his boss's boss to discuss an urgent sensitive situation. The manager in question said, "Would an hour from now be okay?"

In conference, Oscar said: "I'm not here to tell tales out of school, but to talk about a serious problem we're having in our department. Jason, my boss and your subordinate, needs help. You're the logical person to get the process started. His drinking problem is hurting the performance of our entire department."

"How serious is the problem?" asked the executive.

"So serious," replied Oscar, "that we might as well not have a boss. Jason is gone or unavailable about two-thirds of the time. You can't depend on him anymore."

However risky this maneuver sounds, it often works. Jason was demoted to a technical position in another part of the company. A company doctor encouraged him to attend a clinic for alcoholics. Today he is a nondrinking alcoholic who has not had a drink in over 18 months. He regards Oscar as having saved his career.

Combating Sexism

7 "Why should I have to do things to get ahead that my male colleagues don't have to do? I resent the fact that a woman sometimes has to approach her job differently from the way a man does just to gain the same amount of recognition or any other goodies the company has to offer. Why should I go along with an injust system?"

These comments made by a middle manager in an insurance company during a management development workshop seem reasonable enough—but they deal with the world as she would like it to be rather than as it exists. Despite many recent advances made by women into higher-paying and more responsible jobs, some subtle and overt job discrimination against women still exists.

A woman intent upon climbing the organizational ladder must, therefore, use two broad sets of strategies to achieve her goal. First, she must make good use of the unisex strategies (those that apply equally well to males and females) described in the beginning of this book. Second, she must make judicious use of strategies designed specifically to combat sexism—the belief that males and females should play distinctly different roles in work organizations (and in society in general).

A cautionary note. A woman will need to exercise some selectivity in choosing which of the antisexism techniques presented

in this chapter are best suited for her individual style of operation. Should a woman reader's career already be proceeding
with the pace and direction she desires, she might use these
tactics as a checklist to see if there is anything she might use
for even further advancement.

HAVE A BATTLE PLAN AGAINST SEXIST PUT-DOWNS

As a starting point in your fight against sexism on the job,
you will do well to have a six-part battle plan. With practice,
these strategies will come to you almost automatically.

1. *Confront the sexist thinking.* Many people remain sexists because they are unaware that their thinking is laced with sexism.
Confronting a person with the sexist aspect of his or her opinion, belief, or attitude can prove valuable in starting the process
of change. The key principle is for you to focus carefully on the
sexist aspect of such a person's statement. Specifically, you
want to communicate that a statement of his or hers implies
that different rules apply for males and females in the situation
at hand. Here it is in action:

Male controller to female budget analyst: "Say, I'm not sure we can
let you out on the shop floor. When the fellows at the machine
see you, they won't be able to concentrate on their work."

Budget analyst to controller: "Perhaps, but I haven't noticed the
women in the office unable to concentrate on their work when
you sit on their desks. I think you have as much sex appeal as
I do. Why is my situation different?"

2. *Counter with a question.* Asking a person a specific, well-
focused question is a marvelous way of jolting his or her thinking. Asking the right question is a more effective way of helping
someone remove his or her sexist blinders than calling them
"old-fashioned" or "sexist." Perhaps the most well-intended
sexist slur is to tell a professional or management woman that
she "thinks like a man." Here is the type of question you might
raise the next time you receive a sexist compliment of this
nature.

Male executive: "Bev, I must say you think like a man."

Bev (a female executive): "Which particular man? A welder? A dishwasher? A physicist? A marketing executive? It makes an all-important difference to me. Could you please be more specific?"

3. *Fight prejudice with facts.* A relevant fact in response to a sexist put-down is a valuable tool in combating everyday sexism. Keeping abreast of feminist literature is a good way of having a ready supply of facts. At a minimum, read at least one book containing statistical facts about women at work. Should you be applying for a new position, you could then deftly handle a situation such as this:

Personnel manager to job applicant: "You seem well qualified for the job. We might be interested in hiring you, but quite frankly we need somebody permanent in this job. You'll undoubtedly leave us once you have a baby."

Job applicant: "I disagree. Should my husband and I decide to have a child, I could very well be back within two months. Over 12 million mothers in the United States hold full-time jobs. My situation would hardly be unique."

4. *Avoid oversensitivity.* Not every comment that alludes to a woman's charm, physical attractiveness, or other apparent feminine quality should be interpreted as a sexist put-down. Sexism does not underlie every gesture made toward the social rather than the professional role of a woman in business.

Assume a male purchasing agent at his first meeting with a saleswoman for industrial solvents is struck by her physical appearance. Here are two ways of her handling the situation:

Oversensitive reaction from sales representative: "My appearance has nothing to do with industrial solvents. Your comment sounds male chauvinistic to me."

Constructive reaction: "Thank you. A compliment is always welcomed. I've come here to talk about your requirement for solvents."

5. *Avoid the overkill.* When your rejoinder to a sexist comment approaches the intensity of a vicious counterattack, you may lose the advantage you hoped to gain. Look for a rejoinder that

jolts but does not alienate your sexist adversary. Assume a coworker says to Marian: "You know Marian, I wish you would quiet down a bit in meeting. I kind of dislike agressive women."

Less effective rejoinder: "I get the distinct impression that your masculinity is threatened when you have to deal with females on an equal footing."

More effective rejoinder: "Okay, you may dislike women being on an equal footing with men. But you may have to live with it. More and more women are learning that it is perfectly accept-able to express their opinions on an equal footing with men."

6. *Mock the opposition.* Quick-witted women can sometimes circumvent sexist thinking and behavior by gently mocking a statement made by a sexist. As with any other strategy for overcoming job discrimination against women mentioned in this chapter, *try what you think will work best for you.* If humor is your forte, try gentle mockery as a way of getting a person to see the illogic of his or her sexist antics. Here is a sample approach.

Senior vice-president of a casualty insurance company: "I'm sorry Cindy, despite the fact that you are well suited to the invest-ment field, we would prefer not to appoint you portfolio man-ager. Off the record, many of our policy holders would object to having a woman manage the financial fate of this prestigious company."

Cindy: "You might be making a serious strategic error. Just think. Last year the value of stocks in your portfolio declined 12 percent. If I had been in charge, people could have blamed the decline on women's intuition instead of faulty financial management."

USE REJOINDERS TO SEXIST PUT-DOWNS

Now that you have a general battle plan, on to 25 specific rejoinders that can be used while applying for a job or in an actual job setting.

1. *Employment interviewer to applicant for a managerial position:* "The next time we get a call for a woman executive, we'll be in touch with you."

Rejoinder: "Perhaps I didn't make my intent clear. I am looking for an executive position. It doesn't matter to me whether the prior incumbent of the job was male or female. Besides, is it legal in this state to hire an executive by sex?"

2. *Future manager to female job applicant:* "Oh, and one more thing to remember. Knitting is not allowed on company time even if there is not work to do in the department."

Rejoinder: "That's an interesting rule. What rules does your company have about what we are *not* supposed to do when the work is slow? By the way, is it just knitting or all hobbies that are taboo during normal working hours?"

3. *Company recruiter to female business school graduate:* "You will be pleased to know that our company has some very interesting jobs for women."

Rejoinder: "Fantastic, but I would be much more interested in knowing what interesting jobs in your company are *not* open to women."

4. *Sales manager to candidate for sales job:* "I'd like to hire you for this sales opening, but some of the wives would complain if there were a woman attending the sales convention with their husbands.

Rejoinder: "It sounds like that's more of a problem for the salesmen than for the company. Can a modern company allow policy to be dictated by a handful of women with old-fashioned beliefs?'"

5. *Job interviewer:* "Will your husband let you work an occasional Saturday morning?"

Rejoinder: "Definitely. My husband and I have a marvelous agreement. We have mutually agreed to allow each other to eat, sleep, play, and work as we see fit providing we use mature judgment. Why don't you give my husband a call?"

6. *Employment interviewer to middle-aged job applicant:* "Madam, are you still capable of having babies?"

Rejoinder: "Thank you so much for your interest in my reproductive system. I am capable of both having and *not* having babies. I am also capable of letting my hair grow to knees' length. What information could I give you about my job-related skills?"

7. *Head of department to college professor:* "I understand you just had a paper accepted for publication in the *Harvard Education Review.* That certainly is exceptional for a woman with three children."

Rejoinder: "Why? Ralph Bartow, the most published member of our department has four children. Is it that you think interest in children and career are mutually exclusive? Maybe this is a subject you and I could profitably conduct research about."

8. *Man to a woman at an interdepartmental meeting:* "Before I help you with your chair, Honey, tell me, are you a women's libber?"

Rejoinder (in a loud voice): "Oh, you big gallant man. A handsome sex object like yourself can do whatever pleases his fancy. Before we go any further with our relationship, tell me do you belong to SEAM (the Society for the Emancipation of the American Male)?"

9. *Man at lunch with career woman:* "You're not one of those women's libbers are you?"

Rejoinder: "I'm not very comfortable with labels, but I do believe in the Constitution, the Bill of Rights, Amendments to the Constitution, and the state and federal laws. Does that make me a member of the women's movement?"

10. *Executive to female assistant at performance review time:* "Marlene, you are so capable you could almost be an executive in this company."

Rejoinder: "I appreciate that compliment coming from a company executive. But please tell me, Why the *almost?* What credentials or experience am I lacking to qualify for an executive position? Let me know now if the *almost* refers to something I can't change about myself like my age, nationality, height, number of fingers, or sex. I've heard of a department head opening in administrative services that I would like to throw my hat in the ring for."

11. *Female boss to subordinate who has been quite critical of a male manager's thinking during a recent meeting:* "Don't you realize it's not very feminine to challenge a man's ideas?"

Rejoinder: "I get the impression you equate femininity with being passive. I can't agree that femininity or masculinity has anything to do with intellectual honesty."

12. *Male computer programmer to other members of a small department during a holiday luncheon gathering:* "Listen folks, if Linda weren't here today, I'd really have a story to fit this occasion."

Rejoinder (by Linda): "Joe, relax. Forget your inhibitions about telling sex jokes in front of women. Do you realize that, according to recent statistics, 50 percent of all people engaged in heterosexual acts are women?"

13. *Salesman demonstrating new camera to photo wholesaler:* "Despite the fact that this camera incorporates some of the most modern technological advances in the field, almost any woman can operate it without difficulty."

Rejoinder (by female company buyer): "Your camera seems more advanced than your understanding of human aptitudes. I would say your camera can be successfully operated by people of low mechanical aptitude. Many women are all thumbs when it comes to cameras, but so are many men. You need to do your homework about individual differences among people."

14. *Office manager to newly appointed personnel manager:* "Evelyn, we are planning to have your office painted a pale green. Is that okay with you? How well will it go with your new fall wardrobe?"

Rejoinder: "I appreciate your conscientiousness in taking a survey of wall color preferences before doing the actual painting. But tell me, do you routinely ask male managers how well the wall color matches their tastes? I'm more concerned about the relationship between wall color and employee morale."

15. *Female office manager to female secretary:* "I noticed that the outfit you are wearing today is on the racy side. There are certain standards of decorum we must adhere to in this company. I wish you would conduct yourself in a more ladylike manner."

Rejoinder: "I'm wearing virtually the same outfit some of the young men in this company wear. Is there a move on in this company also to tone down the dress of men?"

16. *Male executive speaking to man from another department:* "I'll have my girl bring you up a sandwich. What would you like? By the way maybe she can also get us some cigarettes. Did you hear us, Ruth?"

Rejoinder (by Ruth, age 43): "While I'm at it, boss man, could either of you gentlemen use new shoe laces, razor blades, or refills for your ball pens so long as I'm going downstairs anyway? I am here to please. By the way does that *boy* with you need his airline reservations confirmed?"

17. *Male chief of surgery to female first-year surgical resident:* "Whatever made you become a doctor instead of a nurse?"

Rejoinder: "That's easy to answer, Dr. Wick. I have known ever since I was a child that I liked medicine. It is common knowledge that the prestige and income of doctors are the highest of any job in the medical field, including nursing. You could say it's just a question of pride and money."

18. *Female secretary to account executive during lunch:* "Tell me, just between us. Why don't you stop trying to compete with men?"

Rejoinder: "Because they have most of the good jobs in this company. When I make my break and find a company where women have most of the good jobs, I'll compete with women."

19. *Boss to subordinate:* "When I get you this raise, you'll be able to buy that fancy clothing you have probably been wanting."

Rejoinder: "Wishful thinking on your part, Harry. Like the two out of three other working women who are single, divorced, separated, or widowed, I need the money for the necessities of life."

20. *Manager to female subordinate at beginning of performance appraisal review:* "Gloria, I'm going to have to give you a below average rating for the year. That also means you won't get a raise. Please don't cry."

Rejoinder: "My reaction is one of anger, not of tears. Incidentally, I have never seen a woman cry because she didn't get a raise, but I have seen a man go off on a two-day drunk because of the same problem. The next time a woman cries in your office during a performance appraisal, could you please call me into the office. I'm writing a term paper called "The Emotionally Unstable Employee."

21. *Principal of textile company to saleswoman:* "Barbara, we *need* the business. Do anything you can. If you have to, sleep with their buyer."

Rejoinder: "All right, Leo, but my call girl fee is $75. I want that added on to my regular commission. If their buyer proves to be a dud in bed, I want my fee and commission doubled. Is it a deal?"

22. *Department head to woman who has just received a promotion:* "Annette, soon you'll be earning as much as any man in the department."

Rejoinder: "Wonderful. It's good to know that our company will soon be complying with the law."

23. *Angry boss to cost estimator:* "If you weren't a lady, I'd chew you out for the mistake you just made. It cost the company $3,000."

Rejoinder: "I'd wish you would give me the punishment I deserve. It's your hang-up, not mine, that you think a woman doesn't want to be held responsible for her mistakes. I deserve the same treatment—good or bad—that you give to male employees."

24. *Male high school teacher to female high school teacher:* "Joan, will you get me a xerox copy of this article?"

Rejoinder: "Okay, John, providing you sharpen some pencils for me. Let's exchange these minor errands."

25. *Male junior executive to female junior executive in company cafeteria:* "I may appear to be a male chauvinistic pig, but don't you really think a woman's place is in the home?"

Rejoinder: "Well stated. You do appear to be a male chauvinistic pig."

PRACTICE GAMESWOMANSHIP

Several approaches to combating sexism in the office are particularly necessary for or well suited to women. Eventually, as the world becomes less sexist, *gameswomanship* will become less necessary. Once more sexist barriers are lifted, these techniques can be replaced with *gamespersonship*. A good tactician will always have the best chances for success in business or work of any kind.

Outperform Males.   Placed in competition with males for more money and better jobs, a woman will find her most logical and effective strategy is to outperform the opposition. Edythe R. Peters of the University of California, Irvine, has lived by this philosophy that she also espouses for other women. She notes, "All the arguments in the world are not as effective as just doing a good job at whatever you do. It makes me angry that we still have to function almost as superwomen simply to demonstrate that we can do whatever it is men are trying to do. But if superwomen are needed, then we will become superwomen."

Humanize Work Relationships.   The ultimate answer to combating sexism in the world of work is to create jobs for people—not for males or females. Women will no longer have to compensate for being female when femaleness or maleness is not an important issue with respect to job qualifications or work relationships.

Mildred, a microbiologist, explains it this way: "When I'm on a project with men, I ease off that preposterous notion that a female scientist has a different point of view from that of a male scientist. I quietly stress the ideas that I am a scientist. Being male or female has nothing to do with my professional decisions. My favorite comment in this regard is 'My reaction to this problem as a microbiologist is . . .' "

Expect Equal Treatment.   People often treat you in the manner in which you expect to be treated. Women who expect to be treated as equal to males often project an image of self-confidence that helps them receive such treatment. The woman who walks into a meeting with a self-assertive, positive air will probably not be asked to serve coffee or take notes.

Asked how she was able to get hired as the first female

consultant in a management engineering firm, Kathy replied: "I just never expected they would not hire me. It was no shock to me that somebody would give me something important to do. As a senior in college, I ran for president of the student association. I did not consider myself a 'girl candidate,' nor did the other students regard me this way. I was simply a competent person trying to bring about some changes in campus life."

Look for the Woman's Angle. Rosalind said to the president of the steel fabricating firm where she worked, "Gary, I think if I took over the office manager vacancy, it could do this outfit a lot of good. As we all know, if Bernie (the last incumbent) hadn't quit, we would have had a mutiny on our hands. Poor Bernie's biggest mistake was thinking that running an office was a battlefield and he was a master sergeant. I want that job both as a source of income and a challenge. Because I have a nice family and a home, I'm not a power-hungry person. I want peace around here, not a day-by-day harangue with the office staff."

By playing the woman's angle—emphasizing that she would be less power-oriented than a man might be in such a position —Rosalind executed a deft act of gameswomanship.

Insurance claims adjusting is another field that is ripe for feminization. Robyn, now a claims manager, explains it this way: "When I entered the field, I pointed out to my prospective employer that a woman's ability to communicate understanding and sensitivity might serve to lower the dollar amount asked for in some claims. I also explained that a sympathetic, responsive claims adjuster might be a good first-line defense against some kinds of claims exaggerations. Many people inflate their claims because they feel that the insurance company is not sympathizing with their problem. At a minimum, a sympathetic woman can leave the accident victim with a feeling that the insurance company cares."

Lower the Tone of Your Voice. Flying out of New York City a couple of years ago, I was seated next to Susan, an ambitious attorney from Legal Services (an outfit connected with the federal government). Her favorite approach to games-womanship can be recommended for a variety of situations. When Susan encounters an ornery judge in a tough negotiating session, she gradually lowers the tone of her voice. Somehow low tones in our society are associated with maturity and forcefulness whereas high-pitched (shrill) tones are associated with less mature and less forceful behavior.

Soft-Pedal Power Tactics.   An absolute last resort to use in your battle against office sexism is to take collective action against your employer or to file a formal complaint of discrimination with a government agency. Power tactics may be justified when a low-key strategy won't work. However, your own career may be severely jeopardized in your firm even if you do create better opportunities for women who follow in your footsteps.

Molly, a computer scientist, offers an admonition—based on her personal experiences—about forming a woman's caucus (one form of a woman's action group):

> Any woman who starts a woman's caucus in her own company is doing a great service for her sisters who were not directly involved in its formation. A woman can almost bet on being sent to a Corporate Siberia if she instigates an action group in her company. No employer would have the guts to fire her outright, but she might be the first to go in the next retrenchment.
>
> But the lot of other women will be improved, making it all worthwhile if you aren't a selfish person and really believe in the cause of feminism.

SENSITIZE YOUR BOSS WITH COMMENTS

Following both the logic and specific ideas presented earlier in this chapter, you can combat sexism at its source by a well-timed retort. Sensitizing works something like the process of inoculating a population against smallpox. Millions of people have to endure a comfortable jab in order to conquer a major social problem.

Presented next is some verbal vaccine to prevent the reoccurrence of a sampling of sexist practices. If one assumes that these comments are gently entered into conversation over a period of time, the sexist boss may develop some insight into what he (in rare instances, she) is doing wrong. At least they are worth a try.

Business conference: "I wish we could make some arrangement other than my having to serve coffee and take notes at every meeting. I don't mind taking my turn, but why should an assistant vice-president also perform the duties of a coffee wagon girl and department stenographer?"

Luncheon setting: "It really isn't necessary to pay for me every time we have lunch together. I see our luncheons as primarily a business meeting. I appreciate your generosity, but I would only feel comfortable having you always pay for my lunch if you also paid for men when you took them to lunch."

Staff meeting: "Please don't ask me to present the 'woman's view' on every issue that comes up in a staff meeting. It would make more sense to me if you asked me to predict how a professional woman might feel about a particular product idea. But what you really seem to be asking me is to present the view of the full-time homemaker with three children. I have no children, and I probably do less housework than anybody in the group."

General discussion: "A sense of humor is a quality to admire in a boss, Mitchell, but your joke about painting the computer pink because I was promoted to data-processing manager made me wince. Once in a while that kind of joke is fun, but why not sometimes direct a joke at a male?"

Confidential discussion with boss: "Sydney, everybody appreciates a pat on the head for a job well done, but I don't appreciate a pat on the buttocks everytime nobody is looking. If patting people on the rear is a company practice and you also did it to the men in the department, I would be more willing to accept it."

Woman's office: "Please don't make such a big production out of lighting my cigarette. If you feel natural lighting my cigarette and it's convenient, do it. But don't feel compelled to stretch across my desk just to light my cigarette. Last time you did that you were almost impaled on my pen."

Boss's office: "I know you mean well, Todd, but please spare me those long patronizing explanations about simple business matters unless you do the same thing for men. For instance, the last time we conferred about a business problem, you spent ten minutes telling me the difference between return on capital and return on sales. One of the reasons I was hired for this job was for my knowledge of business finance."

Secretary's desk: "I've checked my entire body for a serial number that indicates I am your property. Because I am unable to locate such identification and I have signed no papers indicating such ownership, please don't refer to me as 'My girl' when talking to other people in the company. I'm your secretary."

SHARE A JOB WITH A FRIEND

Women are often discriminated against because their lifestyle does not allow commitment to a full-time job. For example, a divorcée with three children at home may find that she needs a high-paying 20-hour-per-week job. Sharing a job is a constructive way of redesigning a job that will allow two women who can only devote part time to a job to have an exciting job challenge. (Part-time work done on the job premises is usually low-paying and not very exciting.)

Two women, Gladys and Janice, share a position as advertising manager in a photographic supply company. An outstanding advantage in such an arrangement is that the company gets an output in excess of the equivalent of one full-time person. Two people working half time will usually produce more than one person working full time, particularly in creative work.

As Gladys explains: "Both Janice and I will admit it. The job calls for coming up with new ideas. Usually, the big ideas pop into view when your mind is fresh. Neither of us comes back to work feeling logy from a two-martini lunch. Also, we have no time to fritter away in water cooler or coffee conversations with other people. I'm a morning person, and Janice is an afternoon person. Gem Photographic Supply gets us both at our peak periods of productivity."

ACT CAREER-MINDED

Successful people exude enthusiasm for their careers by both their spoken words and a variety of actions. An important way of appearing (and, more important, actually *being*) career-minded in a large organization is to request that the company give you a chance to attend a work-related seminar, convention, or trade show. This bit of gameswomanship is particularly effective when you can point to some specific benefit you hope to derive from that company-sponsored time away from the office.

Marlene impressed her boss with a request of this nature: "Dan, I heard that the American Management Association is holding a first-rate conference on management by objectives for administrative assistants. This is something I'm sure we could use around here. I would like to attend."

Nancy failed to impress her boss in making a request for attendance at the same conference: "Dan, I heard that the management club is running something up in Toronto for three days. I've never been to Toronto. How about it?"

Sandy Sports a Career Person's Symbol. In order to act career-minded, you sometimes have to look career-minded. One young, attractive woman in public relations uses a devastatingly simple technique of appearing like somebody of higher than clerical rank. Sandy, in talking about how frequently she was at first thought to be a typist, recounts: "I purchased an attaché case that does not resemble an oversized handbag. I carry it with me continuously. It may sound minor, but from that time on I found fewer surprised looks when I told clients I would be working on their account. It's all part of the game. An attaché case makes you appear businesslike."

GET ASSIGNED TO CREATIVE WORK

Naomi worked her way into the computer science field because she intuitively recognized the career thrust creative work can provide a woman:

> Anyone can sit around and grumble about being a secretary and not go anywhere. I've no sympathy for them. I began in the company at the lowest possible rating in an area that had never had a woman employee in the 26 years of its existence.
>
> Believe me, it was not heaven. In four months I had volunteered myself for other jobs, and people became aware of my creative potential. I moved into a job operating computers. I had programming in school, and I took it upon myself to get books and learn a new computer language completely on my own.
>
> I requested formal training. Now after a little over two years with the company, I am being transferred into a job where I will have a professional standing. I owe a lot to the "movement" and to my genuine desire to succeed.

HANDLE MALE INSECURITIES

"Ben, the head of the shipping department in my company, seemed so nervous and uneasy when I showed him my plan for improving the work flow in his area. I wondered if he were having heart palpitations or some kind of anxiety attack. He became red in the face and started to express anger. It finally dawned on me that Ben wasn't just reacting to the changes that I was proposing for shipping goods out the door. They were bound to improve his operation and make him look better in the long run. The source of his concern was that a woman was giving him advice about running his operation."

Lisa, a systems analyst in an industrial pump company, made the above comments in a discussion session about handling sensitive interpersonal problems. The scenario she reports is oft repeated in principle as an increasing number of women work their way into key jobs. Career women are sometimes put down, sidestepped, circumvented, or treated with hostility for reasons unrelated to any actions they have taken.

Many of the manifestations of antifemale prejudice they face are products of male feelings of insecurity. Men—certainly not all—feel insecure in the presence of a competent woman. A man of this predisposition has pangs of self-doubt when the possibility exists that a woman might in any way take away some of his power, imaginary or real. To combat sexism, a woman has to be able to detect and handle such male insecurity.

The Omnipotent Male Image. An unknown number of men express their insecurities by insisting that in cases of differences of opinion between males and females, the male is correct. Mysteriously, the male is endowed with or acquires a natural superiority over females in matters of judgment over a wide range of topics. One everyday manifestation of this attitude crops up in arguments about petty matters such as which brand of an industrial product should be purchased. Exhibiting his insecurities, the male says to the female, "For crying out loud, we'll do it my way. Men know better."

A counterattack to insecurity of this nature is for a woman to recognize her adversary's underlying need for reassurance while at the same time defending her point of view. Here is how it works.

Male lawyer to female lawyer: "Maggie, I think you're making a mistake in the way you're setting up that schedule of payments on the second mortgage for my client. These are tricky matters, and I've been paid to represent my client, as you've been paid to represent yours. Men usually have a much better grasp of the finances involved in closing a house; so here is the way we should do it."

Female lawyer to male lawyer: "Bruno, you're a very strong person [appealing to his need to assert his masculinity]. I certainly trust your judgment. But this is simply a legal issue in which we have equal experience. My method is quite orthodox, and I think both sides will be getting a fair shake if we use the method I am advocating. Would you be willing to take another look at what I've done?"

A Woman Might Steal My Job. A number of young

women in business have observed that they receive their best cooperation and support from the older, supposedly old-fashioned managers. A meditating reason is that some younger middle managers fear that women will effectively compete with them for the limited number of promotions available. Managers in their fifties are less concerned about being promoted; many have already reached their final placement in the hierarchy. The new generation of less sexist managers (junior executives or management trainees) are supportive of women. The middle group of managers—those in their late twenties or early thirties —are the most fearful that women might take their jobs.

What to Say If This Should Happen to You.   When it is apparent that a male manager fears that a woman may somehow steal his job and is, therefore, being uncooperative, it is crucial that a woman allay his concerns. A frontal attack such as "Don't worry. I'm not trying to steal your job" might be too obvious.

Assume that you (the female reader) are being interviewed for a job by a man. You sense some concern on his part that you could conceivably wind up taking over his job. To allay these fears, you might casually remark: "The job you're describing sounds exciting. It's something I would like very much because I need some marketing planning experience for a couple of years so that I can qualify for the job I really want. My ambition is to move to the West Coast as a sales manager. I've heard that working in your region is a good stepping-stone to getting there."

ASK FOR A BIGGER JOB

An effective way of liberating your boss from sexist attitudes about women is to let him know that you are available for promotion. Many women are bypassed in work organizations because managers above them assume they were not interested in more responsibility. There is nothing unethical, unbecoming, or uncouth about taking the initiative in asking for a promotion. Waiting around to be noticed because of your outstanding performance is often a feeble approach to accomplishing your objective of gaining more power, prestige, and money.

Miriam and Her Boss Are Both Shocked. Fired up because of a feminist book about career development she recently read, Miriam stormed into her boss's office one morning. She said with conviction, "I want a promotion to supervisor, and I want it now. I've been with the company four years, and my reputation is outstanding. I've earned a certificate in management from night school. I'm tired of being an administrative assistant when I could easily handle a supervisor's job. If you don't want me as a supervisor, some other company will."

Miriam's boss replied, "I agree you'd make a good supervisor. Why didn't you ever let us know before? We have two supervisory openings in the company right now. When would you like to start?"

Combating the Mid-Career Slump

8 Cliff, the 43-year-old chairman of the Department of Statistics at a small private college, confided to a friend during coffee:

It's getting harder and harder to face my job any more. A day like today is particularly bad. It's registration day, which means I have to face at least 30 students with the same dumb complaints about wanting the introductory statistics course waived. I'll hear the same laments over and over from students that they have a mental block against statistics.

Honestly, if I could do it, I would pass an edict that any student who did not want to take statistics would not have to. Students who do not want to take statistics and then find themselves on the verge of failing wind up in my office complaining that their professor was unreasonable.

But the issue is bigger than the problems of students with statistics. I thought that being a college department head would be a glamorous job. I figured that people would be asking me questions of profound importance that only a statistician would answer. I figured college professors would look up to me. Instead, the only questions I field are about as profound as whether or not I have the right change so that somebody can use the coffee vending machine.

The professors in my department look upon me simply as somebody who should be running errands for them. When I hand out raises, the faculty and staff in my department think I'm just passing on money handed down from higher-level college officials. My faculty has more sorrow than envy for me. Most of them know I don't make much more money than they do. Two of my professors are paid a few thousand more dollars per year than I am.

It's almost getting too late in my career to make a name for myself as a statistician. Besides, there are too many genius types in statistics nowdays. I just cannot compete intellectually with the best of the new crop of statisticians. And "quantitative people" are now found in almost every discipline—not just in departments of statistics. I'm beginning to feel like the athlete who tries to make his mark as a short-distance runner. Every major sport has runners who can run faster than he. The big difference is that they can also play another sport well.

My life at home has also headed down the path toward becoming an unglamorous routine. Althea and I have been married for 20 years. It's hardly a thrill waking up to the same woman for the seven thousandth time. I don't suspect she regards seeing me the first thing in the morning as a thrill any longer. All I have left of my dark curly hair is a smooth top and some gray sideburns. If I bought a hairpiece my friends would probably silently snicker.

"In one sense, Althea is more fortunate than I am. She began in real estate about seven years ago. She still gets a big thrill when she closes a sale. She is much more excited about her work than I am about mine. She's also more thrilled about her real estate than she is about me. I can't really blame her for her feelings.

"My two children are now teen-agers. They are both fine people, but they don't have much to do with me. Linda doesn't dislike me. She and I just don't have anything to talk about or do together. Scott is doing okay by his standards. He and his friends care very little about anything but sports. I've always been unathletic, and it's hard for me even to fake an interest in sports.

"I don't want you to think I'm some kind of depressed character who is ready to jump off a bridge. It's just that I feel as if I'm not headed anywhere in particular and that I've been nowhere in particular. I'd like to change things, but I don't know where to begin."

Cliff is less unique than he might think. Almost any career-minded person in his or her early thirties to early fifties can become entrapped in a mid-career slump. However, once a person recognizes what is happening to him or her, an escape route can often be found.

WHAT ARE SOME OTHER SYMPTOMS OF THE MID-CAREER SLUMP?

Two synonyms for the mid-career slump are the *mid-career crisis* and the *occupational blahs,* which gives some indication of the gravity of the problem. A person has usually fallen victim to the "slump" when he or she begins to ask a lot of questions about the meaning of work and personal life. Beneath it all is a bothersome feeling that one has landed on a plateau that is difficult to leave.

Dr. Theodore A. Jackson, an industrial psychologist who has been counseling managers for over 30 years, uses the term *middle-aged middle-management syndrome* instead of *slump.* Jackson describes it as "the general feeling of discontent and unhappiness these executives have concerning their jobs, the feeling of boredom and restlessness, the sense of entrapment, the absence of any significant challenge, and the vague dissatisfaction with the way their careers seem to have turned out. And it's all wrapped up in an overall distaste for getting up and going to work."

Faith Decorates Her Rear End.   Because the mid-career slump and the middle-age crisis are intertwined, it's not unusual for a person to exhibit the problem both on and off the job. Faith, a personnel manager in her late forties, was basically end played in her career (at least she felt that way). She was paid too much to take a comparable level job in most companies that might hire her. The only opening above her in her company that she could logically aspire to was vice-president of labor relations. Lacking a specialist's degree in labor relations, Faith had no hope of getting that position.

Faith's husband was preoccupied battling his own middle-age crisis. He bought a small red sports car, took up scuba diving as a hobby, and spent many an evening in discotheques watching other people dance. Faith's only child was away at college, which made a flight into mothering unnecessary.

Faith turned toward a younger mode of dress as a way of manifesting her mid-career, mid-life crisis. She outfitted herself with clothing bought in shops catering to the under 21 set. Among her favorite acquisitions were a pair of prewashed, pre-faded, prefrayed blue jeans with "Faith" embroidered across the seat.

Like her husband, Faith frequented discotheques. In addition, she began to spend Saturday afternoons browsing through record stores and Friday nights in singles bars populated by younger people.

Faith Has a Narrow Escape.   A nearly serious accident finally led to Faith's awakening that there were more constructive ways of her working through her existential (Who am I? Where am I going?) bind. Despite the questioning looks of the instructor, Faith took hang gliding lessons. On her first venture into flight, Faith rose four feet above the ground only to come hurtling down with her right leg pinned under her left thigh and her head bumped against a small rock.

While recovering, Faith developed a sensible plan of finding a new life-style. She shifted into a fashionable wardrobe and hairstyle appropriate to her age. She enrolled in a master's degree program in personnel administration. Also, she and her husband joined a rap group for married couples. Said Faith: "Bernie [her husband] and I profited from the group sessions. We suddenly learned that we weren't the only couple questioning what was happening to our lives. Once you recognize that it's natural to be concerned treading water in life, it doesn't hurt nearly as much."

HOW DOES METAPAUSE AFFECT A MAN'S CAREER?

Guidance Professor Dr. Edmond C. Hallberg uses the term *male metapause* to define the period when a man stops and thinks about his identity and direction—very similar in concept to climacteric or "change of life." According to Hallberg, symptoms of male metapause run the gamut from unhappiness at work to fear of losing sexuality.

The metapause-influenced male has subtle physical changes that are magnified by our youth-oriented society. "He's gaining weight. He's not climbing trees with the kids anymore. He may stay in shape, but it takes a lot longer." Many of these symptoms have a spillover on to the job. In his quest for excitement and thrills, the metapause male may exhibit poor judgment that can adversely influence his career.

Hollis Becomes One of the Boys. An inventory control manager, Hollis exhibited some classic symptoms of male metapause. Recently having left his wife of 15 years, Hollis took up mountain climbing in the search for a more adventuresome life-style. One summer he spent his three weeks of accumulated vacation on mountain climbing trips in the Canadian Rockies. Upon his return, he decorated his newly acquired apartment in a singles' complex with posters and bookcases made of brick and pine board. He outfitted himself in leisure suits for his return to work.

On the job, Hollis began to spend increasing amounts of time with people of lower rank and age than himself. He made regular excursions into the plant cafeteria to participate in the coffee break prattle of male and female clerical help. At lunch Hollis would frequently spend his time in conversation with workers and spent many a lunch hour picnicking on the shipping docks with the warehouse workers.

Asked by his boss why he was spending so much time with lower-ranking employees and so little time with management personnel, Hollis replied, "I'm trying to reach the people in this company who make the place actually work. You can't learn about the company by hiding behind your desk with the other members of the establishment. The action is with the troops."

Hollis Could Have Found Another Outlet for His Metapause. What Hollis had to say about maintaining contact with clerical and warehouse workers made good organizational sense. However, he could have found a less radical way of making such contact. Frequent job-related discussions with younger people would have been a productive way of his relating to younger people. Perhaps he could have joined a company bowling league and opted for membership on a younger team.

His leisure suit attire would be acceptable in most companies, but in his conservative manufacturing plant a manager wearing a leisure suit was viewed negatively by upper management. Hollis could have compromised by wearing other youthful attire such as bold plaid suits.

Hollis persisted in becoming "one of the boys" and consequently lost out in a department reshuffling. After a reorganization, his department shrank in size, which intensified Hollis's concern about being on a career plateau. His approach to dealing with his metapause was self-defeating.

HOW DOES MENOPAUSE AFFECT A WOMAN'S CAREER?

Like the male metapause, female menopause can influence a person's judgment on the job. However, because female climacteric has so long been recognized (whereas only recently has the same phenomenon in males been publicized), it is likely to be less shocking (more accepted) to the female system than is the male equivalent. Mid-career crisis is always the combined influence of physiological changes and concern about career progress. When a woman is concerned about physiological changes and career retardation, she could behave just as irrationally as a male with the same problem.

Rita Becomes a Pill.   Having worked her way up from a secretarial job in a travel agency, 48-year-old Rita was now the manager of a downtown office of the same agency. After running the office successfully for five years, Rita realized that she may have reached her final placement in the company. Unless she began a travel agency of her own—a step she thought beyond her financial means—Rita saw no way of advancing in her career.

Things were also not proceeding well for Rita on the personal side of life. Her romance with a lawyer friend was heading toward termination, and she recently underwent a hysterectomy. As Rita became increasingly irritable and unpredictable in her behavior, turnover in her office mounted.

Rita's boss, noticing the high turnover among personnel in her agency (along with complaints from a few irate customers about improperly scheduled travel arrangements), called for a conference. Rita's reaction to the turnover problem was cavalier: "It's difficult to get good help anymore. Many young people would rather be unemployed than stick with a demanding job."

The travel agency president believed that the problems must be deeper than Rita recognized or was willing to admit. He asked her permission to call in an industrial psychologist to investigate the nature of the organization problems that were creating turnover. Rolf, the psychologist, arranged individual and group interviews with Rita and other people in the suburban branch.

After one day's investigation, the nature of the problem was apparent. Ginger, a travel agent, confided to Rolf: "If you want to save this branch, stop wasting your time talking to the agents and the clerical help. Concentrate on Rita. She's the one with the problem. She moans and groans about every step we take. She finds fault with almost every travel package we set up. She's become so negative in her outlook that we've nicknamed her 'Rita the Pessimist.' "

Rita Gets Rejuvenated.   Counseling with Rolf about problems in her branch helped Rita realize that she was allowing her inner conflicts to interfere with her job effectiveness. As she proceeded about her supervisory and administrative work, Rita now tried to ask herself, "How would I evaluate this situation if I were in a good mood?"

The simple plan worked. Rita now carefully monitored her own behavior and was able to regain her former effectiveness. She's now concentrating on building up business in the agency and rebuilding her social life. With this new perspective, the passage of time seemed to help Rita with her problem.

WAIT FOR THE PROBLEM TO GO AWAY

A friend of mine says he enjoys being an internist because 75 percent of his patients' problems would go away even if he did nothing for them. Similarly, some cases of mid-career slump will go away without any planful effort on your part. Nevertheless, this represents a passive approach to working out a major life problem.

One reason that doing nothing sometimes helps you over your slump is that circumstances may change enough to alter one of the factors contributing to your problem.

Serendipity Rescues Gunther. A computer scientist by education and experience, Gunther found that his fast growth had cooled down. In a ten-year period he had received six promotions, but now his head was close to the ceiling. Because he was manager of systems and procedures, the next step up for him would be as a vice-president in a company the size of his present one or as the manager of systems and procedures of a larger company. Gunther liked the company he was working for and also liked his unique location—San Diego. Gunther cautiously explored bigger job opportunities for himself in San Diego, but he did not even turn up a warm lead.

In time, Gunther's concern about his professional future began to spill over into his personal life. He began to project blame onto his wife and children for making him geographically (and, therefore, occupationally) immobile. He even considered having an extramarital affair as a way of adding some spark to his life.

At the low point of his funk, Gunther became privy to an exciting development. Marvin, the vice-president of administration (and his boss), announced that he was leaving corporate life behind. On the basis of an unexpectedly large family inheritance, Marvin was buying an automobile dealership. He confided to Gunther, "I'm recommending you as my successor. You've performed well, and why bring in an outsider and stir up a lot of people for no good reason?"

Gunther came home in an ecstatic mood. All of a sudden, his career was off its plateau. As a consequence, he enjoyed his wife and children more than he had in the recent past. Gunther bought a new boat (to celebrate his promotion, not to express his mid-life slump) and scrapped his plans for an affair. His new job was providing him the extra kicks he was seeking.

IMPROVE YOUR PRESENT SITUATION

Your mid-career slump sometimes comes about because one or two major problems come to influence your total outlook adversely. If you can get down to the root cause and modify that situation, the other parts of your problem may fall properly into place. Improving your present situation is much less risky than revamping your entire life-style. If your solution doesn't work, at least you can maintain a holding pattern until you develop a sensible alternative.

Len Gets Lonely Beating the Bushes.   An outdoorsman all his teen-age and adult life, Len landed a sales job with a manufacturer of hunting and fishing attire. Len's job was quite simple in design. He was the Northwest representative for his company, calling on a couple of hundred sporting goods stores in northern California, Washington, Oregon, and Idaho. After ten years of good performance, Len faced a bothersome dilemma. As he told his career counselor:

> I've carved out a weird niche for myself in life. My job only takes about eight months a year. The rest of the time I'm off to pursue all the outdoor and family life I want. I make about $35,000 per year peddling fishing and hunting gear. Most people think I have it made. In a way I do, and in a way I don't.
>
> It's hard for me to accept the fact that I'll be calling on these same stores for the 20 working years I have left. It gets very lonely beating the same bushes year after year. I tell my friends about my predicament and they tell me to get a different job. Well, with luck maybe I could come up with a $10,000-per-year job in a different field. Besides, I do like the four months off per year to spend at my leisure. It's a lonely, depressing life with excellent fringe benefits.

Len Cures His Loneliness.   After listening to Len's problems, his counselor confronted him with a penetrating observation: "Beneath it all, Len, it sounds as if you are lonely. A person like yourself is perpetually out in the boondocks with very little contact with the home office. What you need is love, understanding, or at least some contact with the home office. Tell them that you insist on a quarterly meeting and at least a biweekly phone call with company officials. Anybody would run into a slump with a schedule like yours."

"You mean if I felt less isolated out in the field, I might be able to pick up my spirits and maybe keep going for a few more years?" queried Len.

Replied the counselor, "That's exactly what I mean. If the plan sounds good to you, why don't you make the suggestions about more contact with the home office tomorrow?"

Len's home office welcomed his suggestion and began a program of quarterly sales meetings despite the expense of bringing people together from all over the country. Len's feelings of alienation and loneliness (the real cause of his mid-career slump) soon diminished. His phone bill and travel vouchers are now higher, but so are his spirits. His company is saving money because his valued contribution to the company will be retained for an indefinite period.

CHANGE YOUR DEFINITION OF SUCCESS

The secret of success is to lower your goals. Although this statement sounds simplistic, it is based upon one of the few *proved* principles of human behavior. Satisfaction results when you achieve a goal *you* think is meaningful or worthwhile. Frustration (or slumps) results when you fail to achieve meaningful goals. Unfortunately for those suffering a mid-career crisis, lowering their goals is not so readily accomplished. My formula won't work unless one is truly happy with his or her lowered goals.

Mike Hears the Truth.   Burly Mike worked his way up the factory ladder from a tool- and diemaker to a plant superintendent. Mike's area of responsibility involved several hundred people, including seven foremen. As Mike approached age 50, he became despondent. He began to withdraw from regular contact with his foremen—a pattern of behavior at variance with Mike's usual person-to-person style of leadership.

Aside from losing close contact with his people, Mike became somewhat delinquent on many of his written reports to top management. Don, the plant manager, insisted that Mike and he go on a weekend fishing trip to work through some problems. By late evening of the first night, the leveling session with Don began.

"Mike, you crazy SOB, what's gone wrong?" asked Don in a paternalistic, concerned tone. "What's happened to Iron Mike, our best superintendent? He's acting like an Ivy League plant superintendent. Somebody who doesn't know that you can't run a plant unless you're in close touch with the foremen. Furthermore, why in hell are your reports late? I know we all hate filling out forms, but we've always been able to count on you in the past."

"Don, you've been honest enough to tell me how things really are. I'll return the favor," responded Mike. "I've been down in the dumps lately. All of a sudden, things are closing in on me. The only thing I see ahead of me is more of the same. I'll be superintendent of this plant until 1990, when company regulations will force me out the door. I want your job. I've got a lot of ambition left. It's discouraging when a man realizes he's topped out in a company that's been his whole life."

"Mike," continued Don, "Let me tell you about your future with us as I see it. Every member of management I've spoken to thinks you're a superb superintendent. We wouldn't take five bright young college graduates in an even trade for Mike. Despite all those good things I've said, we don't see you as having potential beyond your present job."

Mike asked with a perplexed expression, "Why the hell not?"

"Because," answered Don, "you've got two strikes against you. First of all, you lack a college degree. You can't become a plant manager or a front office executive in our company without a college degree. If the founder of our company quit and came back one year later trying to get an executive job with us, he would be turned down. However brilliant old Mr. Stone might be, he is not a college graduate. The second strike is that we see you as a diamond in the rough, a bull-of-the-woods type. That approach goes over big out on the shop floor, but it's not suited for the executive suite. In our opinion, Mike, you just don't have enough polish to be a front office executive."

Mike Realigns His Goals.   Don and Mike returned from the fishing trip on good terms. Mike appreciated being leveled with, and Don appreciated Mike's capacity to accept the truth. Within one week, Don noticed that Mike had returned to his same energetic self. He was back out on the shop floor in belly-to-belly discussions with his foremen. Mike caught up on his back reports, and his new weekly report was handed in promptly.

Don commented, "It's great to see the true Mike back in stride. What's happened?"

Mike answered, "Can't talk for long, Don. When I returned home last weekend, I decided to change my goals. I've decided to become the best superintendent this plant has ever had. If I waste too much time talking to my boss, I'll never make it."

IMPROVE YOUR PERSONAL LIFE

A career person's attitude toward his or her work can be influenced in a positive direction by an improvement in personal life. Although success in social life cannot fully compensate for failure in business life, an improved social life certainly helps the occupational blahs. A total cure for the mid-life crisis, usually requires an enrichment of both career and personal life.

Laird Raises His Frustration Tolerance.   Laird had become irritated, annoyed, and frustrated with his vice-principal position. As vice-principal, he was concerned mainly with discipline problems and minor administrative chores considered too unimportant for the principal, yet too important for the principal's secretary. He applied in vain for a series of principal jobs in other schools. Next he bought himself a quadraphonic stereo set that incorporated all the latest in high fidelity design. Still his annoyance on the job persisted.

Divorced for six years, Laird found his social life was mediocre. Quite suddenly, mediocrity turned into superiority. A 27-year-old woman was hired into the school as a replacement for a retiring social studies teacher. She immediately took a liking to Laird. Although he was older than her father, she regarded Laird's chronological age as a sign of maturity and wisdom.

Laird and Mona (the new English teacher) had an adventuresome time together exploring new restaurants, visiting discotheques, going on picnics, and finally merging households.

Laird's colleagues noticed that he now dressed better, looked more alert at staff meetings, discussed discipline problems with a more objective viewpoint, and looked upon minor administrative chores as challenging problems. As Laird said to the principal over morning coffee, "You're right. My spirits have picked up. Since Mona and I have been keeping company, little things don't bug me as much. Now when a teacher sends me a discipline problem that he or she should have handled, I look upon it as a learning experience for that teacher. In the past, I would have acted annoyed and dragged my heels."

Walt and His Wife Get Enriched. Approaching age 50, Walt had grown stale both in his career and personal life. A successful life insurance salesman (and recently also an estate planner), Walt did not see much change in his occupational future. He expressed it this way: "I've been doing a fair job of selling insurance for over 20 years. My income is fine, and I like the work, but it is getting monotonous. With all the money I'm making on renewals, I couldn't possibly afford to leave the business. But it is getting much harder to canvass for new business. I just don't have the spirit I used to."

Walt's personal life was going about as well as his life insurance selling. He had invested over 20 years in his relationship with his wife. Although there were few peak experiences left in their marriage, it was not bad enough to consider dissolution. Walt explains how an offhand suggestion by his wife became a turning point in their lives:

> Helen mentioned over cocktails one night that a couple we both know had spent a weekend at a Marriage Enrichment Group spon-

sored by the Catholic Church. But it had nothing to do with Catholicism. Somehow this couple came back from the weekend all charged up about each other and life in general. Helen shyly suggested that we ought to try something that worked so well for somebody else.

As a salesman, I'm always open to new experiences; so I told Helen to go ahead and make arrangements. She was surprised by my reply, but she took me seriously. We went away to the enrichment weekend a few weeks later.

My first reaction to the marriage group is that it would be just one big bull session. But after a while, I recognized it had some value. Like most of the people there, I cried and sobbed when I wrote down a list of all the reasons I wanted to go on living and all the good things about my wife. I was very surprised at all the good things Helen had to say about me.

The good feelings persisted long after the weekend was over. Helen and I are closer. I look forward to our times alone together. I feel as if I'm having an affair with my wife, and it's a wonderful feeling. We're now both more sensitive to each other. Because of my fun at home, I'm no longer as worried about stagnation on the job.

FIND SOME OUTSIDE THRILLS

When it appears that you might have to stay with your current job for an indefinite period of time despite your mid-career slump, off-the-job thrills can sometimes be helpful. Exciting hobbies can sometimes serve as a substitute for on-the-job thrills.

Marlene Finds the Right Thrills. Dutiful Marlene had worked as the head librarian in her high school for many years. Although she was well paid and well respected, the occupational blahs were beginning to take hold of Marlene. Finding a new job seemed like a remote possibility for the indefinite future. Marlene noted, "At $19,500 per year, my current earnings are too high to accept a beginner's job in another field. The last time there was a head librarian opening at the local university, the library received 200 resumes."

Marlene tried to withhold her laughter when a good friend

suggested that she take up reading as a serious hobby. Instead she searched for a hobby that was far removed from the main thrust of her occupation. Marlene took to the stock market. Naturally, she took out a few books about the market from her library. She carefully studied the business section of the newspaper every morning. After asking five different people for recommendations, Marlene settled on a stockbroker to advise her and execute her transactions.

As Marlene began to show a profit from her initial investment of $3,000, her enthusiasm for the stock market intensified. As she became increasingly knowledgeable about securities, her life seemed to take on a new dimension that even carried over onto the job. Marlene explains how: "My knowledge of the market now rivaled that of the economics teacher. In collaboration with him, I established an investment section of the high school library. We offered students current books and periodicals about investing. We also collected a current file of annual reports on local and some national companies. My hobby was now infusing some new life into my work."

Willy Gets Overthrilled.   Willy, a well-to-do pediatrician, tired of being a healthy-baby doctor. As Willy described it, "I enjoy the fact that I'm well respected and that I earn an above average income. But how many times in a life time should one person have to tell a mother not to worry about her child's illness and that all babies run fevers once in a while? It finally hit me that I was on a repetition cycle when I made a trip to the hospital to examine a newborn named Julius Schmidt. It was shocking to know that about 23 years ago I went to the same hospital to examine another newborn Julius Schmidt—his father."

As an antidote to his mid-career slump, Willy took up skiing. Willy's mistake was the depth of his plunge into skiing. His *raison d'être* became time on the slopes. He decorated his office with ski posters, and he wore ski sweaters in the office.

Willy's preoccupation with skiing began to impair his relationships with the other pediatricians in his group practice.

Three times in one month, Willy was late for his Monday morning hospital rounds because of a late return from a ski weekend. The next month he missed three days of office appointments because of a torn knee ligament. One of his colleagues commented to Willy, "As pediatricians, we can't afford to have one of our doctors acting in a childlike manner. Please make your choice soon between the practice of medicine or skiing."

Willy's antidote for his mid-career slump proved to be self-defeating. His disenchantment with his career intensified as his colleagues tried to control his off-the-job activities. Had Willy been able to pursue skiing with moderate intensity, it might have given him the extra excitement he needed in his life. Instead, it increased his job-related conflicts.

After his knee injury, Willy did restrain his skiing to the point that it did not interfere with his medical practice, but the damage had already been done. Willy's relationship with his colleagues was less mutually supportive than in the past.

CAREFULLY PLAN A JOB CHANGE

Properly executed, a job change can help a person emerge from a job slump. Frank, an electrical engineer in a large company, recognized that his talents were being underutilized. He spoke to his company about his being promoted from straight engineering to engineering management, but no changes were forthcoming. His company had considerably cooled off in growth, and many capable people were looking for administrative jobs.

Frank looked at the problem this way: "Just because the company has levelled off, it doesn't mean that I should level off in my career. At 35, I can't afford to stay in a straight engineering job much longer."

As an antidote to his problem, Frank registered with a technical employment agency in his city. Within three months the agency helped him gain employment as engineering manager in a small machine screw company. Frank was ecstatic, but six months later he resigned from the screw machine company. He returned to the employment agency, pleading with them to find him another engineering management position.

What Frank Should Have Done. Asked by the employment placement specialist what went wrong, Frank replied, "You didn't tell me the owner of that company was a despot. During the interviews he smiled nicely and told me that I would be in charge of everything in the company that related to engineering. But once I got there, the owner second-guessed me on everything. Worse than that, he ranted and raved like a maniac when something went wrong in the plant. Once when a major machine broke down, he expected me to get on my hands and knees and climb under the machine to repair the electrical wiring. I told him an engineering manager isn't supposed to be a maintenance man."

Frank's mistake was his lack of caution in checking out a new job. An intelligent approach for him would have been to gather as many facts as possible about the machine screw company that made him a job offer. He could have tried to learn the name of a few past or present company employees and have a candid discussion with them about the company. He might have spoken to a few of their customers or suppliers.

Frank made the classic mistake of many people caught in an unfavorable job situation. He grabbed the first job offer that came by. An antidote of this kind can be worse than the problem it was intended to solve.

FIND A NEW LIFE-STYLE

For some people, the only way out of a mid-life crisis is to catapult themselves into a radically new life-style. Thus "heading for the hills," "taking to the woods," or "leaving the rat race behind" have become shibboleths for an increasing number of middle-aged executives.

Rodney's Sensible Plan. Rodney struggled for over 20 years to climb the organizational ladder in a succession of big companies. At 47, he realized that it was not likely he would realize his ambition of becoming a high-level executive. His disenchantment with corporate life gathered momentum until it became a gnawing hatred. Rodney's wife, Cynthia, empathized with his disaffection. A fulltime volunteer, she also questioned the relevance of her life-style.

Both children were off to college and would be graduated within two years. Rodney and Cynthia carefully analyzed their assets and liabilities and decided they were in a position finally to lead a simple life. The equity in their house, alone, came to about $25,000. Six months later a new life-style had emerged for both of them. They are co-proprietors of Rodney's and Cynthia's Tackle Shop in the Adirondack Mountains.

During a holiday visit to his city relatives, Rodney commented about the success of his new life-style:

> Most people think we have dropped out of society, but Cynthia and I think we have finally dropped in. We eke out a penurious existence, but it's fun. The children's college is already paid for. We paid off all our debts before taking the plunge. We have taken on no new debts. Cynthia and I are at the top of the pyramid in our little store.
>
> We both have much more time to think and read and enjoy each other's company than we ever had before. Both of us liked coming up to the Adirondacks for many years before we moved up here permanently; so we knew what we were getting into. Should our desires in life change at a later date, I'm sure we can make the shift to an urban life. We've learned how to adapt to a new life-style.

Averill's Senseless Plan. Averill, like Rodney, grew to despise his business career. He developed the romantic notion that running a small vegetable farm would represent nirvana for himself, his wife, and two adolescent children. Averill and his wife, Abigail, sold their house and used the equity as a down payment on the farm. One year later they had put up the farm for sale and were trying to collect unemployment insurance. Abigail explains what happened:

> I'm not placing all the blame on Averill. I went along with the ill-conceived scheme. What we both didn't realize is that running a farm of any size can be a grueling experience. Averill didn't know

enough about machinery to keep it running without hiring outside mechanics. We couldn't even keep the plumbing in our farmhouse patched together.

Our children had almost no friends. They became increasingly annoyed at us because of our having taken them out of school. My parents kept accusing Averill of having lost his mind. What infuriates both of us the most is that neither of us can get back the comfortable, secure jobs we left behind. Our choices seem very limited right now.

WATCH OUT FOR A RELAPSE

Once you have overcome your middle-aged syndrome, you should be sensitive to signs of a relapse. Take action as soon as that first feeling of discontentment and uneasiness begins to creep into your psyche. Nipping discontent before it fulminates is a good way of taking care of most career (and other) problems.

Mike Enriches His Own Job Mike, the man intent upon becoming a super superintendent (described earlier in this chapter), almost had a relapse of his mid-career slump. He began to notice an uneasiness during the end of each week—a tinge of that "headed nowhere" feeling. Mike's solution was to change the way he conducted his job.

Mike accomplished the modification by trying out a new technique on his job each month. If it worked, he incorporated it into his permanent style of doing business. One month he tried not calling women "girls." It worked, Mike received even better cooperation from his female help than before—although Mike was astute enough to ask each woman whether she preferred being referred to as a woman or a girl. Many of the older women on production jobs preferred to be labeled girls.

Another month Mike tried out a system of evaluation by subordinates. Every person in his command was asked to write him a note anonymously with a constructive suggestion for him as a manager. Mike learned a lot about himself and his operation. His favorite anonymous comment read, "Stop trying so hard to improve. We love you the way you are."

Coping with Change

9 Jim worked as a supervisor in a dairy plant. His company installed an automated ice-cream-making machine, which, when fully implemented, would allow for a sharp reduction in personnel —a consequence that clashed with Jim's humanistic values. Three days after the installation of the machine, a group of executives from the home office scheduled a visit to observe the new ice cream machine in action. Embarrassingly, something went wrong with the ice cream machine that day. The shutoff control failed. Ice cream in three different flavors spewed out over the machine.

A person could have stood knee deep in ice cream for a three-foot radius around the machine. Horrified, the plant superintendent (who served as a tour guide for visiting executives) demanded an explanation from Jim, who argued, "What was I supposed to do? Nobody gave me instructions on how to disengage an automatic ice cream machine?"

What is your characteristic response to job-related changes? Do you exhibit passive-aggressive tendencies like Jim? Do you withdraw and become agitated, resentful, or anxious? Even if your reaction to change is rarely destructive, you can probably benefit from a few strategies for coping with change on the job.

WHAT'S IN IT FOR YOU?

Answering this question about change could improve your attitude toward the change you are facing. A fundamental reason many people resist change is that they believe that the outcome of the forthcoming change will be negative for themselves. Few people object to changes that they perceive as unequivocally advantageous. The individual with a tyrant for a boss is usually quite receptive to a new boss taking over the department—a change that is usually perceived with trepidation. If you analyze an impending job-related change, you may be able to ferret out some hidden advantages for yourself.

Craig Is Optimistic.   Enthusiastic Craig worked as a product planner in a small company that manufactured components for printing machinery. The company sputtered along without any serious setbacks or major breakthroughs. One day the company president announced that the company was being acquired by another company four times its size.

Concern and apprehension spread throughout the small company. Among the most negative rumors was that one-half of the work force would be laid off after the merger was consummated. Craig saw things differently. As he explained to the vice-president of marketing: "Please don't include me among those antsy people who are worried about the take-over. I've read in trade journals about the capability of our new corporate parent. It could be a golden opportunity for the right people. As you know, I like my job in our little company. But I have bigger goals in mind for my career. The merger should give me a chance to show a large company what I can do."

Craig's self-confidence and openness showed through to the parent company. After one year he surfaced to a new position as manager, Advanced Product Planning. His positive reaction to change had served as a vehicle to increased responsibility.

Steve Is Pessimistic.   A social worker in a family counseling agency, Steve learned that from now on the agency would be working under a new system of management. Barbara, the agency head, had returned from a management development seminar. Following suggestions made in the seminar, Barbara planned to run the agency according to a management by objectives system. Under this system, every professional worker would be held accountable for his or her results.

Steve's defensiveness and negative attitudes toward the contemplated change were apparent. He told Barbara, "As a professional social worker, I object to this management by objectives approach. You can't measure what I do for clients as if I were a factory worker doing piecework. I just don't like the idea of my boss's trying to measure what I do. It's an insult to my professionalism."

Barbara countered, "Steve, your attitude is wrong. The purpose of management by objectives is to make sure we as an agency are accomplishing what we think we are accomplishing. Even if you don't love the idea, you have to recognize that most social agencies are moving in the direction of some form of measurement."

Steve persisted in his negativism. He showed no enthusiasm for the new system of management and went through filling out the necessary forms in a perfunctory manner. At his first review session, six months after the management by objectives system was installed, Barbara asked Steve, "How well have you done in reaching your objectives?"

Steve quipped, "You tell me. They are your objectives, not mine. I didn't want the system in the first place." Barbara shrugged her shoulders in dismay. She responded, "Well, Steve, let's just do the best we can in completing our review session. We cannot change agency policy just to suit you."

Steve's Shortsightedness. If Steve had searched for the advantages of the management by objectives system, he would have discovered that an effective person (including a social worker) welcomes the opportunity to be measured. The old adage "Stand up and be counted" has applicability to the office. Because Steve had made an exception to himself, he came to be perceived as a loosely associated member of the agency.

Steve's failure to accept change cost him about 7 percent of his salary. When salary figures for the new year were established, Steve was given a token 2 percent adjustment. The average increase in the agency was 9 percent. Beyond the short-range financial considerations, Steve's reluctance to participate in the management by objectives system was damaging his reputation as a cooperative staff member. We can only guess the true cost of losing a positive reputation in one's field.

ACCEPT SOME ANXIETY AS NATURAL

Anxiety (or tension) is an almost universal concomitant of change or the prospects of change. Both self-confident and unsure people succumb when there is *some* concern when a major life change is imminent. You'll do a better job of coping with change if you accept those internal flutters as normal. The internal feelings of apprehension you experience in response to change or its prospects are as normal as the similar feelings you would probably experience if you learned that the Internal Revenue Service planned to audit your tax returns.

Jacques Feels Queasy.   Having worked for several years as the New England branch manager for his company, Jacques faced his biggest career opportunity. His company offered Jacques the Canadian division presidency. He and his wife were ecstatic. Both French Canadian by birth, they wanted to establish themselves as residents of Quebec Province permanently. As the contemplated date of moving came closer, Jacques became uneasy. Concerned about Jacques's apparent discomfort, his wife, Madeline, asked about the nature of his problem. Jacques replied:

> I feel like a humming bird is vibrating inside my body. I'm battling a constant twitching inside of me. When I sit down to make some concrete plans for implementing the move, I experience a familiar feeling—the one I get while skiing when I peer down a tall mountain just before I get moving.
>
> You could also say the sensation is not too different from the feeling that takes hold before I have to give a talk to a group of people. The strangest thing is that you and I agree that there are only benefits associated with this move. We enjoy the United States, but we love Quebec. I'll be Monsieur Canada for our company. You and the children will be with me. I'll be making more money and I'll have more prestige.

In spite of all these good things, I feel very uneasy. Do you think, Madeline, that I'm really afraid of success? Is it possible I really don't want to become Monsieur Canada for the company? Could it be that I'm dropping out at just when victory is in my grasp?

Jacques's Fallacious Reasoning. Jacques is being unduly critical of himself. True, some people actually fear failure and back off just at the moment of career orgasm. But a more parsimonious explanation may be in order. Jacques is experiencing the typical mixed feelings of anybody about to make a major life change. Jacques should recognize that he is facing two major life changes—both a promotion and a geographic relocation.

Jacques is doing the right thing in talking out his feelings with Madeline, but he should not regard his internal flutters as a sign that he fears success. Once Jacques and Madeline busy themselves in the innumerable details of relocation, his flutters will probably go away by themselves.

GET THE FACTS

Many of the resistances we erect to change stem from our fear of the unknown. When the facts become known, the impending change often seems a little less ominous. Unfortunately, in the absence of facts, people typically distort the true picture about the consequences of change negatively.

Clem Misinterprets the Future. Clem, a salesman for hospital supply equipment, learned that his company's sales program would be shifted somewhat from direct selling to selling through distributors. Overtly upset, he confided to his wife: "Cancel those plans for the new inground swimming pool and patio. Get used to dining out only once a month. Forget about having our daughter's teeth straightened. The company has just pulled the rug out from under me. We're going to be selling through distributors, and I'll be losing most of my commission business."

The next day Clem stormed into his boss's office with the same lament. Despite his discouragement with Clem's immature behavior, his boss confronted Clem with the facts. First, the shift to distributors simply meant that the company would sell low-volume items through distributors. Second, sales representatives would now be asked to call directly only on accounts with big potential. Third, the net effect of these changes would be to increase the earnings of sales representatives.

Clem had no founded reason to resist change in this instance. Had he collected the relevant facts before emoting, Clem would have created a more favorable impression upon his boss.

Doris Hears Some Bad News.   Proud of her position as the first woman industrial engineer in her company, Doris looked forward to a career in engineering and possibly engineering management. Suddenly her optimism was set back. Rumor spread throughout the company that layoffs would be forthcoming as unsold inventory accumulated. A spreader of foreboding tales told Doris: "If I were you, Doris, I'd start looking for a new job right away. A friend of mine in personnel told me that layoffs would begin on a straight seniority basis. And that means that women professional level employees will be the first to go. Second will be the people we brought into our minority group training program. The company is secretly happy about the whole idea. They didn't appreciate being forced to add women and minority groups members just to meet a quota."

Doris Digs for the Facts.   Doris felt slightly uneasy about the prospects of being laid off. She had a child to support, and she had recently put a down payment on a condominium. Instead of beginning a new job campaign or asking her physician for a Valium prescription, Doris took constructive action. She requested (and received) an appointment with the vice-president of personnel and organization development. At the interview she asked, "Mr. Marquis, could you please authenticate or deny a rumor for me? Word is out that there will be layoffs soon and that recently hired professional women will be the first to go. What can you tell me about this situation?"

Bill Marquis answered, "Doris, you are right in one respect.

There will be layoffs. In fact, they will be announced in a management newsletter this afternoon. But the layoffs will not be on a seniority basis. The company is not in serious trouble. True, we have overhired in a few spots, and we're going to do a little trimming down. We will be laying off some people and giving others the opportunity for early retirement. If you are regarded by your management as a person with a contribution to make for the company, your job is not in danger. I'm glad you came to me with your rumor. As an industrial engineer, you come into contact with a lot of people. We couldn't afford to have you contaminating things further."

Doris felt much better after her interview with Bill. Back at her job, she was able to concentrate upon her work. Doris did not have to preoccupy herself with the underlying concern that she might be the next person in the company to lose her (or his) job.

DEVELOP FLEX IN YOUR ATTITUDES

An underlying reason many people resist change is that they perceive change as good or bad, right or wrong, workable or unworkable. Rigidity of this type leads you to welcome some changes as all good and others as all bad. Recognition that you are rigid (if you, in fact, are) must precede the development of flexibility. As you develop the ability to examine multiple sides to an issue, you become better able to cope with change.

Rigid Hanna Becomes More Flexible. Hanna worked on the public relations staff of a firm based in New York City. She had held this position for ten years, deriving considerable job satisfaction for issuing directives and suggestions to company divisions located throughout the United States. A new corporate director of public relations announced to his staff that the corporate P.R. staff would be tapered down in size.

"From now on," commented the V.P., "our community relations work will be concentrated in the field where it should be. Most of you will be offered transfers to the field. I want you out in the trenches with the troops.

Hanna was horrified when told that her new assignment would be as the plant public relations manager in Gary, Indiana. She told a friend, "It's absolutely uncivilized to pitch your tent in a Midwestern industrial town. Where will I have lunch? Where will I shop? Where will I live?"

Her friend retorted, "Hanna, you are being so rigid that you are going to let a great career opportunity get by you. If you can't live in Gary, Indiana, it could very well be your fault— not the town's. Besides, if you profess to know so much about public relations, isn't it about time you practiced your art at the grass roots level?"

Rigid Hanna became more flexible after the confrontation with her friend. After six months of acclimation (including obtaining her first driver's license), Hanna is enjoying her new life as an involved community relations manager at her company's Gary site.

Phil, the Antifaddist, Goes Under.   An enviably successful home developer for a number of years, Phil, nevertheless, tended to resist changes in his field. His firm's speciality was building single unit high-priced houses for speculation. Phil's firm barely weathered the housing recession of the early 1970s. At a conference about business conditions, Marie, the sales manager commented:

> Phil, as I've mentioned many times in the past, we are constructing our own tombstones. If we continue to build so many of these expensive homes, we will be out of business. We're building homes for a shrinking market. Our houses are too expensive for the middle-class market and not in the luxury category that the upper income group demands. Many potential customers have walked away from our homesites, complaining that, although our houses are beautiful, they cannot raise the necessary down payment.
>
> Even when a middle-class couple can afford the down payment, the husband or wife does some rapid calculations about the taxes or utilities for the house. Their verdict is usually, "Let's look for something a little lower-priced." The only logical conclusion, Phil, is to move with the tide. Why don't we shift some of our produc-

tion to the new compact model home that is sweeping the country?

Looking annoyed, Phil responded:

Marie, you want to jump to every new fad in the building industry. These ugly little homes are a passing fancy. In two years the market will be glutted with these stark, little, tool shedlike structures. Besides, they are nothing new. Millions of them were built in the early 1950s.

Why change what we do best? We're in the comfortable, luxury-type home business. As my father used to say, "Shoemaker, stick to thy last." Besides, all change is not progress. Why should our fine company enter the junk home business?"

About one year after that conversation, Phil's firm was in receivership.

Phil Could Have Compromised. Unfortunately for Phil, he lacked sufficient flexibility to save his business. Marie, his sales manager, had her finger on the market pulse. Marketing intelligence about the new trend in home buying was abundant. But Phil's inflexibility acted as a blind spot.

Phil even neglected to weigh carefully a compromise solution that would not have involved a conversion to the stark mini-home. Phil might have considered constructing a luxury compact as the automobile industry had done. The lowered heating and tax bill on his line of luxury homes would have appealed to the luxury-minded buyer who could not afford a spacious home. But Phil lacked enough flex to envision compromise.

AVOID CHANGE OVERLOAD

Some of the worst cases of *future shock* (an adverse reaction to change) come about because a given individual is swamped by a series of major changes in a short period of time. Major changes in life are more readily coped with when a number of them do not have to be managed simultaneously. Two changes coming at once can have a more powerful impact upon a person than the combined effect of the same changes happening one at a time.

Jack Makes Some Major Changes. College Professor Jack worked hard to get ahead as an academic physicist. After ten years of teaching and research, Jack slowly came to the realization that perhaps he was pursuing the wrong path to job and life satisfaction. As he told one of the many job interviewers he spoke to in his search for a new career: "It's been ten years since I received my Ph.D., and I don't think my progress is as good as it could be. I've not made a big splash as a scientist, and my daily work isn't as much fun as I would like. Most of my research has not led anywhere. Many of my students—even some of the mediocre ones—are now making more money than I am. I want a piece of the action."

Jack found a better market for his talents than he had anticipated. Two chemical companies offered him a position. One company made him an attractive offer to become the physicist in residence in one of its laboratories. Another company offered Jack a job as a product planner. He accepted the latter offer because it promised him a new kind of work. Jack would team up with a marketing specialist to help decide what kinds of products the company should be offering in the future.

Jack eagerly planned his move to the company laboratory located in Atlanta. Having lived in the Washington, D.C., area almost all of his life, Jack welcomed the opportunity to explore a new part of the country. Now Jack was faced with two major changes in life—career and geographic relocation.

Jack's personal life also entered heavily into the increasing complexity of the changes confronting him. Antoinette, a legal secretary, divorced mother of two young children, and Jack had been seeing each other regularly for over one year. Jack and Antoinette had lengthy, at times agonizing, discussions about the implications of this move for their relationship.

One night while sharing a bottle of wine, Antoinette and Jack talked the problem through to conclusion. They mutually decided to marry two weeks before Jack's new position was to begin. The two would spend a week's honeymoon camping in the South. Upon their return, they would set up house in Atlanta, enroll the children in school, and Antoinette would seek a job for herself.

Pouring the last two glasses of wine, Jack looked at Antoinette and said, "One more big decision. My old car just won't make it. With all the new family responsibilities plus the camping trip, I'm going to need a new car. Maybe a station wagon would be the best bet."

Jack Gets Overwhelmed.   Two weeks into his new job, Jack showed up at a psychiatrist's office, flooded with anxiety and wondering what was wrong. After listening to Jack's synopsis of the events that had recently taken place in his life, the psychiatrist concluded: "No wonder you feel as if you are falling apart. You have simply absorbed too many life change units in too short a period of time. The human system can only absorb so much shaking up all at once. You should feel better once you have adjusted to all these changes."

What Jack Should Have Done.   However consoling the analysis presented by his psychiatrist, it was not sufficient for Jack to get rid of the discomfort associated with his personal case of future shock. Jack simply took on too much all at once. His best strategy would have been to spread out some of the major changes in his life. Within a two-week period of time, he became a new homeowner, a product planner, a husband, an instant father, a honeymooner, and an Atlantan.

Perhaps Jack could have moved to Atlanta alone. Antoinette and the children could have joined him once he had adjusted to his new job. Marriage was not a precondition for his employment. To simplify matters further, he might have postponed his new car purchase!

AVOID THE PROCRASTINATION TRAP

A generally ineffective, yet widely practiced method of dealing with change thrust upon us is to procrastinate until the situation worsens. Many people faced with the necessity for making a major work-related change delay taking any action. Instead of mobilizing to face the challenges, the change-over-whelmed person freezes.

Edwin Becomes Immobilized. Edwin's company pros-pered for many years because of its exclusive patent on a small electric motor that was used primarily by automobile manufac-turers in windshield washer assemblies. Seventy-five percent of the firm's business centered around shipments of these useful, reliable motors. A patent for these motors was issued in 1960, granting Edwin's company a 15-year exclusive on their manu-facture. After 1975, it would be open season for any company that wanted to compete in the production of this type of small electric motor for windshield washers.

As the years went by, Edwin held causal conferences with his engineering staff about the importance of developing a new high-volume product for the company. However, there was little commitment behind Edwin's utterances. By 1971, Ar-mand, his sales manager, pleaded with Edwin to accelerate a new product development program. Edwin replied, "Not a bad idea, but we don't want to rush into production with a product of little proved value."

By 1972, Ralph, the manufacturing manager, joined in Ar-mand's plea: "Edwin, the day for our patent's running out is coming pretty close. Even if one of the bright young develop-ment engineers came up with a useful product idea tomorrow, it would take about two years to have it ready for shipment to customers."

Edwin replied this time, "What you say is generally true. But we can move faster than that if we have to. Besides, how do we know for sure that other people really want to get into competi-tion with us? We may be battling an illusory enemy."

One year later, the management team had their annual dis-cussion about new product development. The furor over the importance of offering the public a new product intensified. Edwin replied, "As president, I have to be a moderating influ-ence. We're acting as if we might be going out of business tomorrow. You've been telling me this for several years, yet our sales have shown a steady increase."

Armand explained, "Edwin, our sales increase is due more to inflation than any marketing breakthroughs on our part. If we don't get off our corporate behinds soon, we'll be liquidating our machines and furniture by 1976."

"Okay, fellows," answered Edwin, "next year I promise to form a new product development committee that will really grab this problem by the horns. Just tend to the shop in the meantime."

Edwin did form the new product development committee in 1974, but he did not heed the recommendations of the committee. By 1975 orders for the new motors began to dwindle as the company's customers learned that a Japanese distributor was now able to supply the motors at a much lower cost. Other competition also emerged: a Detroit-based job shop that had attracted national attention because it hired only physically handicapped employees began to manufacture and sell a similar line of motors.

At that point, three of Edwin's top people left the company in recognition of its forthcoming demise. At the end, Edwin was forced into liquidation. He had no company and no product to sell.

Why Did Edwin Procrastinate? We never know unequivocally why one individual will take a problem-solving approach to a contemplated major change, whereas another individual (for instance, Edwin) will freeze and do nothing. Perhaps Edwin could not tolerate the painful thoughts that his prized contribution to the world—a tiny electric motor for windshield washers—would soon be in public domain. By doing nothing, he was perhaps unconsciously denying that other companies would be infringing upon his prized contribution.

BECOME A SUCCESS GRADUALLY

Sudden success can represent a shocking change to the human system. Some recipients of sudden (and unanticipated) success manage their good fortune effectively. Others are overwhelmed by the sudden burst of money and/or prestige, winding up more dissatisfied than they were before the arrival of instant success. The people who seem to handle success the best are those whose success derives from many years of dedication to the task. Big success does not overwhelm them because they have accumulated a variety of minor successes along the way.

Rudy Gets a Big Cash Award.   Working as a shipper in the potato chip department of his company, Rudy had one satisfaction most people don't receive in their jobs. He was able to see his company's products displayed in most of the grocery stores and supermarkets in his area. When Rudy and his children went food shopping, they could point with at least a modicum of pride to the potato chips that Rudy helped pack.

Tricia, his 14-year-old daughter, commented to Rudy during one of their supermarket expeditions: "Dad, it upsets me to see so many of your beautifully bagged potato chips get crushed by thoughtless people. The way the bags just lie there, most of them get tossed around and damaged. Why don't you put them on a wire rack the way the candy makers do?"

"Not a bad idea, daughter," commented Rudy. I'll give it some thought."

Tricia's simple suggestion (which has now been implemented by many manufacturers of potato chips) kept surfacing in Rudy's mind. Two weeks later he took home a blank from the company's suggestion box. In lieu of his usual evening of an after-dinner nap and two hours of television, Rudy stayed in the kitchen to work on Tricia's suggestion. He labored over the suggestion until he thought it worthy of consideration by the suggestion committee. Rudy furnished a simple diagram in addition to the written description.

One year later, Rudy's life took a sudden change. The suggestion committee of Supreme Foods decided that Rudy's (or, really, Tricia's) simple suggestion merited an award of $12,575 (on the basis of new sales it generated since its acceptance). Containing his urge to tell everybody he knew that he was now rich, Rudy rushed home from work. Mary, his wife, and Tricia were already there.

Rudy shouted gleefully: "We're rich. I'm a success. Rudy, the old shipper himself, has become the biggest suggestion winner of the year at Supreme Foods. Mary, no more cleaning other people's houses for you. Tricia, you helped me with the suggestion so you can have a new bedroom set. We're going to fix up this apartment so that it looks like a respectable place to live. Mary, let's you and I go shopping and get some decent clothing. No more dressing like poor folks for us."

Rudy's $12,575 did not last long. He made a down payment on a car, purchased an outboard motor boat for $2,000, bought $4,000 worth of new furniture, $3,500 of new clothing, and put $1,500 down on a mutual fund. The rest he spent in restaurants, airfare, and resorts.

Wasn't Rudy's Behavior Normal?   True, most people who come into sudden wealth bathe themselves in unaccustomed luxury. But Rudy elevated himself into a life-style that he could not afford once the initial supply of cash had been depleted. He had to discontinue his mutual fund investment program because he could not continue the monthly payments. Rudy was forced to sell his new car because of the $175 monthly payment. The instant infusion of money into Rudy's life put him in a temporary state of euphoria. Spending large amounts of money was a way for Rudy to make up for past hurts of being broke.

Once the money was spent and Rudy faced installment payments he could not afford, an ugly sick feeling developed inside him. Mary suffered, too, because she could not get back her regular house-cleaning job. Instead, she worked for a series of households less desirable than her previous assignment. Only the furniture remained as a useful memory of the suggestion award. The clothing Rudy and his family purchased was uncomfortable because it seemed more appropriate for wealthy people. Eventually, Rudy even sold the boat because he could not afford its storage costs.

Had Rudy been accustomed to success in the past, he might

not have been overwhelmed by sudden, temporary success. Rudy was not unlike the prize fighter, singer, or novelist who makes the complete cycle from obscurity to wealth and fame and back to obscurity in a two-year period. Rudy needed a manager, but who would want to help a shipper in a potato chip department manage a suggestion award?

RECOGNIZE THAT CHANGE IS NOT IRREVERSIBLE

The mistaken notion that most changes are irreversible is yet another reason why change makes people anxious. If you can emotionally accept the fact that something can be done to reverse change (for instance, it is *possible* to remarry a spouse from whom you are separating), the threat of change seems less ominous.

Garth Goes into Private Practice.   After ten years of dedicated service as a corporation lawyer, Garth decided to enter into private practice. He rented a small office in an old downtown building in a section of town where most of the corporate attorneys were located. As Garth phased down his company job, he prepared for his new future. He dutifully took care of ordering stationary, developing a mailing list for announcements about his new venture, selecting office furniture, and hiring a legal secretary and answering service. Garth's law office was to open in 30 days.

One morning, in the midst of preparing for the move, Garth had the irresistible urge to speak to a treasured acquaintance— an elderly law school professor. Flattered to hear that Garth sought his counsel, the professor agreed to meet him for lunch. During their meeting, Garth divulged his concerns about the upcoming future:

"Professor Lindstrom, I'm getting cold feet. What does a lawyer do when the phone doesn't ring? I mean if nobody calls me for legal services, what do I do? I can't canvass for clients by telephone. I can't advertise. It must be a horrible feeling to think that you might have no business and that you might not be able to pay your secretary or your landlord or even your answering service. What good is a lawyer without clients? What do you do for business? This is something we never talked about in law school."

Professor Lindstrom Imparts Some Wisdom. "Garth, my talented young lawyer," said the professor, "you are creating problems for yourself that are entirely in the realm of conjecture. You are assuming you will be a failure, that nobody will want you, that there is no need for a one-man law firm who can afford to charge lower fees than a large firm and that corporation law is really an unnecessary discipline. Even if all these untenable assumptions were true, you are forgetting one more fact of life in corporate law. You can go back at any time and work for a large corporation. Your only loss will be a few months of wages, the small overhead costs you have accumulated, and a minor hurt to your pride. You are putting yourself through needless anguish. Relax and look forward to the challenges that lie ahead."

PART III

IMPROVING
YOUR JOB SKILLS

Communicating
Your Way Ahead

10 Pat, a college placement specialist, received a telephone call from Myron, the director of the junior executive training program at a large retail chain: "Pat, I need your help. Our business is booming. We could use five more young people for our program. We see all sorts of growth in the near future."

"But, Myron, we're running a little thin on retailing majors. I think most of our graduates have jobs by now."

"Pat, don't be naïve. We don't care about what a student's major is. That's almost irrelevant in all but the most technical fields. If a young man or woman can communicate with people, he or she will make out okay in retailing."

An oversimplification on Myron's part? Maybe, but an overwhelming reason many people are held back in their careers is that they do a poor job of communicating their ideas to other people. Communication is the basic process by which most work is carried out in organizations.

Note that the career advancement strategies described earlier in this book all require reasonable ability to communicate with people. As a case in point, praising people can only be done through communication. Unless you have good communication skills, almost all other success strategies are a waste of time.

GET INSIDE YOUR PROSPECT'S HEAD

A fundamental truth of communication between people is that the other person is going to accept your proposition (one purpose of many forms of communication) only when you offer to satisfy an important need. Suppose you had a severe stutter, nibbled on your fingers while you stammered, and spoke with a combination of monosyllables and sign language. Yet, despite all these communication handicaps, you were the advertising manager of a $100 million family business. You would be able to get your message across to an advertising agency you wanted to handle your account. If they *needed* business, they would hear your message.

Although few situations are as obvious as the example just cited, your message has the best chance of being received when it explains what you can do for the recipient. Your job is to figure out what the receiver of your message needs. Then you have to convince that person that your proposition can take care of that need.

Tam Tries to Hustle Up Some Business.   Industrial Engineer Tam was encouraged by his boss to develop some new contacts for the department. Tam's boss reasoned that unless his corporate industrial engineering group developed some new clients, they might be subject to a budget cut for the forthcoming fiscal year. One of Tam's first appointments on his new mission was with Horace, a plant manager within the corporation. Tam explained to Horace: "Horace, I appreciate this chance you have given me to tell you about the services our group performs. We are doing a lot of things that might be of interest to you. Did you know that we have the latest methods of determining whether or not your plant is operating at top efficiency? Within two months after we begin, we can give you an accurate report of how your manufacturing methods stack up to other plants in the corporation. We can usually also furnish you a report on which supervisors are doing the best job."

"Very interesting," responded Horace, "but what other kind of work are you fellows up to? We don't have much of a need for an efficiency study right now."

"Too bad, Horace. You might be overlooking something of immense value. But we do have an ecology audit in the planning stages. We could tell you how good a job your plant is doing from an ecology point of view. We interview everybody, including the town mayor and the local health authorities."

"Tam, maybe Dick, our personnel manager, can take you on a plant tour. It's been great of you to come all the way out here. By way of appreciation, I want you to have a complete tour of the plant. Be our guest for lunch at the cafeteria."

What Tam Might Have Tried. Tam was being a conscientious industrial engineer but a naïve psychologist. Horace was resisting his propositions because Tam wasn't offering to solve a problem that Horace thought was important. He might have figured out what Horace needed by a direct line of questioning. After the usual exchange of pleasantries, the conversation *could* have gone this way:

"Horace," Tam might begin, "we're in the business of trying to be helpful to the divisions in the corporation. Our group has different techniques to solve different kinds of problems. What management problems are you facing that you would like help with?"

"The way I see our problems, Tam, it's simply top management's reluctance to spend money on this division that is creating problems. I'm damn proud of our management team. But you can't create miracles with antiquated machinery. If your studies could prove that our people are fine, but our machinery is obsolete, that would help us out of our biggest bind."

"Horace, I could never guarantee that our results would dovetail with the conclusions you want us to reach. However, if you let us in to do a feasibility study, at least we can figure out in broad brush strokes what our conclusion is likely to be. Considering when this plant was built, I suspect you are right about some of the machinery. And there is no reason to believe that your work force is any less effective than the work force at any other division."

"Tam, you're making a lot of sense for somebody from the home office. When do you think you would be able to get started on that feasibility study?"

Tam was receiving an important lesson from Horace, the veteran plant manager. Many executives hire consultants to help them prove to somebody else (or to themselves) that their judgment is sound. Recognizing this need, Tam could have adapted his strategy accordingly. Unfortunately for Tam, Horace proceeded to hire an outside consultant of his own to help prove his point that the machinery in the plant was obsolete. Horace was willing to listen to a consultant if the consultant focused in on his real problem. Tam's thrust dealt more with what Horace could do for Tam than what Tam could do for Horace.

DEVELOP YOUR FACE-TO-FACE COMMUNICATION SKILLS

In a discouraged and perplexed mood, Scott finally brought his problems to the attention of a career counselor. He expressed his concerns in words like these:

> My problem is that I don't seem to be getting anywhere in my company. I'm close to 30 years old with seven years of industrial experience. By my age I should be a second level manager instead of working by myself as a financial analyst. It would be unfair to attribute all my slow progress to hard times. My boss is a man who began to work with the company three years after I did.
>
> I've done a conscientious job of preparing myself for management work. I've always been a hard worker. I graduated in the top 10 percent of my class in high school. At college I majored in accounting and did quite well, receiving an almost A minus average. During my first four years of employment as an accountant, I attended school at night in order to pick up a master's degree in my field.
>
> While on the job, I waste very little time. In fact, I often take

home work with me. I try to be cooperative with everyone in the office; my attendance record is very good; my lunch hours are within reason. Management tells me I'm doing a fine job and that if I keep up the good work, I'll be kept in mind for promotion at a later date.

About two years ago, out of curiosity, I confronted my boss at the time and demanded to know why I wasn't being promoted. He told me that I should improve my public speaking. I didn't really see the relationship between public speaking and first line management, but nevertheless I joined Toastmasters for two years. Many of the brief talks I gave were rated highly by other members of the club, but I'm still in my same job. I'm beginning to wonder if management isn't telling me something.

Where Scott Went Wrong. Scott's lament is heard repeatedly in today's demanding work organization. Realizing that his career progress was retarded, he logically asked his boss for an explanation. Scott's boss suggested to him the most overworked remedy for improving promotability—developing one's public speaking skills. Personnel managers have a weekly chuckle over the number of people who are urged by their managers to enroll in a public speaking course.

True, Scott may have been excluded from promotion because his communication skills required development. However, developing his skills as a public speaker was hardly the correct remedy. Unless you are a highly placed executive or on the public relations staff of a large organization, your job rarely requires you to make large-group presentations. Scott's real need was to develop his ability to express his ideas in belly-to-belly contacts or in small groups.

Scott's Preferred Course of Action. Scott was encouraged by his career counselor to embark immediately upon a program of improving his one-to-one and small-group conversational skills. Scott purchased a tape recorder for this purpose. Daily he conducted imaginary conversations into the machine. He interviewed himself about projects in the department and made fantasy presentations to management. As instructed by his career counselor, Scott listened carefully for any systematic mistakes he could find in his presentations.

Within several months, Scott decreased markedly the frequency of his vocalized pauses and his apologetic, self-effacing comments. For instance, Scott learned to stop making comments such as "I may not be the best qualified person to solve this problem, but . . ."

As a supplement to his tape-recording exercises, Scott was also encouraged to use innocent bystanders in his quest for improved face-to-face communication skills. When he had the opportunity to converse with a sales representative on the phone or in his doorway, Scott tried to speak in a confident, polished manner. He looked upon meetings with sales clerks in department stores and bank tellers as imaginery meetings with company executives.

As another vehicle for improving his interpersonal communication skills, Scott capitalized upon his membership in a stamp collectors' club. At meetings he made an effort to articulate his views whenever they seemed to have merit. Scott volunteered to serve as club treasurer, which gave him the chance to make a treasurer's report at every other meeting.

Asked by his career counselor six months later about his career progress, Scott commented: "I'm finally getting a small promotion, which could be related to my improved speaking communication skills. Whether or not there is a cause and effect, I feel more confident. I think when I begin my new job, my new boss will have a much different image of me from the one my old boss had. He will see me as a person who can get his ideas across. My old boss gives me some credit for having improved, but I doubt he can change his image of the old me."

WRITE SHORT, PUNCHY MEMOS AND LETTERS

Although not ordinarily considered as specialists in verbal communication, executives generally are effective letter writers. Even if they have talented secretaries and administrative assistants composing letters for them, executives at least know what letters to *approve*. In contrast to executives and a small percentage of verbally skillful lower-ranking personnel, most people in work organizations write difficult-to-follow, ambiguous memos and letters. Your reputation will be enhanced if memos and letters going out under your signature are punchy and unambiguous.

Emily Dislikes What She Reads. Emily worked on the auditing staff of a public accounting firm. Barry, her immediate boss, was a specialist in conducting audits of inventories held by client companies. A major purpose of the inventory audit was to insure as far as possible that a client's actual inventory (at the time of the audit) equaled its stated inventory. Rather than conduct the inventory, a representative from the accounting firm would supervise the conduct of the inventory.

Barry came to note that inventory audits did not receive the same careful attention accountants gave to auditing the financial statements of clients. He mailed an internal memo to all professional members of the firm:

To: ALL STAFF MEMBERS
FROM: BARRY L. WINTERS
RE: CONDUCT OF INVENTORY AUDITS

Ladies and gentlemen, a problem of serious consequence to us all has recently come to my attention by means of personal observations in the field. It has become my considered judgment that we —each and every one of us—must come to grips with a problem that has gotten out of hand because of lassitude and carelessness on our part. A close scrutiny of our approach to conducting inventory audits suggests that we are as guilty as our clients of shoddy, sloppy, careless, and lackadaisical inventory-counting practices. Nay, a janitor's lunch box cannot be classified as "miscellaneous inventory," nor can a badly worn chair assigned to the lady's powder room be considered "slightly marred, to be reduced for clearance" inventory.

We must indeed keep abreast of irregularities in inventory accounting and immediately bring these to the attention of the principal assigned to the account. Please input to this problem within a two-week time frame or prior to a vacation, whichever date occurs sooner.

(SIGNATURE)

Three weeks later, Barry had not received any replies to the memo (which he thought would elicit about a 90 percent reply).

Emily Revamps the Memo. "Barry," said Emily with tact, "the returns on your memo may be slow in coming because of its complexity. A few of the recipients may not be sure if they are required to take action. Could I have a try at rewording the same memo?"

"No objection on my part, Emily. My ego doesn't bruise easily."

Emily rewrote the memo, receiving constructive suggestions from about 75 percent of the staff. It read:

To: ALL STAFF MEMBERS
FROM: BARRY L. WINTERS
RE: CONDUCT OF INVENTORY AUDITS
SECOND REQUEST

Just the other day a janitor's lunch box and a women's room couch were included in an inventory audit we supervised. A few more mistakes like that, and *we'll* be audited. Could we have your suggestions within two weeks (or before you go on vacation) about improving our inventory audits?

(SIGNATURE)

Barry was so pleased with Emily's performance that she received an outstanding rating on her next formal review. Aside from this recognition, Emily was assigned supervisory responsibility on the next inventory audit assigned to the firm.

BE A RATIONALIST, NOT AN EVANGELIST

The major purpose of many forms of communication among people is to present information in such a way that your listener will accept your point of view or buy your proposition. In work organizations, a professional, forthright, enthusiastic presentation works the best in most circumstances. When you beat the drums for your side too hard, the result is often suspicion about your motives. How would you feel if a cardiologist pleaded with you that he or she were the only person capable enough to handle your case? Or that, if you refused treatment from him or her, you would be doomed?

Ray, the Evangelist. Ray was a computer science executive in a large company. In the throws of reorganization, his company was deciding whether to consolidate most data processing under one roof or to have a number of smaller data-processing units in the field. Ray believed quite strongly that a large centralized data-processing facility would serve the organization (and himself) the best. Drew, another computer science executive in the company, favored the decentralization of data processing.

Ray and Drew separately prepared reports on the problem of consolidation versus decentralization. The reports were distributed well in advance of the meeting. Ray spoke first at the meeting:

> Gentlemen, you have read my report. Need I say more? There is no way I will submit having our firm thrown back to the Dark Ages of data processing. As a truly modern corporation we must have a data-processing facility that does us proud. We want something up-to-date, sophisticated, and with an avant-garde flavor. We want to attract some of the country's best computer talent to our company.
>
> Gentlemen, think of the future. Where will we be in the year 2000? Will we be known for our data-processing technology, or will we be a big, clumsy, calcified follower? I beg of you, the fate of computer science at our company is in your hands. And for those of you penny counters, centralization is likely to be less expensive than the duplication and overlap caused by having a swarm of data-processing facilities in the field.

Drew, the Rationalist. Drew took a more moderated approach:

> What my colleague has to say about the potential benefits of consolidation has some merit. But I'm a little more concerned about data processing serving the corporation than the corporation serv-

ing data processing. If computer scientists envy our computer equipment, fine. But that is certainly a secondary consideration.

As I have noted in my report, when large corporations totally centralize their data-processing facilities, there is a pronounced tendency toward empire building and the preparation of reports rarely used by operating people.

I also think that each division location should have its own data-processing facility that is responsive to local needs. Maybe we can have some centralization by having the divisions share time on the most expensive, biggest pieces of equipment. Whichever way the committee votes, try to keep this point of view in mind: What can computer science best do to serve the interests of those parts of the company where the work actually gets done.

Drew's objectivity and professionalism (*professionalism* in its most basic sense means that the client's interests are kept paramount) impressed the other committee members. On the basis of Drew's low-key rational argument, Ray's plan was interpreted as an attempt to establish a large data-processing institute on company premises for himself and his subordinates.

DOCUMENT YOUR ARGUMENTS

We live in a documentation-conscious world. Even if the skeptic does not investigate the source of your documentation, he or she finds documentation convincing. In the world of science and scholarly literature, documentation is expected to underly each major point. In the world of business, where intuition prevails (despite the advances of management science), documentation is impressive. If you find some suitable documentation for your arguments, you will increase your ability to persuade people. Printed documentation is generally more impressive than its oral counterpart.

Fay, the Franchise Skeptic. Fay and her colleagues were participating in a two-day conference on the feasibility of a new direction for their company. As a marketing executive, Fay carried considerable clout. The group pondered whether or not the company should set up a nationwide franchise of "Euro-

Fashion Centers." If they did so, almost any town of greater than 20,000 population would be eligible to establish a local Euro-Fashion Center. An individual buying into the system would have to invest a minimum of $15,000. The franchise would include assistance on running the store from company headquarters. All its stock would be bought exclusively from the company.

Fay saw some problems with the plan: "Gang, I dislike playing the role of the devil's advocate, but I see something scary about a franchise operation. The United States is rapidly becoming glutted with franchise operations. Pick up any copy of the *Wall Street Journal,* and you'll see what I mean. They have an entire page filled with advertisements for franchise investors. We could be making a drastic mistake by adding to the confusion."

Others at the meeting listened to Fay, but were not entirely convinced by her impassioned argument. Donna, who had originally developed the concept of Euro-Fashions as a franchise operation, said to the group, "Fay's position seems good on a logical basis, but do we have the true facts? You'll hear from me again tomorrow on this point."

Donna Digs for the Facts.   That night Donna raced through her back issues of *U.S. News and World Report* to locate an article she had read several months ago about the growth of franchising. Donna found precisely the article she wanted. Her memory was correct; the article contained U.S. Department of Commerce statistics on the growth (and decline) of different type of franchises. Her documented argument swung the group over to her point of view. She said:

> Back to the discussion about the world's being glutted with franchises. Fay's point is convincing in some ways, but I want to shed some additional light on the problem. Franchises have been growing rapidly in some areas and slowing down in others. For instance, franchises in recreation, travel, and entertainment are up over 100 percent. The only franchise operations actually to slow down are gasoline service stations and auto and truck dealerships. The rate of

acceleration for many of the franchises seems to be slowing down
—but a distinct growth trend is still apparent.

Surprisingly, very little activity is reported in the franchising of
the kind of speciality boutiques we have in mind. But retailing in
general shows a 13 percent increase. The conclusion I reach is that
there is still plenty of room left in the market for a well-conceived
high-fashion boutique.

Donna's homework paid dividends. The group swung to her
point of view. Donna is today merchandising coordinator for a
growing chain of Euro-Fashion outlets. Fay came out slightly
less well in the shuffle. She now works for Donna.

ROAD TEST YOUR IDEA BEFOREHAND

A simple, but infrequently used technique of improving the
salability of your ideas is to road test them before making your
final pitch. Road- (or field-) testing your ideas beforehand is
essentially documenting your ideas by conducting some fresh
research of your own.

Colin Road Tests in the Cafeteria.   Recently, the management development committee of an insurance company invited
me to lunch to discuss a presentation to their management staff
at a forthcoming evening meeting. During lunch the group attempted to decide which of several topics would be best suited
for their group. One member felt a talk of job motivation would
be best; another voted for the topic of professional obsolescence. Colin waited for the other members to express their
opinion; then he spoke:

> Just out of curiosity about which topic would captivate the most
> interest, I went to the company cafeteria this morning during the
> coffee break. I spoke to about ten men and women. I asked them
> which talk they would actually attend. Even if a talk is great, it can't
> help us unless we have a big turnout.
>
> It seems that the people I spoke to are tired of hearing about
> motivation. What intrigues them was the talk about career people
> and their families. From the little evidence I collected, I would have
> to vote for that talk.

Surprised, the committee head commented, "I'm pleased that you conducted your little survey. I'm with you. Does anyone else second the motion in favor of the talk about problems created by successful spouses?" "Aye, aye," said the committee.

COMMUNICATE WITH YOUR BODY

An important way of getting your message across to other people is to use body language to supplement spoken or written language. It is important to use cues that people who have not studied body language can interpret. For instance, it may be true that tucking your hands under your armpits means you are closed to further suggestions, but does your receiver understand that cue? Uninterpretable communication is wasted communication.

One industrial organization lagged behind competitors in new product development, as reported in my book *Fundamentals of Organizational Behavior.* One antidote selected by the president was to appoint a new product committee composed of representatives from a cross section of the company. It was chaired by the executive vice-president. The next highest-ranking member was the vice-president of engineering. The lowest-ranking member was an inspector from the electronics assembly area. As in any group meeting, a good deal of body language was displayed.

Member A yawned. He felt many of the ideas being generated had been suggested many times in the past. Furthermore, as he verbally communicated later, not everybody on the committee was qualified to serve.

Member B tapped his fingers and shuffled his feet. He was a new product planner. The fact that this meeting was necessary implied to some extent that he was not doing his job—a situation that raised his anxiety level.

Member C maintained a smile even during the more somber moments of the meeting. She was the only female engineer in her department and was enjoying the opportunity to demonstrate her capability to a cross section of the organization. Her smile did not necessarily imply total acceptance of all the ideas brought forth in the committee. (Therefore, C should have held back on her smiles at those times when she was not in agreement with the issue at hand.)

Member D occupied the chair closest to the chairman. During the meeting he inched his chair even closer to the chairman. At a minimum, this implied an acceptance of the chairman and perhaps an attempt to curry favor with him.

Member E spoke with his eyes. This man directed his gaze away from the committee chairman whenever tentative assignments were thrown out to the group such as, "We need someone to review in the trade magazines what new products using our technology have been brought out in the last several years." As in other relationships with people, E does not want to take individual responsibility for things; yet he would be unwilling to confront the chairman with this attitude. His solution is to look the other way.

REMEMBER NAMES AND FACES

Communicating with a person is facilitated when you remember his or her name. Rarely have I met a successful executive who has not honed his or her ability to connect the right names with the right faces. Most systems for remembering names, facts, and figures are readily forgotten because they require continuous practice. What do improve your ability to remember people's names are a few, basic, time-tested principles. Nobody intent upon climbing the organizational ladder (or communicating effectively with people) can afford to forget people's names consistently.

Hello, Giuseppe Zavaglia. At a business meeting, Joe was introduced to a new designer on the staff, Giuseppe Zavaglia. Joe said, "Hi, pleased to meet you." The next day the two men passed each other in the halls. Giuseppe said "Hi, Joe, how are things going?" Joe replied, "Oh, just fine. Say, I've forgotten your name."

Joe was giving misinformation. He did not forget Zavaglia's name. He never learned it. Upon meeting Giuseppe, he should have said. "Nice to meet you, Giuseppe Zavaglia. I'll try to remember your name." At the end of the meeting, he should have said, "So long, Giuseppe, I enjoyed meeting you." Two quick rehearsals are an effective way of learning somebody's name.

I Can See That Little Stein on Your Head. A widely practiced simple memory device for remembering names is to make an absurd association between that person's name and a familiar object. Assume that Peg meets Teena Stein, one of the young women working in her department (Peg has been newly appointed as the boss). Peg would like to remember the names and faces of as many of her subordinates as quickly as possible.

As Peg looks at Teena, she silently says her name and conjures up an easily remembered image: A woman with a small (tiny like Teena) beer stein (same as Stein) perched on her head. As long as Peg doesn't call her new subordinate "Teena Beer" on their next meeting, her system will work.

John Smith Meets Jim Brown. At a management development conference, John Smith was introduced to a potentially valuable contact in another company—an individual of average height and appearance named Jim Brown. What could John do now? He met a number of people at the conference; there was nothing apparently distinctive about Jim Brown's name; he realized that people were forever forgetting his name because it is hard to connect the name John Smith to any one person in particular.

Trying out one of the principles learned in a memory book, John Smith tried to make some kind of absurd link between the simple name Jim Brown and *this particular* person. Within eight seconds John Smith had the necessary association. He made a mental image of the most famous Jim Brown of them all (the former football great and sometime actor) tackling this average-looking Jim Brown. The association worked well enough so that at the closing banquet John Smith remembered Jim Brown's name—even though name tags had been discarded for the evening.

IMPRESS PEOPLE WITH YOUR VOICE

Of equal significance, be careful not to impress people unfavorably with your voice. Listening objectively (as best you can) to yourself on a tape recorder will be helpful to you in monitoring extreme voice characteristics of volume and pitch. "Squeaky" is a bad nickname to acquire if you're trying to impress people in a work environment. "Froggie" isn't a helpful nickname either. Besides, an artificial attempt to develop a gravelly voice can do permanent damage to your larynx.

Pace is another key voice characteristic that can influence your effectiveness in communicating with others. Extremely rapid speech makes you appear insecure. Rapidity connotes insecurity because the unsure person is afraid to let another person make a contradictory comment. Extreme slowness, aside from irritating impatient people, makes you appear indecisive. But some speech characteristics are even more irritating than those already mentioned.

Alfie Should Have Tried a Dry Run.   "There you have it, ladies and gentlemen," concluded Alfie, "my suggestions for getting the community on our side. With enough advance publicity, my plans for the Community Day should be a big hit." A few of the members present clapped mildly, but the two most influential members of the audience had left, looking visibly irritated with Alfie's presentation.

At after-work cocktails, Alfie asked Jody (one of his coworkers): "Let me have it, Jody. What do you think really went wrong in my presentation today? When the top brass left, I could have died up there. What happened? Did I have bad breath or something? Was my fly open?"

"At the risk of losing the friendship of a valued coworker, I'm going to tell you what went wrong. Just don't get defensive, Alfie. What went on was worse than bad breadth. The three top executives were getting so wet from your spray that they felt forced to move. I recall the president looking perplexed when you first sprayed him. By the third time your saliva hit him, he looked nauseated. Next time try a dry run."

AVOID OVERCONFORMITY IN SPEECH

An amusing phenomenon in many organizations is that the most successful members have comfortable, natural patterns of speech, whereas many of the lower-ranking aspirants to bigger jobs show rigid conformity in speech. In an attempt to impress people with their command of "in" or "buzz" words, they risk sounding immature and vacuous.

Sterling Maps Out Some Strategy. Sterling applied for a job in his own company as a financial analyst who would overlook the business dealings of the marketing department. His prospective boss asked Sterling if he had any general ideas about his approach to such a job.

Eagerly, Sterling replied: "First of all chief, I'd shake up those peddlers across the street. I'd zap right where it hurts—in the old pocketbook. What we need around here is a healthy R.O.I. (return on investment), and those hustlers aren't giving it to us. Okay, so they see me as a whistle blower or a cop. I'm not here to win a popularity contest. We're in business to make a profit. It's that simple. If they think we bean counters should get out of their sandbox, they have another thought coming. The name of the game is spend less than you take in. Any other input you need?"

Sterling Could Have Used Common Business English. Sterling created a negative impression upon his prospective boss because of his pseudosophisticated business language. Sterling should use business terminology, but not to the extreme that his speech sounds contrived. He might have said: "I would try to implement a financial control system that would help the marketing department realize when a particular course of action was unprofitable. Everybody in business realizes that you need both a profit and a sound return on investment. Perhaps if we alerted marketing when they priced an item too low, they could make the right adjustment. I recognize that this kind of business activity is not likely to be well received by all. However, that is the nature of my work."

COMMUNICATE WITH YOUR DOOR

A curious form of nonverbal communication reported on by the management adviser Auren Uris in *Nation's Business* is the use of doors to communicate messages. Properly used, it could give you another mode of getting across to people.

Cliff Uses a Subtle Maneuver. Working away busily at a report requiring heavy concentration, Cliff peered through his door to determine the source of chatter he overheard. Outside his door were three clerks conducting a postmortem on the previous weekend's major football game. Rather than alienate the intruders by telling them to go away or be quiet, Cliff tried something less obvious. He simply arose from his chair, tiptoed to the door, and closed it gently. Simultaneously he motioned to the three people to continue with their conversation.

The three visitors offered their apologies. As a bonus for Cliff, they chose a new sight for their next hallway conversation.

Holly Tells the World He's Available. New in his post as dean of applied science, Holly wanted to spend as much time as possible talking to faculty, staff, and students. Yet he didn't want to violate college norms by interrupting professors with their work by scheduling formal meetings with them. Holly thought that hanging around the campus to encourage interaction with students would be unprofessional.

His solution was close to ideal. Holly kept his door wide open with his desk plainly in view. The number of people dropping by to see him quadrupled. Gradually, Holly was faced with a different problem. His open-door policy was working too well. Holly needed to decrease his number of visits without breaking down communication channels.

Holly Backs Off. As an antidote to his new problem, perceptive Holly kept his door ajar. By doing so his message to the world was, "I'm willing to see anyone on nonroutine matters. I'm working, but I can be interrupted." Had Holly put that sentiment in writing, it probably would have been interpreted by others as an indication of withdrawal.

MAINTAIN A FRIENDLY, LISTENING POSTURE

Meaningful communication is two-way communication. Therefore, to communicate well you have to improve your listening acuity. The single most effective way to increase the amount of valid information you receive is to maintain a friendly, listening posture. Be easy to talk to, and other people in the organization will provide you much of the information you need to get your job accomplished. In contrast, if you act like an interrogator or autocrat, you may shut yourself off from vital information.

Arthur Stays Misinformed.   As the head of new customer development in his bank, Arthur began to realize that his bank's performance was poor. In comparison to other banks in his area, First Traders Bank was performing poorly. In order to discover what factors underlay the difficulty in attracting new business, Arthur decided to speak to bank personnel. Among the questions he asked were

1. What's going on down here?
2. What isn't working out in your branch?
3. Why are you people falling behind in attracting new business?

Arthur's line of questioning yielded scant information. People reacted self-protectively to his questions. For instance, when one branch assistant manager was asked the third question, she replied, "I didn't know we were falling behind."

How Arthur Should Have Proceeded.   Arthur needed information about sensitive matters. He should have acted concerned, but not accusing. A question such as "How can we in top management help you attract more new business?" would probably have helped elicit the information Arthur needed. A question such as "What problems are you facing in attracting new business?" might also have been productive.

Perhaps Arthur should have sent somebody else on this fact-

and-attitude-finding mission. His basically authoritarian, demanding personality does not lend itself well to receiving information from other people.

REHEARSE AWAY YOUR FEARS

People have an almost universal fear of talking before an audience. People who are effective speakers owe much of their success to practice. As mentioned earlier in this chapter, public speaking ability is a requirement of very few jobs—yet you want to perform effectively when you have to face an audience.

Aside from being familiar with the fundamentals of good speech making (outside the scope of this chapter), a major hurdle to overcome is fear. If you can overcome your fear of facing an audience and if you are interested in what you are talking about, you can probably do a passable job.

Zane Feels He's Going Insane. Lois, wife of veterinarian Zane, confided to Gertrude—a speech teacher friend:

> Zane is about to flip his lid. I mean the man is climbing the walls. He's supposed to give a talk to the state veterinary medical association about rodent control, and he is ill. He wakes up at night in a cold sweat. He's more irritable than an impounded dog. He has stomach cramps, headaches, and now a rash on his face.
>
> Zane thinks that perhaps I should give the talk for him. But that wouldn't work because I couldn't answer technical questions about rats and related subjects. Besides it's Zane's paper. He's being such a baby about the whole matter. He doesn't want to fail in this assignment, and I don't want him to fail. Some of the biggest names in veterinary medicine will be there.

Astute Gertrude replied, "You may have come to the right person. I may be able to help Zane. I do a lot of speaking for the Zero Population group aside from teaching speech."

Zane Practices in the Kennel. Gertrude conferred with Zane that evening. She explained to him that fear of speaking to *people* is normal. Gertrude then recommended that Zane try out his talk to the animals in his kennel: "Just look at the different pets as if they were distinguished members of the audience. As you make an important point, smile at that nice poodle. Establish eye contact with a basset hound."

Zane did rehearse his talk to the animals twice. He reported a vast improvement; yet he still felt acutely uncomfortable. Gertrude made another suggestion: "Now that you've given the talk to a live audience, try the best possible way of overcoming that nagging fear of presenting to an audience."

"And what is that, Gertrude?"

"See if you can practice your talk a couple of times right in the auditorium where you will be giving it. Look around at the empty chairs as if they were members of the audience."

Zane discovered that the auditorium could be made available to him at night. He gave his ten-minute talk three times in one evening of rehearsal. By the third presentation his fear and apprehension had been reduced to manageable proportions.

Gertrude's simple system, effectively used by many beginning speech makers in the past, also worked for Zane. He did a professional job of presenting his research on rodent control.

FIND A LOGICAL BRIDGE TO YOUR AUDIENCE

The most frequently used approach to warming up an audience is quite often the poorest way. Beginners in public speaking think it necessary to tell the audience a canned joke. Even if the joke is executed well (infrequently the case), it rarely accomplishes its purpose of establishing a communications bridge between you and the audience. After the joke is told, the audience quite naturally reacts with some degree of laughter. Once the joke is completed, the audience slumps back into their chairs. You have told your joke, but you have not established a bond with the audience.

How Do You Establish Rapport? The most effective speakers find some logical bridge between themselves and the specific interests of the audience. A witty comment of this nature performs the function of a joke (warming up the audience). In addition, it gives you some intellectual respect—what you really need to get your message across. Once the audience perceives that you empathize with them, your chances of reaching them are improved. Here are three examples.

Paul, addressing a local chapter of the National Association of Accountants on the evening of April 15: "First of all, let me compliment this group on your sense of timing. There must be 20,000 people in your county screaming for help with their income tax forms tonight. It's April 15, and here you are hiding out at a professional meeting."

Dan, a personnel manager, speaking to a group of security guards: "I must say you fellows are on your toes. My brother-in-law came to see me the other day. He called me from the security office that he was being frisked and detained until proper identification could be made. If I were in your shoes, I would do the same thing. He's a very suspicious-looking character."

Margot, a clothing manufacturer's sales representative, speaking to a group of designers: "Thanks for letting me in here to speak with you creative types. Without your designs I'd have nothing to sell but my personality. And the gross from that wouldn't be enough to keep my parakeet alive."

MAKE SURE YOUR MESSAGE REGISTERS

Communicating with people on or off the job has the central purpose of trying to register a message. If the message doesn't register, the communication cycle is incomplete. Unless you are an extraordinarily effective communicator (whose message gets across practically all the time), you need to look for some indication that your message has registered. If it has not registered, try again.

José Asks If He Was Heard. Army Captain José is an effective communicator because he keeps communicating until he is confident that his message has registered. After informing his troops (a reserve unit) of what needs to be accomplished (or any other message), José routinely asks at the end of the meeting questions such as: "How did you interpret my instructions?" "Could we summarize the points we've agreed upon?" "What agreements have we reached on who is to do what?"

Sylvia Interprets Body Language. Real Estate Agent Sylvia believes that a person's facial expressions and body motions mean as much as what they say in a sales situation. Sylvia's job is to rent luxury apartments, working out of a resident office in a large complex. She explains how she knows if her message is registering:

> We get hundreds of people who are just out for a Sunday afternoon or an early evening of fun. Among this group of fun seekers are a small percentage of legitimate prospects. I try to spend as little time as possible with the time wasters, short of being rude to them. Any casual looker could conceivably send around a friend who is a legitimate prospect.
>
> After about 20 minutes of taking a person on a tour, I tell him of her directly that he or she could move in within 30 days or sooner if necessary. I then watch carefully their body or eyes. If the prospect moves toward me or develops an intrigued, excited glance, I know I've got a live one on the hook. But if the person tightens up his or her body or turns away, I know I've got a time waster on my hands.
>
> That's the way I operate. My business is basically all communications.

How to Work Harder and Shorter

11 At a social gathering an editor in a lawyer's publishing company commented, "The strangest thing I've discovered on my job is that the only lawyers who seem to have time to write lawbooks are the busiest, most successful lawyers. If you needed a book written in a hurry, the best person to ask would be somebody in the league of F. Lee Bailey."

What this editor had to say about lawyers applies to people in virtually every field. Successful people manage time better than do their less successful counterparts. If we assume that you really want to make better use of time—that you are motivated to be better organized—you are invited to capitalize upon some time-tested, easy-to-apply suggestions.

Anybody who implements the suggestion offered in this chapter will become a better manager of time. The payoff is that you will be able to accomplish more than other people doing your kind of work without having to spend more hours working.

TRY WORK COST AVERAGING

According to the stock investment strategy of dollar cost averaging, you invest the same amount of money in a particular stock at different points in time. When the stock goes down in price, you get more shares for your money. When the stock rises in price, you get fewer shares for your money.

Similarly, in work cost averaging, you invest a constant expenditure of energy every working day. The payoff is that you develop a precious supply of bonus time that you can use for forward planning and thinking creatively about your job. For instance, if you find yourself with an afternoon of discretionary time, you can figure out ways of doing your job more effectively. Such improvements should ultimately enhance your reputation wherever you work.

Skip Is Overwhelmed. Likable Skip finally sold his service station at a loss because it was ruining his family life: "Even though people need gas all year round, this type of work was too seasonal. During the spring and early winter, we were absolutely swamped. I couldn't afford more than two people in help, and we were always behind. During our busy season, especially in March and December, I was working 80 to 90 hours per week. My wife just couldn't take it, and neither could I. But what I'm doing now might be even worse for my homelife. I'm a senior mechanic in a big shop. I like the work, but I hate working for somebody else. It eats away at my pride. I'm becoming a grouch at home."

How Could Skip Have Used Work Cost Averaging? Skip could have found ways to even out some of the work load in his service station. He might have tried keeping a telephone roster of his regular customers. During the nonrush season, he might have telephoned all of them, suggesting that they have their cars serviced before the rush. If offered the chance, many people would prefer to have their cars serviced at an earlier time than usual.

By having his customers spread out over different servicing cycles, Skip could have cut sharply into the peak-and-valley nature of his business. One novel approach for Skip would be to encourage his customers with radial tires (who thus don't use snow tires) to have their cars serviced outside of the winter changeover months.

By working reasonably hard every month. Skip could have

avoided the fatiguing (and family-wrecking) 80- to 90-hour-per-week months. Customers cannot be mandated to switch to Skip's preferred schedule, but even a slightly better balanced work load would have helped Skip survive.

MAINTAIN AN UPDATED LIST OF CHORES

Few people are so innately well organized that they can make good use of time without preparing a list of activities that need doing. The executive planners commercially available are essentially orderly systems for allocating your time among various activities. Many of these planners suggest allocating your time into 30-minute chunks. In addition to time allocation, such planners serve as convenient record-keeping devices for luncheon engagements, expense account items, and important dates.

The World's Simplest System. Whether you choose to record your list on an index card (my favorite) or in a leather-bound (or genuine goatskin) VIP planner, the principle is the same. Prepare a list of activities required for your job for one day, several days, or a week at a time. As each activity is performed, it should be crossed off the list—a marvelously therapeutic feeling for many people.

Separate lists for business and personal activities are highly recommended. Otherwise, your list could conceivably read:

1. Make tender offer on smaller company.
2. Call vice-president of marketing for lunch.
3. Fix crib spring.
4. Make business trip arrangements to Philadelphia.
5. Meet with citizens' pollution committee.
6. Pick up flea powder.

SCHEDULE SIMILAR TASKS TOGETHER

Management consultant Chester Burger advises managers to discharge similar tasks in the same block of time. By doing so, you develop the necessary pace and mental set to knock off the chores in short order. When you flit from one type of task to another, your efficiency may suffer.

Larry Was Being Strangled by his Job. A claims manager in a health insurance company, Larry admitted that his job was providing him too much stress. As he added more working hours to his day, his problems still did not go away. His feelings of helplessness only increased. As he explained his problem to an adviser,

> Sure, it's easy to say if I were better organized, my job wouldn't be so harassing. But the truth is that my job is harassing; so I become disorganized. I can't control the phone; I can't control personnel problems; I can't control irate policy holders who insist on speaking to me.
>
> With conferences to attend, letters to write, phone calls to make, and phone calls to answer, my day is pretty well gobbled up. Above all, I want to get out of this bind. I want to be on top of my job.

Larry Regroups His Work. After consultation with his adviser, Larry figured out what he was doing wrong and how his job efficiency could be improved. Larry developed an almost rigid schedule of performing similar tasks in blocks of time. For instance, he set aside the hours of eleven to twelve each morning for telephone conferences with policy holders. Other people in his department took care of routine inquiries from people with complaints.

He used the first 30 minutes of each working day to issue directives and requests to people in the company. In this way, much of the work that needed to be accomplished by other people in order for Larry to do his job was set in motion early in the day. By late in the afternoon, Larry often had the information requested by the early morning calls.

Larry found that conferences with subordinates and peers could be handled comfortably by scheduling them between the hours of 2:30 and 5:00 P.M. Although he had become a tightly scheduled manager, Larry still met with superiors at their request. Larry's biggest revelation was the reaction of other people in the company to his new schedule: "I found that other people respected my new schedule. If somebody wanted to see me, I could forthrightly say to him or her, I deal with problems of that kind after 2:30 in the afternoon. Would tomorrow at 3:00 P.M. be okay?' The usual reaction was positive. In the past, I thought a manager had to be available to anybody, anytime. No wonder my job was controlling me."

CONCENTRATE ON IMPORTANT TASKS

Many of the caveats offered in this chapter tell an individual how to become more efficient. *Effectiveness* is also very important. In order to become effective in your job, you have to concentrate on tasks where superior performance could have a big payoff on performance. For example, no matter how quickly you took care of making sure that your store paid its bills on time, it would not make your store an outstanding success. However, if you concentrated your efforts on bringing unique and desirable merchandise into the store, it could have a big impact on your business success.

Raymond Breaks out of the Ski Repair Shop.   Modern ski shops sell a wide range of sporting goods and sports clothing— a relatively recent trend. Several years ago, Raymond worked as the manager of the repair department in a thriving ski shop. During the nonskiing season, Ray helped with the sale and repair of bicycles and performed miscellaneous maintenance chores around the store. Raymond became preoccupied with the idea that somehow the ski shop where he worked should become a truly year-round store.

He devoted one hour per day to developing ideas and collecting information about additional merchandise lines for his store. His boss was skeptical but granted Raymond the time. After six months of investigation, Ray shocked his boss in a positive way with a detailed marketing report on the diversification of the ski shop into a two-season (winter and spring-summer-fall) store. He notes:

> My boss was particularly impressed with the logic of my ideas.
> I wrote and phoned other ski shops that achieved success with

diversification. I did the same for the failures. At my suggestion, we basically turned to a ski, tennis, and bicycle shop. But we also threw in a very important addition. We called this the "hot sport" department. Whatever fad came along that seemed to hold promise of at least a two-year run became a candidate for that department.

Skate boards are a perfect example. We had the most solidly stocked skate board department in town. A promotional stunt I thought of was to have a couple of good-looking fellows and girls clad in bathing suits skate outside the store. We set up a small ramp on which they could perform tricks. We sold hundreds of skate boards that way."

Raymond's creativity paid off. The store prospered, and his boss developed enormous trust in Raymond's business judgment. Because of this, Ray was offered a chance to buy into the business. His focus on important tasks—instead of shuffling around inventory and tending to store maintenance during the off-season—represented a breakthrough in his career.

Mannie, the Minutia Man. Compulsive Mannie was the vice-president of administration in an earth-moving equipment company. In general, his duties involved total responsibility for the running of the internal aspects of the firm. Mannie was in charge of people who did the accounting, personnel work, and data processing for the company. At age 55, after 25 years with the firm, Mannie was urged to take early retirement. He protested: "You're cutting me off at the point of my biggest contribution to the company. There is nobody reporting to me who is seasoned enough to take my place. You'll have to go outside the company to fill my spot. The risk is that such a maneuver may create morale problems at the department head level."

Mannie Miscalculated. He was not missed; he was not even replaced. According to the president, "We really didn't need Mannie around anymore. At his salary level you expect much more than somebody who keeps track of what a handful of competent people are doing. He called a lot of conferences that filled no apparent purposes. Worst of all, he was getting in other peoples' hair with his incessant demand for copies of everything. I felt Mannie had no legitimate contribution to make to the company. He was doing a lot of things that could be done by a clerk or that didn't really need doing. The company runs much more smoothly without him. Why add another layer of management unless it fills some important purpose?"

SPEND ENOUGH TIME ON PAPER WORK

Although it is fashionable to decry the necessity of having to do paper work in responsible jobs, the effective career person does not neglect paper work. Paper work essentially involves taking care of minor administrative details such as correspondence, personnel reports, and completing questionnaires and other forms. Unless paper work is efficiently attended to, a person's job may get out of control.

Ideally, a small amount of time should be invested in paper work every day. Nonprime time (when you are at less than your peak of efficiency, but not overfatigued) is the best time to discharge paper work).

Michelle Loves People. Michelle, the child-loving school social worker, found herself temporarily without a job—an uncomfortable situation because she and her husband made equal contributions to household finances. She disagreed strongly with the reasons she was given for not having her contract renewed:

> The man in charge of pupil personnel activities tells me he did not renew my contract because I did not keep up-to-date records on the children I saw. My point is that keeping records interferes with my relationship with children. Why should a social worker spend her time filling out forms? My job is to interact with children and with parents.
>
> I can make my biggest contribution to the school district by providing personal help and advice to children, parents, and teachers. I'm not paid to be a paper shuffler.

Michelle Is Mistaken. Michelle has a compelling story from an emotional standpoint. The vision of a school social worker counseling with a child or parent seems more palatable than the same person digging his or her way through paper work. Nevertheless, careful record keeping is an important part of any job. Her school administrators need records to justify Michelles's job. Mental health workers in the community may need to refer to her records. Should Michelle ever leave the school, other social workers working with the same child's family may find information about past consultation invaluable.

Lastly, because Michelle did not keep usable records, she was perceived by the administrative staff as disorganized. With a reputation for disorganization, her advice and counsel were unlikely to be sought by the administrative staff.

HARNESS YOUR NATURAL ENERGY CYCLES

The old saws "I'm a morning person" or "I'm a night person" have scientific substantiation. People vary somewhat as to their hours of peak efficiency. A week of charting should help you determine the hours at which your mental and physical energy is apt to be highest (or lowest).

After you have determined your strong and weak energy periods, you should be able to arrange your work schedule accordingly. Tackle your intellectually most demanding assignments during your energy peaks. Avoid doing creative work or making major decisions when fatigue has set in. It may be all right for a 25-year-old intern to patch a wound in his or her twenty-third consecutive hour of work, but for most of us crucial tasks demand a fresh outlook.

Tony Gets Embarrassed. A financial specialist, Tony worked for a commercial loan company that lent businesses money essentially by buying their accounts receivable at a huge discount. Generally, companies that could not raise cash through banks dealt with Tony's company. Intent on improving his own cash position, Tony worked long hours—often to the point of severe mental and physical fatigue.

Dutifully, Tony would prepare summaries of his visits to clients and prospective clients. When traveling, Tony would often dash off a typewritten note to the home office or prospect he visited on the trip. (He carried a small portable typewriter with him.) Tony often took care of such paper work when his level of concentration was impaired.

One Friday morning, Tony's boss, Vince, called him into the office: "Tony we've got an irate client on our hands. The client is threatening to sue us for defamation of character. It looks as if you sent him a note intended for me, and you sent me a note intended for him."

"Let me see," asked Tony inquisitively. He gasped at the incontestable evidence in front of him. Tony had mistakenly sent a memo to the client that read, "Vince, this outfit looks like a bunch of turkeys. I think some of their accounts receivable are worthless because they shipped a lot of defective merchandise."

On the other hand, the memo to Vince read, "Dear Mr. Duerr [the client executive], we will give every consideration to your credit needs. We have to weigh each request for funds carefully. I'll be in touch as soon as I review your file with the home office."

DON'T NEGLECT PERSONAL LIFE

As just suggested, a helpful guideline in learning how to work harder and shorter is to back off from your heavy work schedule when the effort no longer seems worth the yield. At some point, even the most work-addicted individual is squeezing very little productivity out of his or her efforts. If long working extralong hours has the effect of making you grouchy and if your job requires that you be extrapleasant with people, lop off a few of the extra hours. In some situations, extra hours put into work could more profitably be invested in personal life.

Laird, the Work-Addicted Biologist.   Single again after ten years of marriage, Laird threw himself into his work with vehemence. Reasoning that the last couple of years of his marriage had interferred with his productivity, Laird was working extra hours to try and develop his name as a researcher. He poured over journals in his field and carefully prepared a report describing his research activity over the past year. Laird set up a work schedule for himself of ten hours per day, six days per week. Sunday afternoons he spent with his son.

Laird confided to an old friend: "I'm finally at peace with myself. I've thrown myself into my work, and I'm moving ahead. I have no more time for golf or dating, but it's worth it. At last I can see an optimistic professional future for myself. When I wind up this report I'm doing now, I'll begin to make some visible progress. I'm on the fourth draft of it right now."

"Laird, old buddy," retorted his friend, "you're not fooling me. You're spinning your wheels. Your kind of work can't be done more than about 45 hours per week. Time after that is just wasted motion. You're escaping from the human race, but I doubt you are really enjoying yourself. You need to get your life in proper perspective."

Laird Takes Systematic Action.   Laird heeded the suggestions of his friend because preconsciously he wanted to improve his life-style. Laird established improving his social life as his first priority for change. Among his most fruitful approaches to a better personal life was to ask one of the department research assistants for a date. Several months later, a mutually rewarding relationship had developed. Laird began to spend more time with her, including arranging three-way get-togethers with his son and himself and his new romance. According to Laird,

> I found that my productivity did not diminish because of my personal life. The quality of my work showed a definite improvement as I backed off a little from my torrid work schedule. I found that reviewing a research report more than three times was futile. Many of the changes that I was making in the fourth revision actually weakened the report.
>
> I cut my work schedule down to about nine hours per day plus Saturday morning. By Saturday morning I was looking forward with great anticipation to seeing my boy and Roxanne [the research assistant]. Monday mornings I felt refreshed after a weekend of romance and fun.

My new work schedule made a lot of sense. I was almost as productive although working about 25 percent fewer hours. Because I was less fatigued, I had enough energy left over for personal life. Maybe working so hard in the past was simply a way to escape the challenges of building a new social life for myself."

IDENTIFY AND PLUG TIME LEAKS

Many a landlord or homeowner has scurried around in recent years to identify and plug water or heat leaks. In years past the money saved from stopping drips or drafts was rarely worth the effort. With the substantially increased cost of energy and water these days, plugging leaks has become profitable. The cost of wasted time has also been inflated enough to justify your identifying and plugging time leaks. By putting more of normal working hours to good use, you can increase your output without increasing your number of hours worked.

Smug Hank Doesn't Think He Wastes Time. Told during a management development conference that most managers waste a lot of time, Hank said the lecture was wasted on him. "You're telling me nothing new. As a manager, I'm well aware of the importance of time. I could rightfully say I waste almost no time during the day. Sure, I eat lunch, and I occasionally gaze out the window, but that's normal. I'm a person, not a robot."

Hank Gets Unbraided. George, a colleague of Hank's, raised his hand. When acknowledged by the conference leader, George said: "I take it this is an open conference. I have a different version of how Hank wastes time. Please don't misinterpret what I have to say. I'm a fan of Hank. I just want to point out that I agree with our leader. Even a model of efficiency like Hank does his share of time wasting. Do you mind, Hank, if I tell the group the ways in which even you waste time?"

After receiving a quizzical look coupled with an approving gesture from Hank, George proceeded with his analysis:

Just like the rest of us, you waste a lot of time. Think of the 15 minutes you spend near the elevator while you gather together your little luncheon group. I bet if you ate in the company cafeteria with only one other person, you'd save 30 minutes on lunch alone.

When I visited your office, I couldn't help but notice that you signed two very brief letters that your secretary had prepared from your dictation. That's a big time waster. Why call a secretary into the office for a one paragraph letter? Why not write out the reply yourself directly on the inquiry? I would think only the most important of letters should consume the amount of time required to dictate and then reread them when the dictation is completed.

I'll give you another example of what I'm talking about, Hank. I think you're too friendly a manager. You spend too much time with people either in your office or in their offices. Why not use the phone more? You could save a lot of time that way?

I'll end my analysis of Hank with a comment that will put things in perspective. The reason I've picked on Hank is that he's a damn fine administrator. If Hank wastes some time, think of how much time the rest of us waste.

Kelly Hides Away.   Kelly, a program coordinator in a college of continuing education, is another example of a time-conscious person. Her dilemma was that she worked in a modern building with office landscaping. In order to save money, her college used movable partitions in place of walls. Unfortunately, people did not respect a closed partition. Whenever somebody wanted to talk to Kelly, they just barged past her partition. Kelly hit upon what proved to be a workable solution:

> It became increasingly bothersome to me to be frittering away so much time in idle conversation with people. I tried posting a sign on my partition indicating when I would be free for meetings with people. The arrangement didn't work. In a college, people just don't respect your privacy. Somehow people don't believe that thinking is working.
>
> I decided that I would spend every Tuesday and Thursday morning in my apartment doing my serious thinking for the week. It worked out beautifully. I got to look forward to Tuesdays and Thursdays. The solitude was magnificent. I could see that the quality of work I turned out at home was better than the quality of work I did in my noisy office.
>
> Perhaps if I worked in a bank, my boss wouldn't allow me to

work at home. But a college is a much looser type of arrangement. Also, my boss is efficiency-minded himself.

CLEAN UP EVERY SIX MONTHS

An orderly desk, file cabinet, or attaché case does not inevitably indicate an orderly mind, but it does help most people become more productive. Less time is wasted, and less energy is expended if you do not have to hunt for information that you thought you had on hand. Knowing where information is and what information you have available is a way of being in control of your job. When your job gets out of control, you are probably working at less than peak efficiency.

Even the most orderly career person should clean out his or her work area every six months. Two hours devoted to office housekeeping may give you some hints as to whether or not you are taking care of all the things you should on your job. You might be surprised as to what has filtered down to the bottom of your inbasket.

Ben Cleans Up.   Disorganized Ben was creative, but average with respect to productivity. He and his two brothers ran a small contracting business that they inherited from their father. Bogden Brothers contractors took whatever general work came their way, such as house painting, light carpentry, and hauling. Ben's approach to new business consisted mainly of answering the phone—if somebody wanted something done, Ben and his brothers would take care of it.

Inspired from time to time, Ben would jot down an idea on a sheet of paper, in his wallet, or on his desk blotter. Learning about the "Clean up every six months" suggestion in a management course for small businessmen, Ben decided to give this simple idea a try. He went back to his office and gave it a thorough housecleaning. Ben describes what happened:

> That little housecleaning escapade must have resulted in $15,000 worth of new business for our firm. And they were all my ideas that I had never done anything about. I came up with about eight ideas for new services that I had forgotten I had dreamed of.

One of the ideas was to contract out on cleaning up pigeon droppings off statues and awnings. The work wasn't glamorous, but our reputation for that kind of work spread. Another approach was to go from house to house in old neighborhoods and clear attics of rubbish. Another profitable item was a house exterior cleaning service. Many people don't realize that cleaning the outside of a house can improve its appearance.

As an offshoot of my inbasket cleanup, I've developed an orderly new file for business ideas. Now I won't have to hunt through the office to retrieve ideas I jotted down in miscellaneous places. I'll know where my good ideas are filed.

GUARD AGAINST PROCRASTINATION

A major time waster for many people is procrastination. Recognizing that you are procrastinating can sometimes help you remedy the situation. (One writer I know is an exception. He knows he's a procrastinator, but his insight doesn't help him. One of his favorite methods of procrastination is to run one more errand before he digs into serious work. Walking to the store for cigarettes is his most frequently used stalling tactic.) It will help your time management to figure out what form your procrastination takes.

Merwin Gets Another Opinion. Asked by his boss whether the company should hire its own maintenance staff or use subcontractors, Merwin became tense. He knew the results of such a decision could become visible to others. If outside maintenance were performed poorly, Merwin would be blamed for making a poor decision. He also reasoned that if internal maintenance people were frequently subject to criticism, any criticism of them would also be a criticism of his decision.

Merwin asked his boss for more time, because "this is a trickier problem than would appear on the surface. Before I rush into a commitment, I'm going to collect some more facts. My plan is to establish a maintenance committee. They should be able to provide me with some concrete suggestions in two weeks."

Two weeks later, Merwin was still working on the formation of the committee. What Merwin failed to recognize was that the appointment of a committee was a stalling tactic. As long as the problem was under study, Merwin could not be blamed for making a wrong decision. (Unfortunately for Merwin, as long as his fence straddling lasts, he cannot receive credit for making a right decision.)

Vivian Tries a Diversionary Tactic. A major problem faced by department store executive Vivian was the gradual decline of business in her store's downtown branch. Vivian had heard top management discuss the necessity of studying the long-range viability of downtown locations. Vivian regarded the future, not as tomorrow, but as a vague point in time some years and months from now.

In lieu of dealing with the future, Vivian turned her energies to dealing with more pressing problems. To adjust for the declining business, she ordered substantial cuts in staff, which she believed would increase the store's profitability despite a lowered sales volume. After mapping out that strategy, Vivian made some elaborate plans for a series of Festival Weeks in the store. Each Festival Week would have its unique ethnic motif, such as a storewide promotion on goods from the Netherlands.

Asked by her management what progress she had made in forecasting the future of her store, Vivian replied, "I'm dealing with so many urgent here-and-now problems that I haven't had time to crystal-ball the future. As a frontline executive, I think my job is to keep those cash registers ringing."

True, Vivian is responsible for maintaining an acceptable volume of business, but, at her level in the organization, she has to be concerned with the future as well as the present. Her plans for cutting back the staff and instituting Festival Weeks could be sound business ideas. However, they still represent diversionary tactics—activities to keep her so busy that she does not have to confront the major decision facing her. As long as Vivian procrastinates, she cannot be fully effective in her executive position.

Frank Flits. "I'm sorry, Mr. Belleville is away on an important business trip," said Frank Belleville's secretary about 25 times in one day. Frank had left for a conference in Miami Beach that was scheduled right around labor contract negotiation time. Because Frank was vice-president of manufacturing, his opinion would be figured heavily into decision making about the new labor contract. In his absence, his assistant vice-president was asked to make bigger decisions than his job demanded.

Frank's flight from heavy problems—another variety of procrastination—had its counterpart at home. His former wife notes:

> Frank had an uncanny knack of being called away on business when the pressures mounted at home. I think he invented a labor strike the day we moved into town. I was left with all the tough chores that have to be done the first few days in a new town.
>
> One week all three of our children had gastroenteritis. Not even an experienced nurse would want to contend with three retching children by herself. But Frank found an emergency to contend with 300 miles from home. He did phone me, encouraging me to keep my chin up through the whole ordeal. When he did return home, everything was under control.
>
> I don't think that Frank wanted to avoid helping me take care of the children. I think he didn't want to be around to help me decide whether or not the children should be brought to the hospital.

Frank's pronounced tendency to avoid making decisions by leaving the scene eventually flawed his career progress. He was demoted to a manufacturing planning assignment, where his analytical skills could be put to good use. As a person who generated facts for other people to ponder, Frank performed admirably. He no longer had to face major decisions.

DISPOSE OF DISTRACTING PROBLEMS

Effective time utilization requires good concentration. When you are preoccupied with a personal or business problem, it is difficult to give your full efforts to the task at hand. The solution is to do something constructive about whatever problem is sapping your ability to concentrate (as discussed in the chapter about job stress).

Roth Is Hounded.   A busy ambitious lawyer, Roth rounded out his business activities with the ownership of a six-family building located in a run-down area of town. Roth ran the building successfully as an absentee landlord for three years. Eventually, the building produced a multitude of problems for Roth. Three of the tenants were seriously delinquent on their rent. In a drunken rage, one of the tenants did considerable physical damage to his apartment. Garbage began to pile up in the halls and backyard. Large dogs owned by the tenants began to create sanitation problems. The Fire Department cited Roth for having 12 fire violations in his building. Similarly, the Department of Building Codes cited a number of violations.

Roth described the gravity of the problem in these terms:

> I began to realize that 95 percent of my worries stemmed from that horrible building. In the past I was able to realize a modest profit along with a substantial tax write-off from the property. I still had the tax advantage, but the profit was quickly evaporating. Now I was stuck with a building that was giving me anguish, but no money. I received telephone calls from tenants, neighbors on the block, the Fire Department, and the city inspector. One major mechanical problem after another popped up.
>
> I put the house up for sale at the same price I paid for it, but I had few lookers and no takers. The only legitimate offer I received was for $5,000 below what I paid for the building. And, considering inflation, that would have been an effective loss of $8,000. So there I was, stuck with a harassing problem that was eating away at my ability to concentrate.

What Roth Should Have Done.   Roth was damaging his most valuable asset—his ability to do high-level professional work—by clinging to a miserable, distracting business activity. Selling the house at a $5,000 real loss (or an $8,000 paper loss) would have been a bargain. Roth could have used this loss to offset some of the high taxes he was paying on his $30,000-per-year income. Clinging to the notion that a dollar loss is always bad (or a sign of weakness), Roth was only damaging his legal career. His preoccupation with his real estate problem was adversely influencing his ability to concentrate—a tip-off that Roth should have accepted his one firm offer on the building.

If his only offer fell through, Roth should have kept lowering the price of his building until a buyer was found. *Some* market always exists for a six-family building—in any section of town.

GET RID OF TIME-WASTING VISITORS

An unknown number of people in all kinds of work places, including business, hospitals, schools, government agencies, and even churches, are essentially either lonely or lazy people who are looking for somebody to help them pass away time. Leave your door open to such visitors, and you will be dragged down to their level of horrendous time management. Seeing your door open (or room on your desk to set upon), one of these chronic time wasters will share with you his or her weather prediction or review with you last night's television variety show.

A reliable barometer of a time waster is his or her opening comment, "Are you busy right now" or "What are you doing right now?" Some exceptions exist, but a time-conscious person will ask for an appointment or specify precisely how much time he or she needs from you.

What Can You Say to a Time waster?   For defending yourself adequately against the casual visitor without appearing grossly discourteous, a couple of closing lines may be in order. Choose from among these time-tested conversation enders:

1. "Could you come back later? I'm working now."
2. "Could we talk about this after work?"
3. "Sit down. I can spend up to four minutes with you. My next appointment is in five minutes."

Improving
Your Job Creativity

12 A popular myth in our culture is that people can be accurately classified as creative or uncreative. In truth, creativity is like height, intelligence, and strength. People vary considerably in these dimensions, but everybody has *some* height, *some* intelligence, and *some* strength.

A less widely entertained, but still existent myth about creativity is that it can only be exercised in a limited number of fields such as science, the arts, and photography. An accurate analysis reveals that creativity can be exercised in any field and in almost any setting—including a child's playpen or your office.

If you accept our dual premise that (1) almost everybody has the capacity to exercise some creative thought and (2) that creativity can be exercised on almost any job, you are mentally set to improve your job creativity. By doing so, you may be able to extricate yourself from the lifelong purgatory of performing routine chores for a living.

WHAT IS YOUR CREATIVE POTENTIAL?

A logical starting point in improving your job creativity is to obtain a rough indication of the amount and type of creativity you already possess in undeveloped form. By running through several exercises similar to those required in actual tests of creativity, you could achieve two worthwhile outcomes. First, you could determine how readily you respond to creative assignments. Second, you could conceivably begin to develop the mental set of a creative person.

Test Your Flexibility.   Write down ten uses for each of the following objects:

1. An ordinary red brick.
2. A paper clip.
3. A pencil eraser.
4. A household spoon.

Do not accept "I can't think of any" for an answer. Force yourself to think of the required ten, but giving yourself a five-minute maximum time for each item is realistic. At the outset, creative thinking is difficult work.

What Answers Did Other People Give?   A guidance counselor thought of these uses for a red brick: "doorstop, bookend, paperweight, grind up and make stones for an aquarium, use to settle marital disputes, put behind rear wheel of car when fixing flat, step for reaching on top of refrigerator, insulator for putting pizza on table, newspaper weight when reading at beach or lake."

A college student thought of these uses for a paper clip: "tie clip, abortion instrument for very small girl, ear cleaner, roach clip, bookmark, typewriter key cleaner, temporary screw driver, cocktail stirrer, tooth pick, money clip."

A purchasing agent thought of these uses for an eraser: "something to play with while tense, earplug, toy for kitten, small wire insulator, pellet for harmless gun, poker chip, goldfish bowl decorative float, something to have to catch with, low calorie chewing gum, place in mouth in lieu of smoking."

A shoe salesman thought of these uses for a spoon: "screwdriver, plant and gardening tool, child spanker, shoehorn, sharpen and use for weapon, toy for infant, discharge electricity before shaking hands with another person on thick carpet, drumstick, use as catapult for small objects by pressing quickly at large end, postman signal for rural mail box."

How do I Interpret My Answers?   If you were able to arrive at close to ten uses for each object (other than repeating the obvious, such as using a paper clip for a tie clip and so forth), you show good creative potential. If the entire task left you stymied, you need work in loosening yourself up intellectually. Keep on trying exercises of this nature (and read the rest of this chapter).

Test Your Ability to Think of Consequences.   Another distinguishing characteristic of a creative person is his or her ability to anticipate consequences of unfamiliar events and occurrences. Anticipate at least three of the consequences if the following things were to happen:

1. We all had a third arm sticking out from our stomach.
2. The law of gravity did not work on Monday.
3. Weeds became the only digestible food for human beings.

What Are Some Typical Answers to These Unlikely Events?   The "third arm" question elicits responses from mature adults such as these: "Tailors would go crazy modifying shirts, sweaters, and overcoats." "A person could grab the other guy by the belt while punching him with his other two hands." "Shop lifting would be an even bigger problem. People could be lifting goods while distracting a sales clerk with their other two hands."

The "law of gravity" question troubles people, yet brings forth responses such as, "People would have to stay home on Mondays to hold on to their belongings." "All cars would have to be off the streets of San Francisco on Sunday night. Otherwise, they might roll up the hills." "You could do all your cleaning on Mondays because it would be easy to lift up heavy furniture."

The "weed" question puzzles and concerns many people. A sample of the answers: "The A & P would go out of business forever." "People who owned old vacant lots would suddenly become rich. At the same time, all the grass-people from the suburbs would be cursing themselves for having spent so much of their lives getting rid of weeds." "Every pet in this country who wanted it would be fed a diet of the best table foods—at least, until the supply ran out."

What could it mean if I were unable to think of any of the consequences to these hypothetical events? You are probably too rigid in your thinking. You need considerable practice in taking a suppositional point of view. You are not alone. Many other people are suffering from a "hardening of the categories."

Do I Have the Personality Structure of a Creative Person?

One tentative indication would be your responses to the following test, which is similar in design to an actual test of creative personality. Our test is for illustrative purposes only. Proceed with caution in mind.

Directions. Answer each of the following statements mostly true or mostly false. We are looking for general trends; therefore, do not be concerned if you answer true if they are mostly true and false if they are mostly false.

	Mostly True	Mostly False
1. Novels are a waste of time. If you want to read, read nonfiction books.	——	——
2. You have to admit that some crooks are very clever.	——	——
3. People consider me to be a fastidious dresser. I despise looking shaggy.	——	——
4. I am a person of very strong convictions. What's right is right; what's wrong is wrong.	——	——
5. It doesn't bother me when my boss hands me vague instructions.	——	——
6. Business before pleasure is a hard-and-fast rule in my life.	——	——
7. Taking a different route to work is fun, even if it takes longer.	——	——
8. Rules and regulations should not be taken		

too seriously. Most rules can be broken un-
der unusual circumstances.   ____ ____

9. Playing with a new idea is fun even if it
   doesn't benefit me in the end.   ____ ____

10. So long as people are nice to me, I don't care
    why they are being nice.   ____ ____

11. Writing should try to avoid the use of
    unusual words and word combinations.   ____ ____

12. Detective work would have some appeal to
    me.   ____ ____

13. Crazy people have no good ideas.   ____ ____

14. Why write letters to friends when there are
    so many clever greeting cards available in
    the stores today?   ____ ____

15. Pleasing myself means more to me than
    pleasing others.   ____ ____

16. If you dig long enough, you will find the
    true answer to most questions.   ____ ____

Scoring the Test. The answer in the *creative direction* for each
question is as follows: 1—Mostly False, 2—Mostly True, 3—
Mostly False, 4—Mostly False, 5—Mostly True, 6—Mostly
False, 7—Mostly True, 8—Mostly True, 9—Mostly True, 10—
Mostly True, 11—Mostly False, 12—Mostly True, 13—Mostly
False, 14—Mostly False, 15—Mostly True, 16—Mostly False.
Give yourself a plus one for each answer you gave in agreement
with the keyed answers.

How Do You Interpret Your Score?   As cautioned earlier,
this is an exploratory test. Extremely high or low scores are
probably the most meaningful. A score of 12 or more suggests
that your personality and attitudes are similar to those of a
creative person. A score of five or less suggests that your personality is dissimilar to that of a creative person. You are probably more of a conformist (and somewhat categorical) in your
thinking—at least at this point in your life. Don't be discouraged. Most people can develop in the direction of becoming
more creative individuals.

LOOSEN UP EMOTIONALLY AND INTELLECTUALLY

All methods of creativity improvement are based on the underlying principle of getting you to loosen up emotionally and intellectually. As long as you remain a tight individual, it is difficult to give free rein to your creative potential. Later we will examine a few formal methods designed to loosen up your thinking. For now, we will concentrate on the kinds of experiences that could achieve this effect—although they are not designed specifically for creativity training.

Cora Becomes a Groupie.   Employed as an assistant to the general manager of an industrial company, Cora felt she was running out of innovative ideas. Assigned to the task of developing a new productivity campaign for the plant, Cora could only think of conventional, much-used approaches. Partly as a way of relieving her work-accumulated tensions and partly as a way of opening herself up to new experiences, Cora joined an encounter group.

Cora Gets All Shook Up.   The encounter group met one night a week for three hours. By the third week, Cora noticed that her thinking was becoming more expansive and free floating. Unexpectedly, she arrived at a solid idea for the productivity campaign. She explains how:

> By the third session, we were really emoting. Nobody seemed to be holding back anything. One fellow was talking about the way he hated being oppressed by his company and his boss. One of the girls was telling how she was frightened by the prospects of having so much responsibility thrown on her on the job and at home.
>
> One of the other fellows in the group said he would like to have sexual intercourse with two of the group members—me and the guy next to him. The wonderful thing was that he was actually encouraged. I was getting high on all the honest expression of feelings running through the room. My mind started to work in an uninhibited manner. I was seeing relationships I never saw before. I could feel barriers to my thinking falling in front of me.
>
> At the high point of my high, an idea for a productivity campaign

seemed to jump into view right in front of me: "Three silver dollars for $3 million."

My idea was to give everybody in the plant three silver dollars on any month that our shipments reached $3 million. It was a simple gimmick, but our plant personnel liked simple gimmicks. The general manager loved the idea. So did his boss when the campaign helped push us over the $3 million mark for the first time in the plant's history.

Glenn Needs a Creative Idea.   A stock market enthusiast, Glenn had an inside tip on an excellent investment. In order to cash in on this opportunity, Glenn needed $6,000 in a hurry. His cash on hand was down to $45, and he was extremely hesitant to disturb the $7,000 he had tied up in other stocks. Glenn thought about borrowing from loan companies, but he concluded that the high rate of interest on such loans would make investing the money into stock unduly risky.

Glenn Has Two Martinis.   Having heard from a friend that martinis should receive partial credit for most of the great innovations in advertising, Glenn decided to think through his problem with a gin-soaked brain. As the martinis began to take effect, Glenn became more adventuresome in his thinking. His mind seemed to persevere on the thought that any bank in town would lend him $3,000 but no bank would lend him $6,000. He figured that his personal debt ceiling (considering his income) was that $3,000 figure.

Suddenly, Glenn realized that his real problem was to borrow $3,000 from two banks without letting them know that he was borrowing money from the other. Glenn's martini-induced solution was to apply for the loans almost within the same hour. In that way, he would not be lying when he listed his indebtedness as zero. He could not be in debt until the loan from the other bank was granted.

The plan worked. Both banks extended Glenn a $3,000 line of credit. Within eight days he had his $6,000 and his investment. Glenn's investment in stock was profitable enough to pay back both the principal and interest within the three-year term of his loans.

DISCIPLINE YOURSELF TO THINK CREATIVELY

No matter how much time and money you invest in courses of study or training programs to enhance your creativity, you will not become more creative unless you practice habits of creativity. People labeled as creative discover many of their best ideas in everyday settings. While walking the streets, taking out your garbage, getting your hair cut or coiffed, cleaning your garage, or waiting in line at the bank, look for ideas that could be put to use on your job.

Self-discipline is the underlying method that enables you to cull useful ideas from everyday happenings. You have to discipline yourself to stay alert to useful ideas or combinations of ideas. Once you have developed the mental set of looking for creative ideas, a few ideas may begin to emerge.

The Missing Birth Certificate. During the last decade, horizontal file folders became widely used in offices. A key feature of horizontal filing cabinets is that they conserve space while simultaneously enhancing office decor—they don't look like omnipresent vertical filing cabinet. Allegedly, this useful development was the brainchild of a man looking through his chest of drawers for an old birth certificate. To allow himself more space in the drawer, he had arranged his envelops sideways.

He took his simple idea of a horizontal file folder back to his boss at the office furniture sales company where he worked. His boss, in turn, contacted a major supplier of office furniture who liked the idea. An important innovation had begun, and the inventor of the new filing cabinet received a substantial financial settlement.

Jacob Cashes In on an Idea. Many years ago, a storekeeper named Jacob Ritty was on a transatlantic voyage. He was fascinated by the device that recorded the propeller revolutions of the ship. Ritty reasoned that the same principle could be applied to keeping track of money received by a retail store. The eventual result was a machine that came to be called a cash register.

Lester Has No Time to Think of Ideas. A purchasing agent in a large office, Lester was admonished by his new young boss, Henry: "You're running things in a very routine manner, Les. I suggest you think up some improved ways of running your operation. You've got to become more creative."

Lester responded, "No disrespect to you, sir, but let me tell you something very basic about my job. There is no time to be creative. Dreaming up some wild eyes to improve things would be a luxury. As things are now, I'm doing the work of two people. I simply cannot take on any more work."

How Lester Miscalculated. Rigid Lester was making the classic error of many harassed people. Instead of thinking of ways to do his job more creatively, Lester stayed in the same rut, doing things in an uncreative way. Lester was tightly scheduled on the job; yet there was more time for creative thinking than he realized. Instead of spending so much time lunching with sales representatives, he might have spent a few more lunches in solitude. While alone in a luncheonette or on a park bench, Lester might have concentrated on a more creative way of doing his job. At a minimum, he could have discussed his dilemma (being so pressed for time) with the sales representatives he met. As travelers from company to company, they might have had some constructive suggestions for Lester.

CONDUCT PRIVATE BRAINSTORMING SESSIONS

Brainstorming, as originally developed by Alex Osborn in the later 1930s, is a technique for group members spewing forth multiple solutions to a problem. Thus a group of six people sit around a table generating new names for a dog food. Anything goes, however bizarre it sounds at the time. A few examples are: "Bow Wow Chow," "Pet Steak," "Canine-Fine," and "Boxer Bagels."

Repeated experiments have demonstrated that good ideas do come out of groups—but better ideas come from private brainstorming sessions. The creativity improvement techniques described earlier will help you develop the mental flexibility so necessary for brainstorming. After you have loosed up your mental processes, you will be ready to tackle your most vexing job-related problem.

An important requirement of private brainstorming is that you set aside a regular time (and perhaps place) for generating ideas. (Count the ideas discovered in the process of routine activities as bonus time.) Even five minutes per day is much more time than most people are accustomed to thinking creatively about job problems. Give yourself a quota with a time deadline.

Hal, the Hardware Store Man. Hal was a part owner of a hardware store. He had agreed to take on the assignment of thinking of an effective way of raising some quick cash for his store. Hal allowed himself six days to find a solution to this problem. His proposed solutions were: (1) pawn some expensive merchandise, (2) borrow money from a bank or loan company, (3) establish a fix-it service for minor household repairs, and (4) hold a garage sale for damaged or slow-moving merchandise.

The garage sale idea proved to be a winner. Hal and his co-owner were able to raise several thousand dollars in needed cash and simultaneously clear some of the clutter from their store. As a result, Hal increased his confidence in his ability to think creatively about job problems.

Elaine Had a Vacancy. Property Owner Elaine had a vacancy in the bottom half of a two-family house located in the city. Although the house was physically attractive, Elaine was forced to charge high rents in comparison to other houses in the area. The taxes on the house were high because of its size and solid brick structure. Of more significance, Elaine had made only a small down payment on the property, thus mandating high monthly payments for principal and interest. Another factor contributing to Elaine's problems in renting her property was a high unemployment rate in her city.

Elaine advertised her duplex for rent in the newspaper for several weeks. She received a few phone calls, and a few people looked at the apartment, but nobody agreed to move in. Elaine's concern mounted as her next monthly bank payment became due.

Elaine Free Associates. An action-oriented person by nature, Elaine was provoked by her concern into action. She decided to make a list of all the desirable attributes of her duplex in the hope of making it more alluring to prospective renters. Among the items on her list were: walking distance to buses, walking distance to church and temple, allow pets, new hot water heater, high ceilings, natural wood staircase, and stone cellar.

Elaine pondered to herself, "None of these are unique features. For instance, who really cares if the hot water heater is new? Maybe it might make a difference to a plumber, but most people take things like that for granted. Being close to transportation and other conveniences would apply to almost any house in the city. Come to think of it, the one item my city house has that most city houses lack is a garden. The last tenants had a tomato and cucumber garden blooming before they left. The tenants can't appreciate it now because it's February, but it would be worth mentioning."

Elaine rewrote the ad to read: "Magnolia Street, double house, 4 bedrooms with real garden, $350 plus utilities, 244–4048." Within two days, brainstorming Elaine had rented her apartment to a fine ecology-minded family that was attracted by the garden feature.

USE THE PERSONAL ANALOGY METHOD

Synectics, developed by William J. J. Gordon of Synectics, Inc., has proved to be an effective method of improving creativity. Among its many components is the personal analogy method. According to this novel method, members of the creativity training group imagine themselves to be one of the problem objects. For instance, "if you were a pool outside a motel-restaurant, how would you prevent drunks from jumping into you at night?" Personal analogies can also be done individually.

Ted Gets Called on the Carpet. Maintenance Manager Ted was called into his boss's office for a serious conference: "Ted, we've gotten a number of complaints from building tenants that our carpeting looks shabby in a few key places. What the people are complaining about deals mostly with a few high traffic pattern areas. They say our carpeting is shabby, but what they really mean is that the carpeting is worn out near the water coolers, receptionist desk, and elevators. Figure out an inexpensive way to take care of this problem."

Ted Makes Believe He's a Carpet. Having been through a company-sponsored creativity training program, Ted decided to put the suggestions to work. He thought to himself, "If I were the carpeting on the floor, I wouldn't want to be replaced entirely every time I became a little shabby. I'd want to stay put, the best I could. I wouldn't mind if I were improved a little, but I wouldn't want to be replaced entirely."

Ted arrived at an obvious solution. He suggested to his boss that the company purchase carpeting squares—similar to tiles —for the high traffic areas. As the carpet became worn, new squares could be put into place with a minimum of expense. When the building needed carpeting throughout, the square concept could be used on a larger scale. In this way when heavy furniture was moved, the damaged carpeting immediately under it could be replaced with a brand new piece of carpeting.

Alison Goes for a Ride. Alison, a design engineer in a company that manufactures zippers, was faced with the problem of developing an inexpensive zipper that would not break long before its attached garment was ready for the rag pile. Using the personal analogy method, Alison pretended she was a zipper.

She ruminated, "If I were a zipper, I'd hold on for dear life when I was first put on the track. I'd also hold on tight when I was unzipped." Alison did not solve the problem entirely with her first modification of the existing zipper. But she found the right track. She developed a larger and surer gripping mechanism to help the zipper from derailing when yanked. The additional cost was only three cents per zipper.

BE CURIOUS

Curiosity frequently underlies creative ideas. The person who routinely questions why things work or why they don't work is on the way toward developing a creative suggestion to improve upon what already exists. Many new ideas for products and services stem from the curious attitude of their developer. An office supervisor in a plumbing supply company encouraged his company to develop a new mechanism that would help stop leaking water closets. His suggestion stemmed from his curiosity as to why so many places he visited had troubles with leaking toilets. The resultant product is built upon a new principle: It uses water pressure to replace the troublesome floating bulb arrangement found in most water closets.

Brad Wonders If Things Could Be Different. Brad, a college administrator, noticed that many of his neighbors talked about some day returning to college to work toward an advanced degree in business administration. Yet their talking about this idea did not lead to action. Brad asked a few of these people why they had been unable to return to school. All replied that the time constraints imposed on a commuter (his questioning took place in a New York City suburb) made working toward an advanced degree almost impossible.

Brad's curiosity was aroused. He rode the commuter train on several different days to observe both the type of people who rode commuter trains and their behavior while on the train. A conclusion Brad quickly reached was that these people generally made constructive use of their time by reading or self-study.

Brad's Curiosity Leads to a New Program. A flash of insight hit Brad. Why not offer a couple of degree courses on one of the morning trains? A substantial amount of class credit could be earned in five 45-minute class sessions. His school bought the idea after a formal survey of commuters indicated that they would enroll in a master's degree program that could be earned in part while commuting. At this writing, the commuter school is still in operation.

FIGHT THE SUGGESTION BLOCK

A creative individual must find an environment in which to express his or her creativity. If your organization throws up intentional or unintentional roadblocks to your creative expression, you will not function as a creative person. Many a good idea is buried because a business or other organization encourages conformity in thinking and supresses creativity. At times, you may have to fight such suggestion blocks. Once you are listened to and your idea works, forthcoming blocks may be easier to overcome.

David Gets Blocked.   David worked for a stable, conservative company. For 30 years they had manufactured automobile and truck radiators. Gradually, as the competition became more intense in this field (including more car radiators being made by companies themselves), the future of the firm became more uncertain. As business prospects worsened, the company planned a substantial reduction in the work force.

Prior to implementing the cutbacks, the president initiated a series of product development meetings. Most of the staff members were skeptical because whatever new production suggestion emerged from the meeting was usually vetoed by the president as being too costly or impractical.

Despite this mood of pessimism, David brought forth his latest idea: "Let's do something that will simultaneously help us with the dual problem of having to lay off marginal employees and attract new business. We could run a subcontract recycling operation for our biggest customers. We could agree to haul all of their rejected metal products to a central location of ours. We could tear the products down and give them back all the valuable components such as copper and aluminum. It would be a low technology operation that could run with our least physically and mentally strong individuals. My plan would not only be doing a social good by recycling rejected parts, we would also be making constructive use of people who might stay unemployed if we let them go."

As had happened in the past, David's suggestions were rejected as impractical. "We're not in the business of curing the problems of society. Besides, the operation you talk of wouldn't fit our company's image."

David Gets His Own Division. Not giving up easily, David made another approach at the president and the executive committee. He suggested that the company start a small recycling division with him as general manager. An aging facility on the outskirts of town could readily be converted into the recycling center. David asked that he be given two years to turn a profit and one year to break even. Seeing this as a practical way of getting rid of some of his most pressing personnel problems, the president finally consented.

David had overcome the suggestion block without having to leave behind ten years of seniority with his company. His recycling operation is running in the black. Of profound social significance, David's division gave top priority to hiring physically and mentally handicapped people to meet its human resource requirements.

BORROW CREATIVE IDEAS

A leading management text lists duplication—copying the success of others—as a type of creativity. Knowing when and which ideas to borrow from other people can help you behave as if you were an imaginative person yourself. Many useful ideas brought to the office are simply lifted directly from others or a simple combination of them. An effective career person does not steal confidential ideas from others, but he or she looks for useful ideas that are public information. Giving others credit for the borrowed ideas, enhances, rather than diminishes, your status.

Preston Fills Up Some Vacated Service Stations. On vacation in Connecticut, Preston noticed a unique use of an abandoned service station. It had been converted into an attractive outdoor farm market. Chatting with the owner, Preston discovered that this farm market operated nine months per year. Also of significance, the rent was low because the market was glutted with vacated service stations looking for sublessors.

Returning home to Ohio, Preston convinced his boss (the owner of a small chain of all-around-the-clock grocery stores) to diversify into at least one farm market. To his boss's and Preston's surprise, they had a choice of several fine locations throughout the city. With low rent and a public demand for natural foods, the store met with immediate success. Preston had successfully borrowed a field-tested idea. Now that he is in charge of the farm market, his income has jumped considerably.

MAINTAIN (AND USE) AN IDEA NOTEBOOK

You will rarely capitalize upon your imaginative ideas unless you keep a careful record of them. A creative idea inserted into your mind for future reference may become obliterated by the press of everyday business. An important suggestion kept on your daily log of errands to run or duties to perform may become obscured. Because it is creative ideas that carry considerable weight in propelling your career forward, they deserve the dignity of a separate notebook. The cautious or forgetful person is advised to keep two copies of the idea book: one at home and one in the office (If you work at home, keep the second copy in the glove compartment of your car.)

Dennis, the Cynic. At lunch, a young manager was complaining to me about the futility of self-development courses. "They are all the same," he contended. "They tell you a lot of things that are basically common sense. The last time I heard a lecture on self-development, the speaker told people in the audience to keep a diary. I've kept a diary, but I'm not any better off today for having done it. Neither is anybody else I know."

Dennis's Mistake. Without his realizing it, Dennis is passively resisting the potential benefits a diary (or more specifically an idea book) can have for an individual. By his keeping a diary and not referring back to it as a source of useful ideas and suggestions, Dennis is only wasting time. He is operating in the same manner as the calorie counter who records how many calories he has ingested but does not allow the amount recorded to influence his intake.

A number of successful people keep their idea book with them even while sleeping. Many a good idea comes into focus as a person phases into or out of sleep—when your mind is relatively free of distractions. When so inspired, you can reach for your pencil and notebook. However, proceed unobtrusively, or your bedmate will think you are a work addict. Why add to the hassle of trying to manage your career and personal life effectively?

PART IV

JUGGLING YOUR CAREER AND PERSONAL LIFE

Handling Problems Created by a Successful Spouse

13 Many people who are successful on the job fail at home because they do not have the desire or skill to be successful at both. It takes a good deal of sensitivity and juggling to manage effectively the physical and emotional demands placed on you when you try to score in your career and personal life. Trying to become successful in business sometimes creates even greater problems at home than those created by the person who has already succeeded. He or she may be able to relax more, thus creating fewer problems for loved ones.

Because a chapter is included in this book about the problems created by successful spouses, it does not mean that (1) every successful career person creates these problems or that (2) unsuccessful people do not create problems at home. My intent is to provide a close look at the problems some career-minded people create at home and to suggest a few remedies.

PHYSICAL ABSENCE BREEDS DISCONTENT

A husband (and now, in many cases, a wife) whose work takes him away from home because of long hours and travel usually precipitates small or hugh amounts of discontent at home. A natural expectation most people have of marriage is to receive steady love, sex, and companionship. A physically absent spouse cannot fulfill these expectations. Similarly, a physically absent parent cannot meet the expectations of his or her children.

Charlie, the Peripatetic Advertising Executive. Approaching his thirty-sixth birthday, Charlie was on his way to realizing a 15-year-old dream. The advertising agency he had formed only two years ago was on the verge of profitability. As Charlie expressed it:

> We may not be the biggest or the best advertising shop on the street, but we are recognized and we will be profitable. I am on the verge of realizing the Great American Dream—running your own profitable business. Hard work and talent have put me where I am today. May average work week is 65 hours, not including travel to out-of-town clients.
>
> Sure I hear a few grumbles from my wife and children now and then. But that's life in the ad business. A nine-to-five life-style is out of the question if you're going to succeed in this line of work. There are simply too many competitors scratching at your clients' doors to back off and relax.

Charlie Misperceives His Home Life. Charlie's analysis of the competitive situation in his field and the need for long hours may be correct. However, his analysis of his homelife was woefully incomplete. As he was soon to learn, his wife's discontent was mounting. As his wife, Vivian, confronted him in unequivocal terms one weekend:

> I wish you success in your business, but I've had it with your neglect. Your chaotic work schedule has forced me into not relying upon you any longer. You're almost never around when the children and I need you. I don't see why you even want to stay married to me. If we were divorced, at least you could commit yourself to a regular time of seeing the children. That would be better than what they have now.
>
> Please don't give me your "I'm going to reform as soon as the agency bills $10 million per year" speech. Don't tell me that from now on things will be different. Things won't be different. You know it, and I know it. I have a job, too, but it doesn't prevent me from living a normal life. The only way out is for us to split.

What Should Charlie Have Done?   Charlie is a prototype of the harried executive. Yet some company presidents struggling to build up their businesses find ways to be physically present at home more than Charlie was. If he really wanted to have a peaceful homelife and yet still build up his agency, Charlie could have carefully studied his job approach.

Charlie might have begun by carefully analyzing his work habits. Maybe there were more time leaks in his typical work day than he realized (as described in an earlier chapter). Maybe he wasn't delegating enough work to other people on his staff. Another logical way in which Charlie might have found more time for homelife would have been to cut down on out-of-town travel. Many executives schedule an out-of-town trip when they could take care of their business by phone.

By just spending about seven more nights per month at home, Charlie could have lessened his wife's discontent considerably. By sacrificing a few quasi-necessary, quasi-business lunches, Charlie might have been able to arrive home at least two hours earlier on many a night.

PSYCHOLOGICAL ABSENCE CREATES PROBLEMS ALSO

A preoccupied career person can create discontent at home even when he or she is physically present. Many career-minded people leave the office, but don't leave their job in the office. It is not unusual for a work zealot to be so enmeshed in a work problem that he or she does not attend to what's happening at home.

Gail Pours Ketchup on her Baby.   Tom, Gail, and their six-month-old baby, Danny, were seated at their picnic dinner table. While enjoying their Saturday night backyard cookout, Gail turned the conversation to her newest project at work: "The implications for the entire corporation are enormous, Tom. It looks like our department is going to get the approval to conduct a human resources utilization audit. I'll be the project director. This will give me a chance to be noticed by many of the top executives in the company."

As Gail proceeded on, she reached across the table for the ketchup. As she gesticulated about the immensity of the project, she inadvertently mistook Danny for her hamburger bun. As the third glob of ketchup settled on Danny's leg, he began to cry.

Dismayed, Tom blurted out: "Dammit, Gail, will you forget your job at dinner time? It's a rare night anymore that the three of us get to eat a relaxed dinner together. You have to spoil it by pouring ketchup on Danny. Don't you even think of what you're doing when you're talking about work? My biggest fear is that you'll let Danny get hurt someday when you're thinking about your job."

Should Gail Forget about her Job?   One of the reason's Gail is so successful is that she is committed to her personnel specialist position. It would, therefore, be unnatural for her to stop thinking about her work. However, she could practice more self-discipline about when she was thinking about her job. It's a practical habit for a career-minded person to delimit thinking about job problems.

Gail might have arbitrarily tried to concentrate on not thinking about her job while Danny was on her lap or while making love to Tom. Job thinking while driving a motorcycle might also be declared off limits.

Tom might have helped Gail. Every day he might have routinely asked her about her job. Given ample opportunity to review job events, Gail might have been less preoccupied with the job at other times. Once a committed person has talked about his or her commitment, preoccupation about the topic generally lessens.

SUCCESSFUL SPOUSES ENGENDER RESENTMENT

When one spouse has more fun and excitement than the other, resentment is often the result. Such resentment may have multiple roots and may be expressed directly at the spouse or indirectly toward his or her work, career, boss, or company.

Sheri Gets Tired of Tuna Fish Sandwiches for Lunch.
Sheri, a full-time homemaker by choice, was married to Ferdinand, a sales representative. Ferdinand's job involved substantial expense account living. Although his out-of-town travel
was not extensive, he dined extensively in town with customers
and prospective customers. Despite his extensive expense account privileges, Ferdinand, Sheri and their three children were
confined to a tight budget at home.

One Friday night, Ferdinand asked Sheri what she was serving for dinner. Sheri answered, "Tomato soup and grilled cheese
sandwiches, followed by canned pineapple chunks and fig
cookies for dessert."

Ferdinand angrily responded, "How can you expect me to eat
food like that? On Wednesday night I had Chateaubriand for
dinner. Today I had eggs Benedict for lunch. And tonight you
expect me to eat the kind of meal they serve in an orphanage."

"Who do you think you are? Do you think I enjoy eating tuna
fish sandwiches day after day while you are out dining in luxury restaurants? You tell me to scrimp and save although the
company pays for your so-called business lunches. You have
the sensitivity of an ox."

What Ferdinand and Sheri Should Have Done.   Both people were overreacting. Ferdinand was losing perspective about
what constitutes good food, whereas Sheri was overdramatizing
her plight. Ferdinand's insensitive comment suggests that he
had no awareness of Sheri's resentment toward his expense
account living. Ferdinand and Sheri were overdue for some
honest dialogue about her feelings of resentment toward Ferdinand's high living. Another topic worth exploring was the
possibility that Ferdinand was putting down the home menu as
a way of asserting his power.

Aside from delving into their feelings, honest dialogue might
have led to a change in behavior. Perhaps Sheri might have
taken Saturday afternoons to dine at restaurants of her choice
with her friends. Ferdinand could have then taken the opportu-

nity to enjoy tuna fish sandwiches with the children. He might have found lunches with no business strings attached to be a refreshing change of pace.

Tammy Gets More Attention than Sylvester.   Tammy and Sylvester met in their senior year in college and were married two years later. Both entered a stockbrokerage business at the same time, but their careers have accelerated at different rates. Quiet, analytical Sylvester gravitated toward a research analyst's position in a large stockbroker firm. Outgoing, alert Tammy moved into the sales end of the business.

Tammy achieved rapid success as a registered sales representative. Her good judgment, combined with her good looks, was a distinct asset in this competitive field. Sylvester plodded along much more slowly in his career. He began to resent the success of his spouse:

> I want to be honest with you and myself. I'm getting jealous of Tammy's success. A conversation I overheard at a party recently convinced me that some people believe Tammy is a business sensation whereas I'm a high-level clerk who assists her.
>
> We started our careers at the same time, but she's the one who is moving out ahead. In the last several months she has received offers from two firms that would like to pirate her away from her present firm. The way stockbrokerage houses are cutting back these days, I feel lucky to hold on to my job.
>
> I admire Tammy for her abilities, but I still can't help resenting all the attention she's getting. After all, I know something about the stock market business too.

How Tammy Could Have Helped.   Tammy did care for Sylvester and his feelings. She likewise cared about her career and enjoyed her success and attention. Sensing that Sylvester's ego needed boosting, Tammy might have tried a thrust of this nature:

> Sylvester, I know you're concerned about my currently making more money than you do. Maybe the public equates success with money and fanfare, but I don't. As an insider, I recognize that you

and I are doing different kinds of work. People like you come up with good ideas for investments, and people like us bring those good ideas to the attention of the public.

In a sense, my success is due to your quiet success. Maybe someday the situation will be reversed. Maybe the state laws will change, and we won't be able to peddle stocks. Maybe people will enter a banklike institution and ask to purchase the stocks chosen by the bank's research department. At that time, you'll be getting all the goodies, and I'll have to find something else to do for a living.

Please don't let my commercial success interfere with our relationship. Would you love me more than you do now if I were less talented and lucky?

CHILD NEGLECT

Performing admirably as a parent and a career person is a challenging task. Many children of successful parents rebel against the life-style required in order to maximize their careers. The child of a career-obsessed parent often suffers from psychological neglect.

Margot Hangs Up on her Mother. At 3:30 one afternoon, 14-year-old Margot received a phone call from her mother: "Margot sweetheart, I'm afraid I won't be able to make it to your class showing of *South Pacific* tomorrow night. I have to make a presentation to the school board. I know that your brother will be able to attend. Try and get in touch with him. Your father said he won't be back from his trip until the end of the week. Let me know right away if your class decides to put on another performance of the play. I'd love to attend."

Before hanging up the phone, Margot screeched to her Mother, "Sure you will, mother. Ever since you became involved in politics, you have no time left for me. It's like not having a mother. The only time you talk to me is when you have something for me to do around the house. I'm your child, not a slave, if you remember."

What Should Margot's Mother Have Done? Caroline (Margot's mother) was caught in the classic conflict of the upward striving individual. She still felt some allegiance toward her family, but she had also developed a growing awareness she had an allegiance to herself. Caroline sought self-fulfillment through her supervisory position in a nursing home and her committee work in local politics.

Her quest for self-fulfillment made her less sensitive to the needs of her children than she was in the past. Her best solution would have been to develop an informal system to assign priorities for family versus career life. When a significant family event was scheduled for the future, Caroline should have organized her work and volunteer schedule to make that event. Knowing the dates of Margot's play two months ahead of time, Caroline could have organized her work to have made her presentation to the school board another time.

Perry, the Absentee Father. Ambitious Perry was one of an army of commuting fathers who rarely see their children during normal work weeks. Perry was headed toward a vice-presidency in a large paper company, headquartered in Manhattan. As he commuted daily on his 25-mile trip from his suburban town to the Grand Central area of New York City, he felt comfort in seeing so many other men participating in the same life-style. When not out of town on a business trip, Perry dutifully left his suburban house at 7:15 and returned home approximately 12 hours later—assuming no emergency meetings were called.

Perry and his wife, Betsy, soon began to argue about his work schedule. Betsy contended, "You are leaving all the child rearing to me. All you do for the children is support them and play with them a little on weekends. I notice that even your weekend play with them is slackening off. After you finish up with your paper work, play golf, or work out at the "Y" and get in your extra sleep, there has been very little time left for Jody and Ivan."

Perry answered: "What can you expect? I have a very demanding job. I'll never become a vice-president if I leave my office at four in the afternoon in order to be home in time to play with the kids. I'll make it up to them when they are older.

Maybe when I'm vice-president, I can sneak home a few afternoons a month."

"By then, the children won't need you around," replied Betsy. "As things stand now, the children are drifting away from you whether you realize it or not."

Perry Makes a Courageous Decision. Tormented by the realization that what Betsy was saying had a strong element of truth, Perry began to question his daily routine. "Why am I a commuter? There must be thousands of well-paid executives in the United States who lead a normal family life. There must be a way for an executive in the paper business to have an exciting job, yet still see his children on almost a daily basis."

Betsy's confrontation and Perry's subsequent self-questioning led to constructive change. Perry began the tedious process of exploring job possibilities outside of large, congested metropolitan areas for an executive of his background. Fortunately for Perry, he began his search internally. His company needed an operations manager in an Oregon paper mill. Perry is still working hard to maintain his success, but he also has more opportunity to see his children than he did in the past.

Perry notes, "It's not that I work any less hard than formerly. It's just that my life is more flexible. When you subtract three hours of almost wasted commuting time from your day, it gives you a lot more time for your job and your family. I'm not the perfect father, but at least now I'm an active father."

FEELINGS OF COMPETITION AND RIVALRY

An unfortunate by-product of doing well in your career is that it sometimes creates feelings of rivalry and competition between you and your spouse. The competitive feelings can be particularly intense when both members of a marital team are pursuing similar goals or performing similar work. As the world becomes more egalitarian, an increasing number of women are pulling ahead of their spouses in income and prestige.

Sandra Takes a Giant Step Forward. Working for a truly equal opportunity employer (a medical insurance company),

Sandra strove for a manager's position in her company. After five years of distinguished performance as a supervisor, Sandra received a promotion to department head. Fred, her husband, extended Sandra his congratulations, but Sandra could not help noticing his double entendres. For instance: "Congratulations to you. It must be nice to be given preferential treatment because of your sex. I've heard that insurance companies are going out of their way to promote women into good jobs."

Several months later, Sandra noticed another uncalled-for dig from Fred. She bought Fred an expensive 35-millimeter camera for his birthday. With a hurt look on his face, Fred commented, "Oh, I wish I could afford to buy you such an expensive present. With my income I can only afford an average gift."

Digs turned to arguments that seemed to arise whenever Sandra discussed her work with Fred. Rather than precipitate arguments, Sandra chose to discuss her career with her friends and avoided the topic in the presence of Fred.

Sandra Was Performing an Unnatural Act. A career-minded person suppressing conversation about his or her career with a spouse is unnatural and unhealthy. A sounder tactic for Sandra would have been to force the issue about rivalry. Perhaps a heated discussion about Fred's loss of self-esteem because Sandra was outdistancing him in the race for career success would have had therapeutic value for Fred. Perhaps he could have realized that his feelings of rivalry were based upon old-fashioned ideas.

The alternative of Sandra's suppressing her favorite topic of conversation could only lead to counterresentment on her part. Equally significant, an unabated series of hostile references to her career by Fred would ultimately create problems in their relationship.

SUCCESSFUL PEOPLE ARE FOREVER SEARCHING

Thorpe established an enviable reputation for himself in his industry. A prominent management consultant, he also operated two small business ventures. Thorpe accomplished as much as two well-organized executives. His income placed him in the top two-tenths of one percent of the people in the United States. His perquisites, such as a company car, airplane, and membership in a country club, added substantially to his real income.

Thorpe planned next to purchase a local radio station. Kristen, his wife, confronted Thorpe with the implications of his proposed venture: "Thorpe, when will your empire building stop? If you take on a radio station, the children and I will never see you. There is absolutely no more room in your schedule for another business activity. As it is, your present work schedule is more suited for a workaholic than a normal person."

"But Kris," rejoined Thorpe, "a person like myself can't stay still. You knew that when you married me. I'm on top now, and I want to stay on top. To stand still in my field is to fall behind."

"Have it your way for now. Somehow I wish you could become a normal executive instead of somebody with an emperor complex."

Thorpe Is Partially Right. Thorpe, the empire builder, should be admired for candor about being a restless individual who thrives on being faced with a series of new challenges. However, if he is serious about keeping his homelife patched together, he should modify his way of finding new challenges. Purchasing another business, which would siphon more time away from homelife, is only one way of finding new challenges. Thorpe might have taken over new tasks on his job while delegating some of his already existing responsibilities to others. Adding more hours to your work week is not the only way of finding new thrills on the job.

Paula Has a Showing.   After years of struggling as an amateur painter, Paula finally created a small market for her paintings. After her first exhibit, several local people commissioned her to do a painting for them. What began as a six-hour-per-week hobby to combat the housewife syndrome became a full-time occupation.

Ward, Paula's husband, began to voice some complaints

about Paula's expanded time commitment to painting. He commented: "I'm all for your having fun, Paula, but I think your hobby thing has gotten out of hand. You're neglecting the children lately because of your obsession with your paintings. I'm beginning to feel left out too. Why don't you do all of us a favor and put your pastime back into proper perspective."

Paula countered: "I have things in the perspective I want. My dream has always been to become a successful artist. Now that I'm on my way, I'm not going to hold back. My plans are to increase rather than decrease the time I devote to my art. Do I tell you that you are out of perspective because you have a full-time commitment?"

Ward's Strategic Error.   Unwittingly, Ward was taking precisely the wrong approach to get Paula to slacken off from her expanding work schedule. By using attacking terms such as "obsession with your paintings" and "put your pastime into proper perspective," he could only alienate Paula. By being supportive and encouraging about her work, Ward might have been able to reach some sort of compromise with Paula about her devotion to art versus her family.

An opening thrust of this nature might have been more effective thrust of this nature might have been more effective than the one Ward actually used: "Paula, the children and I are very excited about your new success. Yet somehow we wish we could see more of you. Do you have any suggestions?"

JOB PROBLEMS SPILL OVER TO THE HOME

A characteristic of ambitious people is that their moods are often directly influenced by events related to their career. A successful career person facing a critical business or professional problem may be emotionally down because of that situation. For instance, an athletic coach with a good family relationship may act in an abrupt and disinterested manner toward his family following the loss of a key game.

Brian's Moods Bother Pam.   Pam, a high school English teacher and free-lance copyeditor, is married to Brian, a prosecuting attorney. As described in my book, *The New Husbands,* Pam reports on what she sees as the biggest problem in their relationship (and Brian does not disagree):

> Brian is a first-rate husband. Our relationship is as good as it was during the two years we lived together. Our big problem as I see it is that Brian's moods are more influenced by his work than by me. If he has won a big case, there is nothing I can do that will annoy him. After an important win in the courtroom, Brian smiles most of the time and has unlimited energy for everything. It works for him even if I'm in somewhat of a bitchy mood myself.
>
> On the other hand, if Brian is in the doldrums because of a political hassle or some other catastrophe about his job, he just doesn't seem to respond to anything positive about our relationship. One Valentine's Day I invited him out to our favorite Mexican restaurant. He sulked most of the evening because it looked as if an alleged murderer he was prosecuting would not be convicted. Brian wasn't insulting—he never is. What concerned me is that Brian couldn't get emotionally up for this special night I had arranged.

What Pam and Brian Might Have Done.   No easy solution exists for this kind of problem. Pam and Brian talking about the problem could be helpful, yet they both show a good awareness of the nature of the problem. If Brian learned better techniques of concentration (such as those sometimes acquired in Transcendential Meditation), he might be better able to concentrate on Pam and leave his job concerns behind. (Improved concentration of this nature would also be helpful to Brian in his career.)

DEALING WITH THE RELOCATION TRAUMA

A career-minded person is often forced into a position where relocating (or staying put) is the best thing for his or her career. A husband might be offered a promotion in a new town, whereas his wife would have to sacrifice a good job if she followed her husband. Even when the wife does not work outside the home, family, social, and community commitments may make relocation a trauma. (For that minority of people who thrive on change, relocation is an exciting challenge and not a trauma.)

Larry Gets His Big Chance. Larry was the controller of a New Jersey company. An executive search firm approached Larry with the chance to become president of a Virginia company. Ecstatic about the prospects of becoming a company president, Larry discussed the job offer at home. Jan, his wife, thought the possibility sounded intriguing. She welcomed the opportunity to live near the nation's capitol and move to a more temperate climate. She believed that, once located in Virginia, she could readily find new employment as a registered nurse.

Randy and Robin, Larry's and Jan's children, bemoaned the prospects of relocation. Randy reasoned that transferring a high school student during the beginning of his senior year was about as considerate as sending him to prison. Robin shared Randy's sentiments, noting that she was entering her last year of junior high school. Larry took his children's attitudes into consideration and listened carefully to his children without committing himself to a course of action.

Larry's Practical Solution. After a series of interviews, Larry was offered the presidency of the company pursuing him. He drew up a package deal to sell to his family. Calling for a family conference, Larry had something specific to offer his wife and children:

> Let me tell you the whole story before you jump ship. The job offer I received looks terrific. We won't have to worry about money anymore if I take the position. I recognize that this move couldn't be more poorly timed. If I were entering my last year of school, I would probably run away from home before relocating.
>
> I'll take all my vacation days by staying in New Jersey for ten consecutive Fridays once May rolls around. My plans are to leave home every Sunday evening and try to get home by dinner every Friday. While in flight, I'll get a good deal of my paper work done. Once school is out, the whole family can relocate. If you folks buy my package deal, maybe the company will bear with a long-distance commuter for a president until midsummer.

Jan, Randy, and Robin and the board of directors at the new company all bought Larry's proposition. As things have worked out, the family have all adjusted favorably to Virginia at home, and Larry has become a first-rate company president.

SUCCESSFUL PEOPLE OFTEN FORGET LITTLE THINGS

Successful career people are noted for their keen memories about business matters. Unfortunately, this keen memory does not always carry over to social and family life. A successful person's preoccupation with the job often means that he or she forgets facts related to personal life such as a planned-for social engagement with his or her mate. Many a busy male executive uses his secretary to remind him of upcoming dates that are important to his wife (such as birthdays and anniversaries).

Rich Misses the Cub Scout Awards Banquet. Hard-charging Rich kissed his wife and son good-bye one Sunday night—not an unusual ritual at his house considering Rich's hectic travel schedule. Before Rich finished his good-bye pep talk, his son, Todd, began to sob: "Dad, Dad, you can't go. Tomorrow night is the Cub's Banquet night. Every other father will be there. You said you would go with me."

The young Cub Scout's mother came to his defense. "Rich, this isn't the first time you've hurt somebody's feelings because you broke a promise. The damage is already done. Go ahead on your trip."

Rich Uses a Mechanical Aid. Rich was in conflict. On the one hand, he was concerned that he broke a promise to his son and was missing out on something very important to a youngster. On the other hand, he realized that his scheduled trip was important. He opted to go on the trip, but to mend his ways. Rich chose a solution that has worked effectively. He now lists his business and social dates on the same calendar. This way when he is planning a business trip, he checks first to see if it conflicts with a very important family date. Also, he tries not to make promises to his family if the promise will have to be broken because of a business engagement.

FIND YOUR OWN IDENTITY

For many individuals, the only solution to handling the problems created by a successful spouse is to be successful—or at least deeply involved in something themselves. Once a married person feels that he or she has an identity outside his or her relationship to a spouse, there is much less cause for resentment. The resentment so frequently harbored by the spouses of successful people stems from envy that the spouse has found something in life so intriguing. Once the resentful spouse develops a similar intense interest of his or her own, the resentment may decrease.

Henry Is Attacked.   During a couples rap session, executive Henry was put under fire by his wife and other members of the group. They agreed that Henry had let work become so all-consuming that it was causing wife neglect. Karen, his wife, was thought to be the sufferer in the relationship. Henry did not let these salvos go without his expressing a counteropinion: "Sure, I sound like a work-obsessed ogre. I agree I have been insensitive to Karen's needs from time to time, but I'm not as bad as the picture you paint. I'm not sure what kind of work most of you are involved in, but it's tough to be the perfect husband when you have a job that could easily consume your every working hour. I think what I'm hearing in this group will be helpful to me in my relationship to Karen, but I still think you people have blown things out of proportion."

Karen Has a Confession.   At a follow-up session to the couples rap group conducted seven months later, Karen had something important to share with the group:

> Folks, so long as this is an open group I'll make a serious confession to you. Henry was right. The reason I thought Henry was overemphasizing work was that I had never experienced the thrill of accomplishment myself.
>
> About one month after we last met, I received a good break in my career. I was asked to work as a research associate for a well-known scientist in my laboratory. I was suddenly turned on by

work. I haven't lost my love for Henry or our son, but I fight to have more free time so I can spend it back at the laboratory.

We have a role reversal in our house now. Last Thursday Henry suggested we drive up to northern Michigan for the weekend. I told him I couldn't go because I wanted to finish up another test run in the lab. Henry told me that even he wasn't that hung up with work. Suddenly, I realized how striving for success and family happiness at the same time can be an agonizing conflict.

Sharing Responsibilities at Home

———•◦◦◦•———

14 When two or more adults sharing the same household (including husband and wife, boyfriend and girlfriend, same sexed gay people, or a small commune) try to succeed in their careers, substantial cooperation is required. Under a more traditional arrangement whereby the husband earns all the money, the division of labor is simplified: the wife tends to do most of the housekeeping and child rearing while the husband performs a few maintenance chores.

When a couple leads a more modern life-style, they have to plan out an equitable and workable sharing of household responsibilities. The alternative to careful planning is awkward situations (for instance, "I thought you were going to pay the gas and electric bill") and hurt feelings ("Why am I the one who is always expected to clean up after the neighbor's dogs?").

USE TWO (OR MORE) DECISION MAKERS IN EVERY HOUSEHOLD

A distinguishing characteristic of modern thinking, dual career couples, is that they share equally in making decisions about running the domestic side of life. Under such an arrangement, neither he nor she has exclusive decision-making prerogatives in any particular area. He may make the decision sometimes without consulting her over some minor matters (such as selection of a plant for the living room). She may make the decision the next time a plant is to be selected for inside the house.

Tilda and Tim Are Confused. A dual career couple, Tilda and Tim believed that households can run smoothly without drawing up formal arrangements of who does what and when. As Tim described his attitude: "I get enough of that stuff in the office. My company is a bug for orderliness. Everybody has a job description and knows what he or she is supposed to be doing all the time. That approach may work well in the army and in the office, but I couldn't see its relevance to running a household."

Idealistic Tim soon had to change his approach. He and his wife, Tilda, learned that such an informal arrangement created more problems than it solved. Tilda gives a sampling of some of the problems they faced early in their marriage:

> We just assumed that because we decided upon a fifty-fifty marriage, things would run smoothly, but they didn't. Just before getting married, we jointly agreed that we needed a new refrigerator. I was hurting for cash because of all the wedding expenses; so Tim agreed to purchase the refrigerator. One day he called me at work from a nearby appliance store. He told me there was a floor sample at a $250 discount, but he didn't want to buy it without first getting my approval. Tim said there were two models left, one coppertone and one avocado.
>
> I told Tim to do what he thought was best and that he should go ahead and make the decision without me. He came home that night to tell me he decided not to purchase the refrigerator without my seeing it. By the time we both went to see the refrigerator floor samples, they were both gone. We ended up spending at least $250 more for a refrigerator than need be because Tim didn't think he should make a unilateral decision.
>
> Another time I was at fault. Tim was away at a convention and could not easily be reached. An acquaintance of mine owned a cottage on a secluded lake in Ontario. She and her family spent a good portion of their summers on the lake. They planned to take a traveling vacation one week and wanted to rent the cottage for

the week they would be away. She offered to rent it to me for $150. I told her I couldn't agree to it without first consulting Tim.

When Tim returned from the convention, he told me that he would be delighted to go, especially because fishing was his favorite vacation pastime. By the time I got hold of that woman, she had rented the cottage to somebody else. By my not making the decision myself, Tim and I missed out on a week of potential fun.

Tim and Tilda Divide Up the Decision-Making Pie. To avoid repetitions of such incidents, Tim and Tilda reached some formal agreements about who would make decisions about what and which decisions should be made jointly. A unique aspect of their agreement was that they would renegotiate their decision-making arrangement each year around the New Year's holiday. The main points of their one-year agreement are as follows:

> Tim and Tilda will have an equal vote on all major decisions such as job relocation, whether or not to have a child, whether or not to buy or sell a house, house remodeling, membership in a country club, the pursuit of an advanced degree for either person, and whether or not an in-law or other family member or boarder should live with us. Also, any purchase over $500 calls for a joint decision.
>
> Tim or Tilda can make any minor decision about the purchase of clothing, home furnishing, or food without consulting the other. Magazine subscriptions, book purchases, car repairs, and choice of wine and so forth fit into this category.
>
> For this year Tim decides where to go on vacation and how frequently we should visit relatives and friends versus being by ourselves. He also can select household plants and pets.
>
> For this year Tilda will decide how much money we should save and invest. She will be responsible for all decisions about what food we purchase for the house and in which restaurants we dine.
>
> However, if either of us violently object to a decision reached by the other, that objection should be voiced and the other person might reconsider. For instance, Tim dislikes Indian food; so when we dine together Tilda should avoid Indian restaurants.

Tilda comments about their experience with this formal arrangement: "At first, we were both skeptical that anything so formal and seemingly artificial could work. However, we were pleasantly surprised. We kept to the agreement, and it seemed that fewer things fell between the chairs. Also, it added an element of surprise to our life. For instance, it seemed romantic now that Tim was back selecting a place for us to go on vacation the way he once did when we were single."

REVAMP THE HOUSEWORK SYSTEM

A career-minded couple cannot make a go of it unless there is a mutually agreed-upon sharing of household tasks. He and she have to agree on what is an equitable arrangement for dividing the countless chores and errands necessary to keep a household together. The old arrangement of his doing chores related to the outside of the house while she tends to inside chores is rapidly diminishing. Modern couples have found more creative arrangements.

Elton and Linda Do Some Job Bidding. Determined to live a nonsexist life-style, Elton and Linda decided to embark upon a new system of sharing household tasks (one they discovered in *Survival in the Sexist Jungle*). In job bidding, every household task is worth an agreed-upon number of points, and each member of the family must earn his or her quota of points. Time-consuming and distasteful jobs earn more points than quick, pleasant, relaxing tasks. A master chart is posted in some convenient location within the apartment or house.

Elton and Linda agreed to choose a particular task for a given week, trying to be flexible about rotating distasteful and not-so-bad, even pleasant chores. Under the system they chose, both needed 100 points to fulfill their weekly quota. Here is the job-bidding chart they used to select their weekly tasks.

Task or Chore	Point Value	Elton	Linda
Wash clothing	20	——	——
Iron clothing	10	——	——
Clean bathrooms	25	——	——
Food shopping	10	——	——
Dust furniture	5	——	——
Prepare dinner	25	——	——

Wash cars	10	——	——
Make up bed	5	——	——
Vacuum and sweep	5	——	——
Clear table/load dishwasher	5	——	——
Empty garbage	5	——	——
Wash woodwork	20	——	——
Pay bills	5	——	——
Drive children to activities	5	——	——
Mow lawn/shovel snow	10	——	——
Prepare breakfast	15	——	——
Window cleaning	10	——	——
Handle miscellaneous tasks, repairs, sewing	10	——	——
Total for each person		100	100

Built into this system is the positive feature that neither person assigns the other a fixed role. As Elton explains it: "I enjoy cleaning windows; so I take on window cleaning more frequently than does Linda. She dislikes the grubby task of clearing the table; so I generally, but not always, clear the table after dinner. We both hate cleaning the bathroom; so we alternate on that chore on a weekly basis."

Junior and Georgia Were Not Getting Satisfaction. A modern couple, Junior and Georgia, tried to cooperate with each other as much as possible on household tasks. Often Junior would sweep, and Georgia would hold the dustpan; Georgia would prepare the main course at dinner, and Junior would make the salad. Junior would dust, and Georgia would mop. The problem they faced was that neither person felt that he or she was accomplishing much. As Georgia notes, "It's not very satisfying to prepare half a dinner."

Junior and Georgia Convert to Total Task Responsibility. As an antidote to their problem, this couple switched to a system that is gaining in use among couples who share housekeeping responsibilities. Under this system, called total task responsibility, the male and female have entire responsibility for different tasks. Switching back and forth among tasks is acceptable (and probably desirable). For instance, the husband might have total responsibility for the den, basement, garage, dining room, and car maintenance. He would be obliged to perform any function he thought necessary to keep the rooms just mentioned and the cars in proper shape. Whatever required doing—dusting, painting, washing, or servicing—would be his responsibility. Nagging by the spouse about when and how to perform these tasks is discouraged.

Georgia describes how total task responsibility worked for her and Junior: "What we enjoy the most is the pride that comes from having accomplished a whole thing. If the kitchen looks nice, I can pridefully say 'I did it.' Because two people are not meddling in the same chore, there is much less second-guessing about how things should have been done. It's the only sensible way for us. No more being somebody's helper on a simple matter for either Junior or myself."

TAKE TURNS BEING INCONVENIENCED

Nobody can escape all the potential inconveniences that are a product of living in a complex society. Ultimately, you have to have your automobile serviced, let the plumber in to repair or replace a leaking pipe, or agonize over a briefcase full of receipts as your tax return is being audited by an Internal Revenue Service examiner. The activities just mentioned are primarily inconveniences because they must be performed during normal working hours.

In the rigidly traditional family, the woman assumes the responsibility for managing these inconveniences, even if she, too, has a job outside the home. The underlying assumption may be that her work is less important than his work. For more modern (less sexist) couples, another solution must be found.

Wanda and Wayne Keep a Diary. Wayne, a construction engineer, earns a handsome income. Wanda, his wife, earns less money but is well paid for her line of work as a bookkeeper. Both their children attend elementary school, adding to the complexity of their running a dual career family. One day Wanda complained to Wayne:

"I'm running myself ragged trying to balance everything. My job is important, but it's very difficult to be a punctual, reliable bookkeeper when I have to take off from work for so many emergencies. So far this month, I've missed a lot of work because of things or because of the children or household emergencies.

"Remember the day both children woke up sick? I had to stay home all day because the day care center would not accept sick children. One week later, a main pipe in our basement broke. You told me that you didn't have the time to fool with it; so I called the plumber. He promised to be there by 9:00. Well, he got there at 11:45 and finished at 12:30.

"I don't want to give my boss the impression that my personal life is helter-skelter. Why don't you stay home for the next emergency?"

"Wanda, that's ridiculous," countered Wayne. How can you expect a person with a job like mine to stay home to take care of a sick child?"

"What's so ridiculous about that?" returned Wanda. You have more leeway as a construction engineer than I do as a bookkeeper. Most of my work is confined to a desk, whereas you're hopping about loose as a goose. I don't appreciate that comment about the children, either. They are your children as much as they are mine."

"Maybe you have a point," Wayne conceded. I'll take care of the next problem. And we'll alternate after that."

"I knew you'd see the light, Wayne. Let's keep track of whose turn it is on a desk calendar. I have one right here from your construction company."

Elliot and Fran Learn How to Deal with Sears. As Elliot walked in the door, he noticed Fran pounding her fists on the table. With a startled look on his face, Elliot said, "What's happening?"

"I'm going mad, absolutely insane. I can't take it anymore. Sears has left another one of their stupid notes that 'You were not home when we attempted to deliver your appliances. Your merchandise has been returned to the warehouse.' I told them on the phone that the only time they could deliver the washing machine was on Thursday morning before eleven. No matter what I do they refuse to accept the fact that not every woman who orders a washing machine is not a full-time homemaker who sits in her kitchen waiting for the Sears truck."

"But it's not only Sears. Any catalog sales company refuses to talk to a man." replied Elliot. "One of them called me the other day, insisting on speaking to my wife. I told them I ordered the drapes, but the clerk just wouldn't listen. After a few angry words from me, she finally did listen."

Fran called back Sears, this time leaving unequivocal instructions with the telephone clerk: "Now hear this. I am not a full-time homemaker. I will not be home all the time, any time Sears wants to deliver my washing machine. Tell your drivers, repeat, tell your drivers, that I will only be home to receive delivery next Thursday morning before 11 A.M. If you don't write my message down on the order slip, I will cancel the order."

After giving the clerk ample time to write down the delivery instructions, Fran said, "Thank you, thank you. It's a pleasure to do business with, Sears. Now could you please read me back exactly what you wrote on the order slip?"

"Mrs. Green says that her machine can only be delivered on Thursday morning. She does housework that morning only."

Please change that last statement to 'Mrs. Green will only be at home Thursday morning. She works the other times.' "

Fran and Elliot finally did receive their washing machine on Thursday morning, and the instructions were written carefully on the order. Elliot and Fran have found their unequivocal messages well worth the effort.

NEGOTIATE WHO PAYS FOR WHAT

Finances continue to be one of the key sources of argument among married couples, however modern in outlook the couple might be. Many of the arguments over finances that occur in one-income families stem from the fact that one person essentially gives an allowance to the other. In two-income families, the modal argument concerns who pays for what. Negotiation and planning are required to arrive at some type of income sharing that will satisfy both parties. No system is argument-proof, but a few logical methods of dividing up household expenses are now being practiced by a wide range of couples.

Bud and Wynette Hassle over Money.   Both in the computer field and both earning above average incomes, Bud and Wynette were not accustomed to the ambiguity created by two incomes. As Bud explains it:

> In my household my father earned the money, and my mother acted as the bookkeeper and treasurer. My father simply handed over his paycheck to my mother. She paid him a small allowance and then took care of all the bills and did most of the shopping. It didn't make much sense for Wynette and me to divide up things that way; so we kind of just let things run a natural course.
>
> The natural course proved to be chaotic. To give you an example, when the gas and electric bill came in, we figured that one month it would be my turn, and the next month it would be Wynette's. But it didn't work out that way. A bill would be unpaid, and each of us would blame the other.
>
> The worst incident happened with a camper we bought on an installment plan. A letter arrived threatening to repossess the camper unless we made a payment in ten days. Somehow we both thought the other person was taking care of the payment. I figured that because I had made the down payment, Wynette would naturally pick up on the next several payments.

Bud and Wynette Shift to the His and Her Bill System. To overcome some of the problems they were experiencing with an ill-defined approach to bill paying, Bud and Wynette decided upon a simple his and her system of mandating who paid for what. Bud paid the rent, furniture, vacations, and all his personal expenses such as clothing, doctor and dentist bills, and his car. Wynette paid for the food, utilities, telephone, dining out and general entertainment, and her personal bills.

Wynette tells about the effectiveness of their his and her system: "After working with this system for about one year, I would say it works quite well in general. It's easy for us to budget our money. We can both save and invest a sizable portion of our paycheck. We each have a separate draw for our own bills. We plan to make one change. The idea of my paying for dining out and entertainment doesn't work as smoothly as we would like it to. I would call Bud a liberated person, but somehow he can't hack my taking him out on a regular basis. Perhaps next year I'll take over purchasing the small ticket furniture items, and he can pay for weekly entertainment."

Odessa and Rob Practice a Graduated System. Working as a nursing supervisor in 1976, Odessa earned about $20,000 per year. Rob, her husband, earned about $10,000 per year as a draftsman. The system of living expense sharing they chose was to create a common pool of money for joint expenses. Odessa contributed twice as much as Rob because she earned twice as much as he did. Odessa explains the system in more detail:

> With the tax system the way it is, I don't take home twice as much pay as Rob. But after you deduct his child support expenses from a former marriage, my take-home pay comes out to about twice his. Rob and I have a daughter of our own, and we contribute a proportionate share of our income for her expenses.
>
> I have heard of working couples saying, "You pay for this" and "I'll pay for that," but that nickel-and-dime approach has no appeal for Rob and myself. The way we handle things, we are both doing the best we can. We both allocate ourselves $150 per month for transportation, lunch, and small personal items.
>
> The only time we argue about money is when there isn't enough cash left in the pool to cover an unanticipated expense. Last month I found out that we needed a new roof on the house. The lowest estimate we could get was $3,000. That left us with a $150 monthly payment that we hadn't anticipated for this year.

Gary and Lucy Work Things Down to the Last Decimal Point. Gary sells mutual funds, and Lucy sells life insurance.

Between the two of them, there is considerable financial sophis-
tication in their household. Aside from the normal problems of
budgeting a joint income, Gary and Lucy both have many tax
deductible household expenses such as office space and a portion of the telephone bill. Gary explains the income-sharing
system they have devised to fit their unusual situation:

> It would be a question of the shoemaker's children having no
> shoes if Lucy and I couldn't decide upon a workable and fair system
> of dividing up living expenses. We both pay for our personal ex-
> penses such as lunches, medical and dental bills, clothing, car pay-
> ments, and hobbies.
>
> I have a list of expenses that I pay for exclusively such as life
> insurance premiums and our mutual fund program. Lucy makes the
> house payments plus food, utilities, and the telephone. We try to
> keep these stable expenses on a fifty-fifty basis during the year.
>
> Around the first week in January we figure out how much money
> we each actually made during the last calendar year. Our income
> fluctuates widely owing to the commission nature of our business.
> Suppose it works out that I made $4,000 more than Lucy (after
> taxes). We would jointly agree on how much of this money should
> be saved or invested.
>
> The discretionary portion of that money would be used to pur-
> chase major ticket items such as a couch or an expensive vacation.
> I would be the person responsible for payment because I made more
> money than Lucy for that year. Lucy has a few big insurance deals
> pending that could send her income skyrocketing beyond mine. I'm
> already thinking of what color den furniture I would like her to
> purchase for me in the next year or so.

BOTH BE ACTIVE PARENTS

A dual career family with one or more live-in children can
function smoothly only when both parents take an active interest in child rearing. Mother and father have to regard spending
extensive amounts of time with their child or children to be an
appropriate activity for their sex. When both couples work, a
parent-teacher conference is as important for the father as it is
for the mother.

Ivan Refuses to Be Called a Baby-sitter. Ivan and his wife, Vicki, were conversing with friends at an evening party. One of the women present commented, "I think Ivan is just wonderful the way he baby-sits for your children. Why this must give you lots of time to yourself. Just the other day I saw Ivan in the supermarket with your children."

Ivan interjected, "Thanks for the nice things you've said about me, Joan, but I refuse to be a baby-sitter. Taking care of your children isn't the same as baby-sitting. A baby-sitter is someone who gets paid for taking care of somebody else's child. It's not something you would do if you didn't get paid. Spending time with my children is as natural to me as spending time with Vicki. I'm no more a baby-sitter than is the children's mother. So although I appreciate your compliment, I don't think I deserve one."

Vicki supported Ivan's statements: "Ivan is leveling with you, Joan. He doesn't look upon time spent with the children as baby-sitting. He's simply being a great parent who loves his children. And you can tell the love is reciprocated. I'll give you an incident that will help explain the quality of Ivan's relationship with his children. Just the other day, little Mary Ann fell down in the playground, scraping her knee pretty badly. She came running into our apartment sobbing and quite frightened. Both of us were seated in the kitchen. Mary Ann ran up to Ivan and held on to him. In most situations an injured child would run into her mother's arms. But Ivan is such an active parent that his daughter sees him as an adult who can play the comforter role."

Bert Takes a Sexist Approach. Hard-charging Bert was headed toward a successful career in the retailing field. His wife, Lisa, a speech therapist, was also committed to her work. Lisa patiently tried to get Bert more involved in the raising of Jimmy, their three-year-old son. One night she confronted Bert about his lack of involvement as a parent: "Bert, you are quickly becoming an absentee father. You pay less attention to little Jimmy than many divorced fathers pay to their children.

I honestly think at times that you forget he is our child."

"Never mind the sarcasm," responded Bert angrily. "I have never forgotten Jimmy is our child. When he grows up a little, I will spend lots of time with him. Have you forgotten the first baseman's mitt I bought him for his birthday? When he's old enough, I'll be playing ball with him regularly."

"But, Bert, Jimmy needs you now. I can't raise Jimmy all by myself and still do justice to my profession. A young boy needs both a father and a mother."

"Dammit, with your schedule as a speech therapist," retorted Bert, "you have much more time for child raising than I do. A man on the way up in the retail business doesn't have unlimited time to play with his child. Besides, I have a lot of things to do around the house. Between my career and my household chores, there is not much time left over for Jimmy."

"How convenient for you and how unfortunate for Jimmy," commented Lisa.

Lisa Makes a Deal.   Lisa reasoned to herself that unless Bert became more interested in child rearing, she would continue to devote more than her fair share of time to raising Jimmy. Lisa recognized that neglecting Jimmy as a way of getting even with Bert was an unpalatable alternative. Instead she attempted a strategic maneuver that would be beneficial to Bert, Jimmy, and herself.

Catching Bert in a particularly good mood (after a successful week at the store), Lisa invited him to join her for a cocktail on their patio. "I have a deal for you, Bert." She said. "This weekend I would like to take over your grimiest, most irksome chore. But first you have to tell me what is the grimiest, most fatiguing chore you plan to do this weekend."

"That's simple," related Bert. "It's cleaning out the garage and washing the garbage cans. It should take me about two hours."

"Okay, I'll make a deal with you. I'll take over the garage and garbage can detail this Sunday afternoon, if you and Jimmy go find something to do together. And that includes changing his diapers as needed."

"That sounds fair to me, I'm willing to give it a shot. Maybe Jimmy and I can go window shopping at a few competitors' stores."

For three consecutive weeks Lisa took over Bert's most burdensome chores while he and Jimmy kept each other company. By the fourth week, Bert had undergone a noticeable change of attitude and behavior. Sheepishly, Bert approached Lisa: "Honey, why don't you go ahead and plan going to that Midwestern Society of Speech Therapists meeting the first weekend in June. I can arrange things so my assistant will take over for me that Saturday at the store. Jimmy and I have been having so much fun together lately on Sunday afternoons that we'd like to try a whole weekend together."

Guidelines
for the Office Affair

15 Whether you are an active participant in extramarital sex at the office or merely a spectator, no business success manual would be complete without a few caveats about this important topic. Artful maneuvering is called for when either you or your office lover are attached to somebody else. An office romance between two single people does not require as much forethought. A few of the suggestions below fit the uncomplicated office romance, but most are geared toward the extramarital twosome (or moresome, depending upon your sexual proclivities).

BE NEITHER AN EXPLOITER NOR AN EXPLOITEE

In 1976 a Supreme Court ruling made it an act of sexual discrimination for an employer to insist upon sexual relations with him (or her) as a condition of employment. Now illegal, it has always been considered underhanded to insist that a woman participate in sex with her boss (or the entire management team) in order to move ahead or hang on.

Clyde, the Sexual Exploiter. Clyde was a life insurance company executive whose exploits are reported in my book *Managerial Deviance*. Recognizing that the majority of company employees were female, yet career opportunities for them were limited, Clyde initiated a career development for women. According to this new program, young women who entered the company as file clerks could move through the steno pool, up into departments, and then into a variety of supervisory and administrative assistant positions.

As coordinator of this program, Clyde had the legitimate opportunity to visit the steno pool periodically and confer with the supervisors to discuss progress of this new career development program. In the process, Clyde also took the chance to observe what entrants to the steno pool appeared particularly attractive. Young women in this category became candidates for Clyde's unofficial, *accelerated* career development program.

Every three months Clyde gave another girl an opportunity to work as an administrative intern in his office (after clearing the appointment with her supervisor). The intern thus had the opportunity to acquire an inside view of the major kinds of administrative decisions faced by the company. She would also have the chance to participate in a variety of special projects, one of which was designed to improve Clyde's morale and feelings of masculinity. "King's harem" was apparently in operation for almost two years before an irate employee's comments in an exit interview led to an investigation and Clyde's dismissal.

How Clyde's Program Worked. Bev, one of Clyde's victims, explains how the unpublicized aspects of the administrative intern program worked:

> Mr. King capitalized upon his charm, power, and the naïveté of the girls who were selected for the special intern program. First of all, a 20-year-old girl would have to be awed at the prospects of working in the office of a top company executive. Add to that the fact that suave Clyde fits a Hollywood image of the successful executive. Well-dressed, debonair, well-mannered, and good-looking, he is very attractive to young girls even if he has a wife and children.
>
> After he got to know you, Mr. King would invite you to lunch and hold no punches about his intentions. He points out that the company has many ambitious and hardworking young women

wanting to get ahead. He prefers to recommend for promotion those girls that he finds very agreeable from a personal standpoint, providing, of course, they are also good workers.

Personally agreeable, in Clyde's language, means that you have an affair with him. Lunch hours were best for Clyde's affairs because they didn't interfere with his home life. He certainly was a gentleman. Champagne or other fine wine and a cute little studio apartment less than ten blocks from the office. I will admit that the setting for his sexual encounters with administrative interns was romantic.

Before I sound as if I'm painting the picture of a patron saint, I have to explain one more upsetting detail. Having sex with Clyde King usually did more for him than it did for you. He made some vague promises to girls that he really couldn't keep. To give you one specific example, he hinted to several girls separately that they might become the word processing manager if they cooperated with him socially.

What Bev Should Have Done.   Bev (another sexually exploited woman working for Clyde) should not have been hesitant to report his manipulative advances to her own supervisor or to the company president. If several women made such complaints, any rational president would have made a thorough investigation. At a minimum, Clyde would have been confronted with his exploitive behavior by somebody in top management. Realizing that his moral behavior was now under close scrutiny, Clyde would have probably backed off from insisting that women offer him sex in order to be recommended for promotion.

Each successive complaint about Clyde would have increased the probability of his demise. However, somebody had to register the first complaint.

A SERIOUS RELATIONSHIP IS WORTH A JOB TRANSFER

Shortly, I will comment upon the inadvisability of having an office romance with somebody with whom you have a formal work relationship. An important exception to this rule occurs when somebody in your office appears to be a long-range prospect. Don't discard the chances for a once-in-a-lifetime romance just because he or she works in your department. Many male executives have married their secretaries. Had either party refused to date the other, the romance leading to marriage would never have blossomed.

Michelle Finds a Romantic Boss. Working in a local office of the General Services Administration (a major branch of the Federal Civil Service), Michelle was an executive secretary. Newly arrived at this rank, she was assigned to a new boss whose position warranted a private secretary. Nelson, Michelle's new boss, was both a capable administrator and a personable widower. Michelle and Nelson felt an immediate attraction to each other. After one month on her new job, Michelle was involved in one of the heaviest romances of her life.

One Sunday night as Nelson and Michelle exchanged words of love and affection, Nelson felt awkward. He said to Michelle, "Today I made breakfast for you at my place. Tomorrow you'll be getting coffee for me back at G.S.A. It certainly is a strange setup."

Nelson Breaks the News. The following Wednesday morning, Nelson asked his administrative secretary (and lover) to come into his office. "Michelle," he said, "my thoughts of last Sunday night will not go away. We cannot continue to work effectively in the office as boss and subordinate if we are sweethearts on the outside. I need a good executive secretary, but I need a fine companion like you even more."

"Nelson, what are you suggesting?" said Michelle.

"As much as I hate to lose you, I think you should be transferred from my department to another. I know another administrator at my grade level who has a secretary working for him at exactly your grade level. We might be able to switch administrative secretaries without having to go through a lengthy bureaucratic routine. Once you have transferred departments, we can openly see each other in the office. I'm not saying we should hold hands in the elevator, but we can at least dine together in the cafeteria without feeling that we would be violating office protocol."

Michelle saw the logic to Nelson's thinking and consented to the department transfer. Last reported, Nelson and Michelle were headed toward marriage (with each other). Michelle was doubly satisfied because (1) her new job was equal in rank to her assignment with Nelson and (2) her romance was able to follow its natural course uninhibited by a superior-subordinate relationship.

HAVE AN AFFAIR WITH SOMEONE OUTSIDE YOUR CHAIN OF COMMAND.

Unless, as just indicated, your prospective lover represents an outstanding long-range prospect, find a lover with whom you do not have direct work contact. For instance, don't have an affair with somebody who has the power to approve or disapprove of your job-related ideas. When the affair is going well, your ideas will probably be well received. Conversely, when your romance is going poorly (or broken off by you), your ideas will probably be poorly received.

A woman having an affair with somebody above her in organizational rank runs a greater risk than does the male. (As work organizations become less sexist, this may be less true.) After an office affair becomes public knowledge and complaints are voiced by people outside the department (there are many prudes working in offices), the woman frequently has to absorb most of the blame and punishment. Often she is quietly ejected from the company whereas the male participant in the romance is only chastised.

Charlene Gets Shafted.   A young accountant is a case in point. A former colleague of hers interprets what happened:

> Charlene had been working in our department for about one year when a new controller, Tom, took over. Within three months she and Tom began to see each other. At the time Charlene was fond

of Tom, but she was also a pragmatic person. She felt that, all things being equal, it's better to carry on a romance with a controller than a junior accountant. It became apparent to everyone in the department that Tom and Charlene were seeing each other.

Other executives in the company learned about the romance. Certainly, they were not opposed to males and females having romances, but they thought that a married executive having an affair with a subordinate could create some sticky problems. A simple solution according to their sense of justice (or should I say injustice?) was to ask Tom to fire Charlene.

Of course, they in no way tried to discourage Tom from continuing his romance with Charlene. From the company standpoint, the couple could do whatever they wanted so long as they both weren't working for the company. My thoughts are that if Charlene were canned, Tom deserved the same treatment.

Charlene Could Have Pressed Her Case. Had Charlene been a more militant person, she could have filed charges of sex discrimination against her company. Both the federal and state governments have commissions eager to listen to and investigate sexual discrimination in its many forms. Had Charlene won her case, she might have felt uncomfortable working for a company that mistreated her, but she would have won a moral victory. Besides, women might receive fairer treatment in the future.

DON'T AVOID OR IGNORE YOUR LOVER

What do you say to the person across the table from you during a business conference when the two of you had sexual relations the night before? An insensitive approach is to ignore the person: it engenders feelings of resentment, hurt, and hostility. A more effective maneuver is to act in a gracious and interested, but not overdone manner.

Melissa Is Ignored. After one year of looking for a logical person with whom to have an affair, Gus (father of three) finally found Melissa, the mail girl. For several successive bowling Monday nights, Gus and Melissa took off on their own while other league members stayed on at the bowling lane bar. Although Gus had no plans of leaving his wife, he valued his newly found girlfriend.

Gus feared that if his relationship with Melissa were discovered by others, he would have to stop seeing her. Toward this end Gus did a skillful job of avoiding Melissa. One day the mail department was overloaded and understaffed, necessitating that Melissa take a later lunch break than usual. Melissa strolled into the company cafeteria. Sighting Gus, she sat down next to him.

Gus barely acknowledged Melissa. He waved in a circular motion with his right hand while he continued his conversation about the Bricklin sports car. Melissa glanced angrily toward Gus and muttered, "You'll pay for this."

Melissa Gets Revenge. Gus telephoned Melissa that night apologetically saying, "I'm sorry we didn't have a chance to talk in the cafeteria today. I didn't want to be too obvious. A married man has to act respectable you know."

Further infuriated, Melissa replied, "You son of a bitch. If I'm good enough to sleep with, I'm good enough to talk to in the cafeteria. Go take a flying leap."

Two days later Gus absorbed the wrath of another woman— his wife. As he walked in the door, Jean said sarcastically: "Look what I have here. A note from a woman named Melissa, who says I can have my husband back because she is through with you. I'm not so sure I want you back."

TRY THE OFFICE NEXT DOOR

An office affair can be considered successful when both parties have fun, neither party gets hurt, their spouses don't find out, and gossip is kept to a minimum. To achieve these ends, try the office next door—particularly when that office is occupied by an enterprise other than your own firm.

Theresa Gets Tired of Lewis's Impotence. Career-minded Theresa worked as an office manager, a position that provided her ample financial and psychic satisfaction. In Theresa's analysis, her only current problem was not enough sex. Lewis, her husband and a person she loved very much, was gradually losing his ability to perform satisfactorily in bed.

Theresa thought about the alternatives open to her: "If I took care of my problem head on, I guess Lewis and I should attend a sex clinic. Or at least *he* should. But I know that kind of talk only upsets Lewis. He assures me everything will be okay once the golf season starts again. He thinks the fresh air, sunshine, and exercise help his sex life. Could be. If I bring up the topic too often, I'll only inhibit Lewis further. In the meantime, my sex drive is increasing. My best solution for now might be to have an affair, providing the right opportunity comes along."

Theresa Looks for the Right Opportunity. Not a believer in fate alone as a way of solving business or social problems, Theresa decided to help fate along. Over the last several months, she could not help but notice an attractive blond architect who worked in the office next door. When they next encountered on the elevator, Theresa took the initiative. She said simply, "I see you often, you must be ——?" The architect happily filled in the blank. "I'm John DeAngelis. What's your name?"

The next day Theresa called the office next door. "Hello, Mr. DeAngelis. This is Theresa Penworthy. We talked recently. My firm has toyed with the idea of having a small suburban building erected to serve as company headquarters. I couldn't say we are ready to buy yet, but could we talk over the possibilities?"

"Why not? That's the business we're in," said John in a warm and enthusiastic manner. John and Theresa began a mutually pleasing affair ten days later. Compassionate John, a divorced father, conducted the affair guiltlessly. Theresa (who claims this was her very first extramarital liaison) was also not plagued with guilt. She reasoned that her architect friend was helping her build a better marriage by satisfying her sexual urges.

Theresa imagined that her sex life with Lewis would again improve, but for now she didn't care.

NO LOVEMAKING ON COMPANY PREMISES

A recent article in *Harper's Bazaar* suggests that sexual intercourse with your boss be performed in locales such as the boardroom, storage, closet, or the film auditorium at the Museum of Modern Art. Note carefully, however, that the smart career tactician takes a shower after sexual relations if he or she is returning to the office. In recent years many younger office and factory workers have used their vans parked in the company or plant lot as the setting for a noontime tryst. Again, the same striking disadvantage; you may need to shower before returning to your work station.

Ben and Barbara Try the Custodian's Closet.   Ben, a middle manager, and Barbara, a senior underwriter, began having lunch together several times per week. One warm spring day, returning from an after-lunch stroll, the couple felt a surge of physical compatability. He said "Let's do it," and she nodded affirmatively, adding, "But it's almost time to return to the office."

"I think I know a place," said Ben. "We'll be back from lunch in no time at all."

A peculiarity of their insurance company was that it was housed in a building originally designed for a high school. Similar to other high school buildings, it contained several hugh broom closets where custodians kept mops, buckets, brooms, and related supplies. (A fringe benefit is that such closets also contain sinks that could almost double as a small bathtub.) Ben had thought of *almost* everything.

Ben and Barbara Call for Help.   Midway through their sexual liaison in the custodian's closet, Ben and Barbara heard a shuffling of feet followed by a double click. Although she disliked the interruption, Barbara quickly cuffed her hand over Ben's mouth and said, "Shh! Quiet, I think I hear somebody." Ben murmured, "I think you're right, but the noise has gone away."

Fifteen minutes later, Ben and Barbara were ready to leave

their microhotel room, having even washed up in the microbathtub. Ben yanked and shoved, but the door would not release. A janitor, finishing his shift, had padlocked the door from the outside. Rather than wait a presumed 16 hours for the janitor to return and unlock the door, Ben and Barbara took turns pleading for help. At first they called out in low tones, "Help, somebody locked us in here by mistake."

As it became apparent, traffic was light in this subterranean level of the company, Ben and Barbara increased the decibel level of their calls for help. Finally, a workman walking by the closet came to their rescue. By the time he had returned with a hammer and chisel, a group of office workers returning from an afternoon coffee break stood by to watch the rescue mission.

As Barbara and Ben escaped the maintenance closet, Ben shook the workman's hand appreciatively and said, "Thanks a million, we were doing an inventory for the company when somebody locked us in by mistake."

Ben's Glibness Could Not Save the Situation.   Ben made the best possible comment, considering the awkwardness of the situation, but it was not effective enough. Tales of the incident raced through the insurance company faster than news about a major fire on an insured's premises. Both Ben and Barbara tried to ignore the subtle barbs and good-natured kidding they received from others.

One week later it seemed that co-workers had finally stopped ribbing Ben and Barbara. A large intraoffice envelop then arrived at Barbara's desk. Inside was a plaque with an inscription: "To Barbara and Ben, who had the courage to take their friendship out of the closet."

LONG LUNCH HOURS TOGETHER ARE OBVIOUS

Two people engaged in an office affair should not repeatedly leave for and return from a long lunch break together for two reasons: (1) By doing so their affair will become common knowledge, and (2) their work performance may be adversely affected. Despite the obvious logic of this admonition, many office lovers continue to participate in 120-minute lunch "hours."

Ruth and Hubert Form a Luncheon Club for Two. Both dissatisfied with their marriages, Ruth and Hubert discovered each other on company premises. First, they found excuses to visit each other's departments to talk over vague interdepartmental problems. Next they began having lunch together. As their relationship grew, they decided upon an occasional room service lunch at a nearby restaurant-motel. Soon these midday get togethers increased in the frequency and duration. On Ruth's birthday, the couple left for lunch at 11:45 A.M. and returned at 2:15 P.M. Ruth and Hubert reasoned that they often brought work home and that, while at their desks, they worked harder than did most people.

Hubert Is Stunned. Ruth and her boyfriend continued their pattern of frequent lunches together, including an occasional lengthy tryst. Both assumed that their socializing during business hours had no adverse impact on their respective careers. Hubert soon learned that he was drawing a false conclusion—a fact he learned in discussion with his boss about being passed over for promotion.

A new level of management was created in Hubert's area. The new manager appointed was an individual with seemingly lesser qualifications. Perturbed, Hubert demanded an explanation from his boss, who obligingly replied: "Hubert, there is no question about your technical competence. You know our systems, and you know them well. It's simply a matter of your office decorum. We in management question your judgment at times. What you do with your personal life is your business, but we prefer that our managers aren't the butt of jokes and rumors. A lot of people have been talking about you and Ruth Ferraro."

"But I can explain everything," rebutted Hubert.

"No explanations are required," said his boss, "You've already convinced us that we made the right decision."

TRY AN OUT-OF-TOWN TRYST

With a little imagination, an office affair can be conducted in a relaxed, nonhurried manner. When an affair is conducted out-of-town, it is much less obvious to office mates and spouses. (Guilt feelings, of course, may be the same both in- and out-of-town.) A high-ranking executive taking a secretary with him on a business trip provides the least suspicious setting for an affair, but few people are authorized to travel with a secretary at company expense. Most junior executives must settle for a transistorized tape recorder as a traveling companion.

Carmen and Betty Do Some Scheming. Carmen's planning skills that he used as marketing manager for his company helped in his extramarital life. A devoted husband and father (while in town), Carmen kept his office romance with Betty, a computer scientist, at a subdued level. A wife without children, Betty was devoted to her husband in most situations. As their attraction for each other grew, Carmen and Betty pondered over what would be a feasible setting for an affair. Neither person wanted to create problems at home.

Carmen approached Betty with his scheme: "Betty, I have more travel flexibility in my job than you do. I have key customers all over the Midwest that I could visit upon reasonable notice. You figure a way to get out-of-town on a trip without your husband, and I'll arrange to make a business trip to the same place.

Betty dutifully poured over her file of information on upcoming meetings in the computer science field. To her delight, an advanced minicourse in computer applications to marketing was being held in Detroit one month later. Betty asked her boss's permission to attend the conference. Appreciating her interest in personal and professional development, he obliged. Betty told Carmen about her upcoming conference.

The next day Carmen excitedly told Betty, "We're in luck. I've just been on the phone with my three biggest customers in the Detroit area. They are all willing to talk to me." Let's make sure we stay at the same hotel. You drive your car to a garage on the edge of town. I'll give you the address later. That way you can park your car, and I'll do the driving. We'll even save the company on travel costs."

Carmen and Betty Forgot One Little Detail.   For Carmen and Betty the conference was a socially and professionally rewarding experience. They enjoyed their extramarital caper and came away from the conference with several new ideas they felt could be applied to their respective jobs. Except for the dutiful call home to his wife and children, Carmen felt completely carefree for the duration of the conference. Shared by Betty, his carefree attitude made them both less attentive to small detail.

Several days after his return from the conference, Carmen's wife had a few angry words for him: "Ah, yes Carmen, I suspect you had quite a time in Detroit. A small package arrived from the hotel addressed to me; so I naturally opened it. Inside was one woman's shoe that doesn't belong to me. Does it belong to a friend of yours? I'm not so sure I want to stay married to a man who has so little respect for his marriage."

Carmen replied with the best defense he could think of for the moment: "You're jumping to conclusions. I don't think any less of our marriage than I ever did. Because the cleaning woman found a lost shoe in my room and turned it over to the motel clerk, it doesn't mean I don't love you."

However carefully worded Carmen's defense, his marital relationship was still hurt by his social activities at the conference. A moralist would say, if he hadn't had an affair, he wouldn't have had the problem. An opportunist would say that if Carmen had been more attentive to detail, he would not have been discovered.

NO BRAGGING ALLOWED

For most individuals conducting office affairs, the affair itself provides ample fun to keep them satisfied. For others, direct and indirect bragging about the dalliance is necessary in order to maximize pleasure. Such bragging is in poor taste and self-defeating. It could lead to an abrupt end to the affair.

Edna Tells It All. It isn't often that a dispatcher on the factory floor has a chance for an affair with the vice-president of manufacturing. Edna was an exception, and she regarded it as a status symbol. One day in coffee conversation with her co-workers, Edna commented: "You girls should know what a gentleman Jim is. Why when he takes a woman on a date, he treats her as if she were a queen. And he can afford to at his vice-president's salary. I mean, Jim is something special."

"How would you know, dearie?" asked Flora, a member of the coffee break group.

"Why, how else would anybody know these things, but through firsthand experience? Of course, that's confidential. I know I can trust you girls."

Jim Feels the Heat. Not having heard from Jim in over one week, Edna telephoned him. She said, "Jim, you haven't called me in a long time. Is there something the matter? Did I do something wrong?" We had such a heavenly time the last time we were together."

"Edna, I can't see you anymore," answered Jim. Word of our friendship got back to my wife. She claims it's grounds for divorce. I don't want to get entangled in divorce proceedings now; so I'm going to be on my good behavior. Maybe if I come home every night for a while, my wife will change her mind. So please don't call me again. Forget you ever met me. Maybe I'll be back in touch when this whole thing blows over."

The Source of the Information Leak. Stunned and disgruntled, Edna wondered how Jim's wife had learned of their affair. Quite simply, Edna's bragging irritated one of her co-workers. Partially out of a sense of morality, but more out of a sense of jealousy, one of Edna's co-workers made an anonymous phone call to Jim's wife. She informed her that her husband was having an affair with a woman named Edna, who worked for him. Confronted by his wife with such a direct accusation, Jim could only wince.

Luann Tries on the Shoe Salesman for Size. Luann worked hard and played around hard; yet her husband was only familiar with her work orientation. As the floor supervisor, Luann had the opportunity to interview all candidates for sales clerk jobs on her floor. Geoffrey, a candidate for a shoe salesman's position, particularly attracted her attention. A well-muscled former member of his college wrestling team, he was looking for work until he could someday find a position as a physical education instructor.

Luann continued her special interest in Geoffrey after he was hired. Her frequent warm greetings were correctly interpreted by Geoffrey that Luann had more than the normal interest in an employee shown by a member of management. The shoe salesman and the floor supervisor began an affair wedged into long lunch hours and early evenings.

One day Luann was returning from lunch when she spotted Geoffrey and a young woman walking arm in arm toward them. Rather than avoid her, Geoffrey walked directly toward Luann and introduced her to his luncheon companion. "Luann I would like you to meet Kay, a good friend of mine."

An uncontrollable pang of jealousy came over Luann. With a vindictive glance on her face, she said to Kay, "Well you may be a good friend of Geoffrey, but he's an even more special friend of mine. He and I know each other intimately."

Kay Is Counterhostile. Although small in body size, Kay was big in mouth. Unknown to Luann, Kay was a clerk in the credit department of the store. She proceeded to tell all her friends and acquaintances in the store that Luann was encouraging young men in the store to have an affair with her. A conversation with a store clerk made Luann realize that she had become the subject of rumors.

Luann was reprimanding a young woman who worked for her for having held hands with her boyfriend while walking across the store floor. Said Luann, "We must maintain a sense of decorum in this store, and particularly on my floor. Whether you are off duty or not, no handholding allowed on company premises."

"Listen to who is talking," said the young woman. "They tell me that the way for a fellow to get ahead in this store is to become your stud."

"One more crack like that and you're fired," retaliated Luann, but verbal retaliation would not rebuild Luann's reputation in her store. Ultimately, the store rumors filtered back to Luann's husband, leading to a nasty confrontation. To maintain peace at home, Luann has ceased having extramarital affairs (at least temporarily).

MAINTAIN A FLEXIBLE WORK SCHEDULE

If being discovered concerns you, the best way to conduct an office affair secretively is to maintain a flexible work schedule. The predictable commuter who is home on the train at the same time virtually every day has little chance to conduct an affair without arousing suspicion because of his or her deviation from schedule. Many an advertising executive, computer scientist, management consultant, or doctor leads a flexible work life.

Lou, the Restless Obstetrician. Good-looking Lou always enjoyed being around women professionally and socially. His logical career decision was to enter obstetrics-gynecology. Happily married, he found frequent conversations with women who gave him a good perspective on his wife's concerns. At mid-career, his professional interest in women turned toward an unremitting desire to have affairs with at least two or three women. One constraining factor that came to mind was his hectic 60-hour-per-week work schedule. Lou thought to himself, "Even if I do line up a few of my patients who would enjoy having an affair with me, when would I do it? I hardly have time for my own wife."

Lou Is Called Away on Official Sounding Business. The solution to his dilemma was remarkably simple. When Lou was able to arrange late night or early morning encounters with a female hospital employee (two nurses aides, one nurse, and an obstetrician at last count), he would have that woman page him at home. Thus his wife heard this call more than once at midnight: "Excuse me, Mrs. Gold, but your husband will be needed at the hospital tonight. We hate to do this to you, but this appointment cannot wait."

PART V

MANAGING
YOUR FUTURE

Finding
a New Job

16 Your professional future often begins with finding a new job for yourself. Whether your job search is voluntary or involuntary, you will need an effective method of landing yourself a new position. You cannot afford to use a slipshod approach to finding a new job for two very important reasons. First, good (well-paying and exciting) jobs continue to be in short supply in comparison to the demand. Second, your competition for these jobs is becoming increasingly sophisticated about job-hunting techniques. Sound advice on career management is much more readily available today than in the past.

Knowing the essentials of job finding is good for your mental health and your job outlook. Realizing that your economic livelihood is not dependent upon the whims of *one* employer makes you less concerned about job security. A spin-off is that you can become more objective (and, therefore, more professional) in your job outlook.

KNOW WHAT JOB(S) YOU ARE PURSUING

Many people searching for a new job will use conventional techniques such as employment agencies, responding to classified ads, or pursuing leads furnished by friends. Others will brave an unconventional approach such as the direct mailing campaign touted in this chapter. In either case, any successful job campaign begins with a recognition of what kind of job or jobs you are pursuing.

Gil Loses His Job. Conscientious Gil was the victim of a retrenchment in his company. After his 15 years of good service, his company decided as a cost-saving measure to terminate Gil. According to their shortsighted reasoning, Gil could be replaced by a junior purchasing agent at half his salary. Despondent at first, Gil began the painful process of searching for a new position. Two weeks into his job search, Gil became even more despondent. He arrived at the doorstep of a career counselor with this tale of woe:

> The market for purchasing agents is murder out there. In our current phase of the economic cycle, companies are holding down expenditures. This means, of course, they are buying less. With less purchasing activity going on, there is very little demand for a purchasing agent. Even worse, to cut expenses some companies are using people from other departments to do much of the purchasing.
>
> I may have to go on unemployment insurance until the next upturn in the economy. It's not something I choose to do, but I'm running out of alternatives.

Gil Broadens His Scope. An hour of dialogue with a career counselor helped Gil take a broader look at himself and his job-getting credentials. His counselor would not accept Gil's lazy thinking that the only value he had to the job marketplace was as a purchasing agent. Asked in several different ways what else he could do besides work as a purchasing agent, Gil arrived at a couple of sensible alternatives. He reflected: "It would be the easiest for me to work as an inventory control specialist. I know a lot about the movement of goods into the factory because of my purchasing experience. But I also know a lot about the workings of the inside of the company. I've become adept at keeping track of valuable supplies. That would make me a natural as an inventory control specialist, which is needed in most companies."

"Fine," responded the career counselor, "but do you *want*

to work as an inventory control specialist?"

"Not at all. So long as I'm unemployed, I'd like to get into sales. I think I'm qualified for sales although I lack direct experience. It seems as if a purchasing agent is really the compliment to a sales representative. Without salesmen, you wouldn't need purchasing agents; and without purchasing agents, salesmen would have nobody to talk to. We're people working different sides of the street."

"What exactly are you saying?" asked the career counselor. "What kind of job are you seeking?"

"To be frank, I believe I would make a very effective sales representative after having worked so many years as a purchasing agent. One decided edge I would have over many sales representatives is that I understand the perspective of purchasing people."

Gil's hunch about the transition from purchasing to selling proved to be correct. He readily found himself a position in industrial selling, dealing with products familiar to him. His businesslike approach to purchasing agents helped him perform satisfactorily as a sales representative.

Hank Will Take Anything. At age 26 after existing on his earnings from a variety of low-skilled jobs, Hank finally decided to enter college, majoring in business administration. He continued to work part-time while he attended school. Toward the middle of his senior year, Hank decided to look for a job. He rightfully believed that his above-average age for a college graduate would be looked upon favorably by most potential employers. Hank dutifully sought out the companies who sent job recruiters to his college campus.

As Hank went from interview to interview, he gave each company representative the same story. "I'm about ready to graduate, and I'm looking for work. I like a lot of different things. Do you have anything for me?"

Hank's letters to prospective employers had the same vagueness. His standard approach was, "I'm a recent college graduate looking for work. I'm experienced in many kinds of jobs, and

I would like to settle down. I'm willing to consider any job that fits my background."

A Better Approach for Hank. Many people who look for work early in their careers do not have one or more specific job objectives in mind. Yet Hank should have taken steps to insure that his flexibility was not communicated as indecisiveness to prospective employers. Hank should have approached them with an interest in one or two specific type of jobs. No one employer had to know that Hank was pursuing different types of jobs with several different employers.

He might have said to one employer, "Because of my varied background, I think I am qualified for entrance into your management training program." To another employer he might have said, "My exposure to different types of businesses has convinced me that I would like to work in marketing. To yet another employer Hank might have noted, "My exposure to several different industries plus my college course work has convinced me that I would enjoy a job dealing with facts and figures. Therefore, I seek a financial analyst's position."

Hank could have made each of the above statements without misrepresenting himself. He was interested in many different phases of business and probably would have enjoyed working as a management trainee, a sales representative, or a financial analyst. Hank was not difficult to please. All he wanted was an interesting job. Yet it was difficult for Hank to be given a chance unless he communicated an interest in something specific.

SHOW HOW YOU CAN HELP THEM

A persistent theme of many self-help guides to finding new employment is "show your prospective employer what you can do for him or her." Most of the alleged magical formulas about sales effectiveness also reduce down to this basic idea. Showing what you can do for them rather than what they can do for you is easier to say than to implement. Once you develop the proper mental state of satisfying their needs rather than yours, you should use this approach at every stage of the job-finding process. (Once hired, retain this mental set. It is a very important career advancement strategy).

Derek Exhibits His Credentials. An MBA from the famous Wharton School, Derek applied for the position of assistant to the president of a plumbing fixtures manufacturing company. Derek bedazzled the personnel manager and the president with his impressive qualifications. His professionally reproduced résumé listed several noteworthy employers, an array of sophisticated-sounding courses, and memberships in a couple of elite clubs such as the Greenwich Yacht Club.

During his interviews Derek talked about his interest in applying advanced techniques of management science to the problems of a medium technology business. He also emphasized how he was looking to broaden his background by taking on a high-level staff job.

Derek Loses Out to Another Candidate. Not having heard from the plumbing manufacturers in three weeks, Derek made a follow-up phone call. Said he, "Hello, this is Derek Gibson. We were talking about my taking on joining your company as assistant to the president. What is the current status of my application?"

The personnel manager noted, "It looks as if that position has been filled. The president and I both were highly impressed with you, though."

"You were impressed; yet you give the job to somebody else?"

"That's right. The person we're hiring doesn't have the same fancy background you do, but he showed us a few examples of how he helped untangle a few messes in the company he now works for. He looks like the shirt-sleeve type who can dig in and solve some real problems for us. We'll let you know if something opens up here more in line with your background."

Derek's Obvious Mistake. His competitor for the position was selected over Derek for this valuable position because the former had the wisdom to show what kind of problems he could solve for the plumbing manufacturer. In applying for this position, Derek assumed that his impressive credentials would speak for themselves. In contrast, the president was more concerned about hiring an assistant who could tackle some of the difficult problems the company was facing. The other candidate presented the company with concrete examples of problems he had solved for a company with similar problems.

Derek, of course, was at a disadvantage in not having worked for a plumbing manufacturer. Nevertheless, he might have asked the personnel manager and the president what type of problems they would want him to work on if hired. He could have then suggested how, if hired, he would approach those problems.

Jody Displays Some Before-and-After Photos. Having worked five years at low wages for a small interior decorating firm, Jody applied for the position of senior interior decorator at the largest commercial furniture store in her city. She learned through a contact in the company that a number of decorators were already turned down for the position and that many more applicants were yet to be interviewed.

Jody worked the "show what you can do for them" principle to good advantage. She decided to construct a portfolio that would go beyond the usual aesthetic displays carried around by most artists and interior decorators. As a standard work procedure, Jody would take photos of a customer's office once a decorator contract had been signed. This enabled her to recollect the unique design problems of each client better. Jody also took some "after" photos for possible use in the store catalogue.

Jody now had the raw ingredients for a before-and-after portfolio. When she applied for the new position, she was able to point concretely to the types of decorator problems she had solved for a sampling of her former clients. The man in charge of hiring for the senior interior decorator's position commented, "If you can convert some of those dumps into attractive work atmospheres, we can find a spot for you with us. Many of our customers have similar problems, and they are hard to please. Yet our budget furniture has a bigger markup than the more expensive lines. We need your talent."

MINIMIZE LYING ABOUT YOUR PAST

Falsifying background information in order to improve one's chances for being hired has become a widespread phenomenon. Because most employers do not verify facts presented on the résumé or during the interview, most lying goes undetected. Aside from ethical considerations, once you are caught, lying will probably lead to your immediate rejection as a candidate. Furthermore, if your falsified information is discovered after you are hired, you may be asked to resign from the position you obtained partially through lying.

Another important consideration in favor of presenting only factual information to prospective employers is that you may be lying about unimportant things. The truth might not be as upsetting to prospective employers as you think.

George Is Self-conscious about Something in his Past. Many years ago George dropped out of high school and took a job as a bag packer in a supermarket. Two months of bagging groceries convinced George of the gravity of his mistake. Yet instead of returning to high school, he took a high school equivalency test (and passed) several years later. As his ambition grew, he decided to attend college. George began his education after high school by attending community college. Studying at night, he earned an associate's degree four years later. As a community college graduate, he was able to gain entrance to a four-year college—even without having a conventional high school diploma!

In his mid-thirties, George was being warmly considered for a position as distribution manager with a large company. His résumé included this innocuous fact: "Graduated from Bryant High School, 1964. Placed in top quarter of class." During a second interview for the position, the personnel manager confronted George in an officious manner: "A very curious fact has surfaced, George. In making a routine authentication of the facts you presented us, we find a dissappointing discrepancy. A call to your high school indicates that you never officially graduated. They do have record of an equivalency test that you took in 1967, but you did not graduate in 1964 as you indicated. It is indeed unfortunate that you presented us misinformation because we would have hired you even without a formal high school diploma. We admire people who overcome an earlier mistake in life. It shows courage."

What Else Can Dale Do but Lie?   An unemployed aerospace engineer, Dale was attending a job-finding workshop. He explained one of his problems to the workshop leader: "For a three-year period in life I just kind of bummed around. I must have had nine jobs in two years. A lot of the jobs were strictly unprofessional, such as box packer and routine construction work. It looks like hell on a résumé to have so many jobs in a short period of time. Yet, you tell us not to lie on the résumé? What should be done?"

Dale's problem is not unique. A careful review of his three-year period of miscellaneous employment shows that it took place *before* Dale graduated from college. As such, it would not be particularly relevant to an employer considering Dale for a professional level job. Dale's recommended strategy is put in an item like this in his résumé:

> 1967–1970:Variety of seasonal and part-time jobs, while saving money for college and traveling throughout the United States. Followed the seasonal work cycle in canneries and construction companies.

A lie for Dale would have been to pretend that he worked for one or two employers during that three-year time frame. His summary statement is both true and understandable. Furthermore, few prospective employers would bother to attempt to authenticate seasonal or part-time employment.

USE THE INSIDER SYSTEM

Anywhere from one to three million job openings will exist this month in the United States, according to Richard Lathrop, director, National Center for Job Market Studies. Even more startling, 80 percent of these jobs will be filled by internal rather than external methods. Only 20 percent of these openings will be mentioned in classified ads or registered with employment agencies. Lathrop notes that employers traditionally fill these four out of five unpublicized jobs in three ways:

1. They fill them with friends or people recommended by their friends.
2. They fill them with friends of their employees.
3. They fill them with people who have applied directly to them without knowing that any opening existed.

Jennie Is Harassed.   An educational research specialist, Jennie found herself locked into an insufferable political situation. As she described it, "Every day is another picky little battle in my office. One faction is trying to fill all the positions with members of the same religious group. Another faction is trying to fill all positions with gay people. In the meantime, everybody who isn't a member of that particular religious sect or gay is being pressured so badly that he or she will leave. I want out as fast as possible. But where are the job openings for educational researchers these days? I can hardly stand it any longer, but I need my job to live."

Jennie Uses the Insider System.   Before circulating her resume around the area high schools, colleges, and universities, Jennie thought she would give the personal contact method (or insider system) a try. She spent an evening compiling a list of everybody she knew in the area who might know of any openings for an educational research specialist.

Once the list was compiled, Jennie telephoned everybody whose name appeared on the list. Given any sign of encouragement, Jennie offered to take that person to lunch to discuss the situation further. Altogether Jennie took nine people to lunch. A fringe benefit from Jennie's job search was that she was able to renew some social contacts whom she had neglected in recent months and years.

Jennie struck gold during one luncheon. An informant, Floyd, noted that the education department of his university just received a substantial grant to develop a program for offering college courses to blind people. "I suspect they'll be needing one or two heavyweight researchers on this contract. I'll give the director a call and see if he's interested."

Floyd reported back that the director was indeed interested and that he would be receptive to granting Jennie an interview. The director and Jennie had immediate rapport for each other. He noted, "Do me a favor and fill out all the tedious forms that are required around here. Also furnish a list of references and have a current vita typed up. I'm pretty sure I'm going to offer you the job. This saves me having to advertise and read through 500 résumés and letters. If I can ram this through without the usual bureaucratic rigamorole, when could you start?"

"As soon as I can be released from my present contract. I would want to tie up all loose ends in my present situation."

PREPARE A LONG LIST OF POTENTIAL EMPLOYERS

The insider system of finding a new job can also involve your contacting a large number of employers in order to obtain a few interviews. (When personal contacts are used to gain entrance to the inside, your ratio of contacts to interviews will be much more in your favor. Friends and acquaintances will not suggest that you contact employers when they are not aware of any openings.)

Whether you are an executive or a high-level clerk, the preparation of a careful list of prospective employers can be your key to landing a good job. I have seen this technique work in the middle of a business recession when an oversupply of managers are looking for positions.

Where Does One Find Such a List? The most direct method of finding a list of potential business employers is to consult a large industrial directory, such as the Dun and Bradstreet or Standard and Poors directories. Directories of this type list companies by industry, geography, and size. Of particular significance is that these directories give you the names and correct mailing addresses of company officers. Most main libraries have directories in their business section. Purchasing one would pay for itself very quickly in terms of convenience and being able to avoid the cost of many trips downtown.

Combing through the directories and establishing your list could consume a full work week. Although the task seems dizzying and discouraging at first, it could be the most important piece of library research you will do in your life. One surprise many job seekers encounter using this method is to discover the large number of companies in the field most familiar to them.

One manager in the food business was let go because of a company retrenchment. He coolly and analytically established a list of 350 potential employers, including consultants in the food industry. His diligence paid off. He left what he felt was an uncomfortable climate (Chicago) for the warm beaches of Hawaii.

What About Jobs Outside of Business? Keep foraging through your library and the reference section of your bookseller. The complexity of today's world has led many industrious people to try to organize an incredible number of lists. You can readily find directories of universities and colleges that list names of people who can be used for job contact purposes. Another worthwhile possibility is to purchase a mailing list from a company specializing in selling mailing lists to direct mail advertisers. Check your yellow pages of both your city and the largest cities. Send for a brochure.

Much of your job hunting can be done in the comfort of your own house or apartment. A careful development of a list will save you extensive time devoted to making appearances in person at inappropriate places. Many people I have polled believe that showing up unannounced at a prospective employer's door is a constructive job-hunting approach. Unless you are interested in raking leaves or mowing lawns, such an approach is taboo.

WRITE AN ATTENTION-GETTING LETTER

Should you contact everybody on your list by mail or simply respond to classified ads, you will need an attention-getting letter to direct attention to your availability. To avoid being treated as junk mail, your letter must be attention-getting in a positive, sober manner. Several years ago a fad developed about using novel approaches to job inquiry letters and résumés. Personnel departments were greeted with menu-sized résumés, orchid-colored letters of introduction, and even special delivery packages with audio cassettes describing an applicant's credentials. One woman sent a telegram to a company that read, "Sally Marcus available for work. Send job offer immediately."

Letters, unlike résumés, must be individually typed—even if an automatic typewriter is used. An automatic typewriter produces letters in bulk, but each with a different address.

What Should Be Done?   A safer approach is to construct a one-page letter of introduction describing what you hope to do for that company, what you have done for other companies, and a few words about your background. Here are two sample opening lines that could be modified to your circumstances:

> 1. Does your company have a few products that would be even more successful than they are if only the cost of manufacturing could be reduced without sacrificing quality? I'm an eager young industrial engineer who gets his jollies squeezing the cost out of good products.
> 2. Would your company be interested in finding a time-tested method of improving your market penetration in my area? Perhaps a sales representative who speaks the language of the local people would be helpful. Fortunately, that person has been located—it is I.

What Kind of Accomplishments Should Be Listed?
Whatever you have done of significance that has made a positive contribution to your organization fits into this category. Thus the accomplishments you include in your letter of introduction should relate to profits earned, money saved, or innovative techniques. Here are a few examples:

> 1. Introduced a return mailer system that reduced the average time in which customers paid their bills from 31 to 24 days. My method

resulted in an estimated annual savings of $7,500.

2. Introduced and implemented a telephone canvass of former and present customers that helped increase our big ticket home furnishing sales by 28 percent. Companion store that did not use this technique only increased sales 5 percent during the same period.

Doesn't Bragging About Yourself Have Its Limitations?

Applying for a job is one situation in life where it is acceptable to speak in glowing terms about your capabilities and accomplishments. However, having a third party endorse your credentials may appear more objective than tooting your own horn. An acceptable variation of the attention-getting letter is to have a third party such as a career counselor or employment agency send the letter, thus endorsing you. Even if you choose this approach, you will be doing most of the legwork involved in getting a job.

DEVELOP A GOOD RÉSUMÉ

No matter what method of job hunting you use, inevitably somebody will ask you for a résumé. A representative of those companies who are attracted by your attention-getting letter will telephone or write, asking for a résumé. In recent years, several job-hunting manuals (including a nationwide bestseller) have suggested that preparing a résumé is inadvisable. They contend you should insist on an in-person appearance, not send a résumé. My experience in helping people get jobs is that the prospective employer insists upon a résumé, particularly when the company is large. Even if you call your résumé a qualification brief or a vita, or a personal background summary, you will still need the same kind of information in printed form.

What Are the Characteristics of an Effective Résumé?

Effective résumés are straightforward, factual presentations of a person's experiences and accomplishments. Two extremes should be avoided. One unacceptable extreme is a flamboyant, overdrawn presentation of your past experiences and accomplishments. For instance, don't give yourself too much credit for accomplishments that were obviously a group effort. (Can you really take credit for having single-handedly saved your company $5 million from your perch as administrative assistant?)

Another common pitfall in preparing a résumé is to include an excess of trivial information. An effective résumé should be confined to two or, at most, three typewritten pages. Delete or pass over lightly information about your working hours, obscure aspects of prior jobs, and minor hobbies and outside interests.

As indicated earlier in the chapter, insure that all details included are factual and capable of verification.

What About Different Types of Résumés? My recommended format combines key features of both the *chronological* and *accomplishment* résumé. It allows for a chronology of your experiences and mention of your work-related skills and accomplishments. No matter how modern your résumé, prospective employers will still insist upon a factual summary of your education and experiences. All any résumé can do for you is to overview your experiences and accomplishments. It is designed to get you an interview, *not a job.*

The format I recommend has worked satisfactorily for many beginners and experienced people who sought jobs. It would be arrant nonsense to state that only this type of résumé is considered acceptable. Use it as a guide unless your prospective employer demands another type. (I would also recommend consulting a few other printed published résumé construction guides.)

RÉSUMÉ

Jason L. Papworth	Born: July 18, 1940
514 Post Avenue	Married; one child
Highland Park, Illinois 60062	(312) 464–2298

Job Objective

Personnel manager, corporate headquarters large company. Participate in full range of professional activities including management and organization development, wage and salary administration.

Job Experience

1974– Plant personnel manager, Rulon Corporation, Chicago. Directed personnel activities for plant of 1,000 people. Duties included responsibility for labor relations, safety, management development, wage and salary administration.
Key accomplishment: Developed supervisory training program that helped increase productivity by 15 percent and reduced turnover by 25 percent.

1970–1974 Personnel specialist, Rulon Corporation. Conducted personnel functions mentioned above as specialist. Served on cost reduction committee.
Key accomplishment: Conducted Hard Core Unemployed Training program that helped company obtain large government contract.

1965–1970 Employment counselor, Papworth-Brown Associates (family business). Placed job candidates and solicited new accounts for firm.
Key accomplishment: Attracted 47 new accounts in five-year period.

1961–1965 Officer, United States Navy. Supervised up to 100 military personnel in a variety of classified assignments. Given highest clearance.

Formal Education

1957–1961 Purdue University, Lafayette, Indiana. Received Bachelor of Science degree in Business Administration while running small restaurant in town. Curriculum emphasized computers and management courses.

1953–1957 Dwight D. Eisenhower High School, Chicago. Honors student; played varsity tennis, basketball.

Skills

Able to handle major functions of professional personnel specialist. Precise in preparing budgets and

human resource forecasts. Effective business conference leader.

Personal Interests and Hobbies
Activities with daughter and wife; tournament ten-
nis player; black belt karate; president, Highland
Park Toastmasters.

CONDUCT A MAIL AND TELEPHONE CAMPAIGN

Armed with a catchy broadcast letter, a backup résumé, and
an up-to-date mailing list, you are now able to close in on
finding a new job. Remember that your goal is to be interviewed
by enough companies in order to be offered a job. Carefully
conducted, a mail campaign should yield about a 15 percent
positive reply asking for additional information (usually a request for a résumé). About one-third of those inquiries should
result in an interview.

Telephone in Ten Days.   After waiting about ten days for
a response from the companies (or other organizations) you
wrote to, begin a follow-up campaign, calling those places at
the top of your preference list. Many of the people you call will
be taken off guard by your call; so you will have to provide a
quick explanation. Here is a field-tested conversation opener:
"Hello, Mr. Klinghammer, this is Angelo Bellasco. Recently, I
sent you a letter asking about job opportunities for myself in
your company. Perhaps it would be helpful if I gave you some
more information over the phone."

The usual response is something like this: "I don't recall
seeing that letter. I may have misfiled it. Why don't you tell me
what you want? Could you send me a résumé?"

Angelo Uses a Bolder Approach.   A slightly bolder approach is, "Hello, Mr. Klinghammer. This is Angelo Bellasco.
Recently, I sent you a letter inquiring about job opportunities
for myself in your company. I'm calling to set up a mutually
convenient time for an interview. Perhaps I can send you a
résumé prior to our interview."

An ideal response from Klinghammer would be, "When did

you want to see us? I think we do have something open in your field."

BE IMPRESSIVE DURING AN INTERVIEW

Your quest for a new job cannot be realized unless you successfully make it through the interview. Seven tips are in order to help you achieve this goal.

Do Your Homework. Gather relevant information about your prospective employer in advance of the interview. One legendary job prospect was turned down by Trans-America Corporation because he thought they were a moving company. To avoid such incomplete (or incorrect) information, read an annual report or several newspaper or news magazine articles about the company.

Look at the Long Range. Carefully analyze how the position you are applying for fits into your long-term career objectives. If it is reasonably true, it is best to point out that your long-range goals may be for continued advancement, but that the job under consideration should keep you happy for the forseeable future. Unless a potential employer is contemplating a period of rapid growth, he or she usually is not really looking for new employees obsessed with the idea of rapid promotions.

Don't Overemphasize Trivial Things. Instead focus on more important aspects of the job. According to work motivation theory, managerial, professional, sales, and technical workers are supposed to be mostly concerned about the guts of a job, not its peripheral aspects. When applying for a responsible position, do not fall into the trap of focusing on such matters as vacation policy, medical benefits, general working conditions, or even salary.

Wage brackets for most jobs are tightly established. The position itself heavily influences the amount of money you will receive if hired. It is more impressive to show concern for what you will be doing rather than how much you will be paid. You want to appear work-motivated, not simply in need of money.

Dress Appropriately. A young man was turned down for

a sales clerk's position in a department store. He later discovered that one of the negative comments made about him during the interview was "questionable appearance." He found this perplexing because he had just invested a substantial amount of money in a suit that he wore to the interview.

The personnel manager defended her position: "He just looked unnatural in that suit, as if he rented it for the interview. Here he was in an expensive suit, but his shoes were badly scuffed, and he wore white socks. I could imagine what he would be like on days he didn't wear that suit."

Don't Worry about Hidden Meanings. Few interview questions are as revealing as you think. Respond in a straightforward and nondefensive way to even the most ludicrous-sounding question. For example, "What kind of an animal would you like to be if you were reincarnated?"

Often the person conducting the interview does not know the rationale behind the question he or she asks—including the last one. Unless your responses are grossly atypical, much of what you say goes unrecorded. However, if asked, "What was your earliest ambition?" do not out of whimsy respond, "Airplane hijacker" or "Arsonist."

Discuss Healthy Weaknesses. Almost inevitably at some place during a job interview, you will be asked to reveal your weaknesses. It is best to think through carefully a couple of your weaknesses that could actually be interpreted as strengths in many job situations.

In applying for a job in a company noted for its problems of customer complaints about quality, you might indicate (if true): "I've been accused of being too compulsive about small details. I've got this thing about any piece of paper leaving my desk without every detail being checked at least twice."

Or in applying for a supervisory position in a company that is having trouble staying within budget, you might comment: "I think I would be more effective if I weren't so impatient. I expect everybody to get results and get them fast."

Reinforce the Interviewer. Frequently, the person interviewing you for a position would welcome the opportunity to talk about himself or herself. At the right moment, ask the interviewer his or her other opinion about the working conditions in the company, the future of the company, or attitudes about how the work ethic has declined in the United States. As the interviewer says something that makes sense to you, subtly respond: "You have a point there" or "It seems that you have given careful thought to this topic" or even, "That's a good bit of wisdom."

Your interviewer is then likely to describe you as "insightful," "intelligent," or "clear-thinking." And who wouldn't want to hire somebody with those attributes?"

DON'T BE CONCERNED ABOUT REJECTION

Almost anybody searching for a new job will experience substantial amounts of rejection. Many more people will not want you than will want you. You may be considered overqualified by some prospective employers and underqualified by others. Some places will tell you a job has just been filled when you know from an inside source that the job is still vacant. Consider rejection part of the game. Matching available people with available jobs is a cumbersome system. People are rejected for both logical and emotional reasons.

Waldo Is a Happy Man.   Addressing a group of unemployed managers and professionals, Waldo spoke with verve about how 275 companies had either ignored his job-seeking letter or rejected him after a job interview. In disbelief, a member of the audience said angrily, "How can you be so happy when you swallowed all that rejection? Don't you have any pride?"

"True, I was rejected or ignored by 275 companies. But the 276th made me an offer. And I was only looking for one job."

Finding
a Second Career

17 "No amount of money is worth living like this. Who needs the constant aggravation day after day? Here I am close to 40, and I'm on my way toward having an incurable ulcer. I'm as good as my last client. My agency would throw me out tomorrow if I couldn't carry my weight for a couple of months. My only reason for staying on is so that I can accumulate enough money to open up a bookstore in New Hampshire someday."

The disenchanted and beleaguered advertising executive who spoke these words is joined by thousands of other men and women who find their present occupation more frustrating than satisfying. Many of these people are finding new careers that provide more satisfaction (yet, usually less money) than their former careers. Others have found disillusionment rather than salvation after switching careers.

If you are convinced that a second career is for you, it may prove to be in your best interest to follow a handful of logical suggestions. Whether you are choosing a second career in response to a mid-life crisis, as a solution to early retirement, or for any other reason, entering a new career will be one of your biggest decisions in life.

THE DIFFERENCE BETWEEN FINDING A SECOND CAREER AND FINDING A SECOND JOB

Finding a second career, in practice, is really a special case of finding a second job. Only the stakes are bigger. A second career usually requires more adjustments and new learning than a new job. Yet the process for simply another job in your field and finding a new job outside your field (a second career) are virtually the same. Everything mentioned in the last chapter about finding a job is equally applicable to finding a second career. This chapter adds a few new suggestions that relate primarily to switching fields.

SEARCH FOR RELEVANT INFORMATION

Many people who would like to start a new career are stymied by a lack of information. They are aware of the type of work they don't want to do (for instance, work similar to what they are doing now), but they lack information about alternative careers. Even retiring military officers often have difficulty finding a second career. The single best written source of information about careers is *Occupational Outlook Handbook,* published by the United States Department of Labor and available in every large library. Volumes adjacent to the *Handbook* on the library shelf usually contain similar information that is also quite valuable.

Bunny Is Disgruntled. As a teen-ager, Bunny invested much time and energy into photography as a hobby. Recognizing that few people can make a living as a photographer, Bunny chose to pursue a career in biomedical photography. After successfully completing a college degree in this field, Bunny found employment. Three years later she decided to make a career switch. Her reasoning followed this line:

> Biomedical photography is more of a laboratory job than one dealing with people. I think the real reason I enjoy photography is that it puts me in contact with people. I enjoy doing some technical work, but I dislike the total emphasis. Besides, a job in biomedical

photography gives me the feeling of being confined to one place. It would be very difficult to switch jobs.

I would like to do something else for a living that's at a comparable level to my present job, but I don't want to go through an extensive, costly period of retraining. But no specific job comes to mind.

Bunny Does Some Library Research.   At the advice of her former college counselor, Bunny decided to scan the entire *Occupational Handbook* to search for a new field that might capture her interest. On the basis of her genuine desire to help people and her positive attitudes toward the medical field, Bunny concentrated on medical service occupations. One hour into the project, Bunny hit upon the occupation of *audiometrist.*

Immediately Bunny conjured up images of herself administering hearing tests to private patients in a busy, aesthetically pleasing private medical office. After reading several articles about audiometry and glancing through one text book on the subject, Bunny decided to confer with a couple of audiometrists. As advised by her counselor, Bunny tried to find out firsthand what a typical work week is like for an audiometrist.

Bunny could not think of any friend who worked as an audiometrist, but she had visited an ear, nose, and throat physician within the last year. During one lunch hour, she visited his office and asked if she could speak to the audiometrist. Rick, the audiometrist on duty, obliged. Bunny explained her fact-finding mission to him and asked Rick if it would be possible sometime to spend an hour watching him in action. Rick said he would have an answer the next day.

When Bunny phoned Rick, he had his answer: "You're in luck Bunny. I want to help you, and so does the other audiometrist in the office, Wilma. She and I will take turns explaining what we do and what we like and don't like about our jobs. We'll also give you the names of a few more audiometrists in town."

Bunny Gets Retooled.   As Bunny learned more about audiometry, she became more intrigued. Particularly pleasing to

Bunny was the fact that she would not have to go through an extensive training program to work as an audiometrist. Her college degree combined with a few courses and some on-the-job training was all that was required to qualify as an audiometrist in the state where Bunny lived.

Attractive and professional in demeanor, Bunny had little difficulty finding employment as an audiometrist's assistant. Working in a large group practice, Bunny seems to have found a satisfying career. Also noteworthy is the fact that she has now developed the skills and confidence to expand her occupational horizons. Should the need rise again to change jobs or switch fields, she would feel equal to the task.

BUILD A SECOND CAREER GRADUALLY

Few people are able to leave one career abruptly and step into another. For most people who switch careers successfully, the switch is more of a transition than an abrupt change. Business executives-turned-college-professors are a case in point. During the last two decades a number of successful businessmen (and a few women) have been able to find faculty or administrative positions for themselves at universities and colleges. Most of these career switchers taught courses part-time for a number of years in order to qualify for a full-time faculty position.

Marty Wants to Shake Loose. An industrial arts teacher in a suburban high school, Marty was becoming disenchanted with secondary education. Gradually, he realized that high school teaching was not the best career for him. He analyzed his situation in this manner:

> I like industrial arts, particularly the creative and craftsman aspects. I also like the students. At least half of them take a serious interest in what goes on in the shop. It's the larger system that I dislike. As a high school teacher, I'm a pawn in a master chess game involving budgets and politics. If the taxpayers decide to vote no on a school budget, industrial arts can easily get chopped. One year we had the ludicrous situation whereby we didn't have the supplies

necessary to do anything but make a few tie racks and plant shelves. Even worse, I know the school system would like me to leave. The administrators know that I'm a good teacher and that I enjoy working with the students, but they also know that with 13 years of experience, I'm expensive. Should I quit, they could replace me with a young man at about one half my salary. Maybe he would be a complete neophyte in industrial arts, but that wouldn't bother them. He could help them balance the budget. I want to be valued for the quality of my work.

Marty Peddles His Wares. As an escape route from high school teaching, Marty began to put his craftsman's talent to work in a direct manner. Marty's speciality was making cabinets and fine furniture. He made a few assorted cabinets for speculation and informed all his friends, acquaintances, and relatives that these cabinets were for sale. Marty sold all four within one week, Word quickly travelled of his skill as a maker of custom cabinets.

Within five months, Marty was devoting 25 per week to cabinet making. Yet he still was not sure if full-time cabinet making could provide him a satisfactory living. To explore possibilities further, Marty rented a converted barn to use as a cabinet-making shop. He hired an assistant, part-time, to work with him on large cabinets and to build independently those orders Marty did not have time to work on himself. Marty renewed his contract for the next school year, while simultaneously devoting more time to his custom cabinet business. So elegant was his work that even his high school principal ordered one—despite the fact that he generally discouraged his faculty from having outside employment.

A New Firm Is Born. As contract renewal time at his school approached, Marty took a careful assessment of his present situation: "I think I can make a break now. With just a little more effort on my part we should have enough customers actually to support a business. Besides, I'm beginning to notice a trend toward repeat business."

Marty then decided to devote full time to his new enterprise and not to renew his school contract. He personally constructed a sign to place over the door of his barn. It read, "Martin McPherson, fine cabinets since 1976."

START YOUR OWN BUSINESS

As with Marty, a second career for thousands of people means opening their own business. Despite the fact that 50 percent of new businesses are dissolved by the end of 12 months and another 25 percent are not around by the end of the second year, the lure is still powerful. The independence and freedom promised by self-employment sounds like the right antidote to the bureaucratic blues experienced by so many people.

If a person had a good idea for a business (or could afford to buy an established one), plenty of capital in reserve, courage, and the willingness to work long and hard, becoming an entrepreneur could be the right second career. For thousands of others, opening a new business has been a devastating way of losing one's life savings and a heap of borrowed money. Consult your lawyer, banker, management consultant, self-employed friends, and the Small Business Administration before taking the plunge.

Peter Finds Nirvana. Nestled in a scenic location of Lake Simcoe, Ontario, lies Peter's Boat Hostel. Peter, the proprietor, dresses to the role with perfection. He sports a faded captain's hat, an ancient pair of blue denims, and toe-showing deck shoes. One would think that Peter was born into the trade of tending to other peoples' boats. An interview with him reveals instead the story of a man who made a successful career switch:

> It's all so simple in retrospect. I was a 50-year-old senior executive in one of Canada's largest oil companies. My long hours of hard work brought me a churning stomach, a wife complaining that I was never home, and accusations of neglect from my children. I think the Canadian government benefited the most. So much of my pay cheque was eaten up in taxes that I hardly felt like a high priced executive. To boot, handling the three mortgages on my suburban home made me feel like a pauper.
>
> Business is great here. I make just enough money to feed myself

and my family. We live in a well-appointed year-round cottage. I've eliminated all the frills like life insurance and a second car. I work about 75 hours per week in season, with no complaints on my part. In place of the old business conferences, I hold rather pleasant chats with the boat owners who do business with me. Life is not without it's problems, but I'm a lot better off than I used to be.

Vivian Invests Her Inheritance. Conscientious Vivian worked in the billing department of a coal company for 15 years. For a five-year period she felt a growing sense of dissatisfaction. As she expressed it, "I'm grateful for my job. My working conditions are more pleasant and my pay much higher than those of many bookkeepers. Despite these favorable features, I still think I can do more in life. I want to be the mistress of my own fate. A bookkeeper's life is too sequestered."

Vivian's solution to her unglamorous occupational life was impetuous. She noted a classified ad in the Business Opportunities section of her Sunday newspaper: "Plant store in prime location. Owner ill, must sell." Following up the ad, Vivian learned that the couple who owned the plant store—located in a relatively new suburban mall—had decided to retire. For only $10,000 in cash, Vivian could have this store, its inventory, and its customers. Vivian's perusual of the books satisfied her that the volume of business made the asking price reasonable."

Within 45 days, Vivian was the new owner of the plant store offered for sale. She plunked down $10,000 of a recent $15,000 inheritance. She invested another $2,000 in new inventory. For the first month traffic flow in the store seemed satisfactory. Vivian had no reason to suspect that her investment was unsound.

Vivian Gets the Isolation Blues. One morning Vivian read the alarming news that a large supermarket located in the mall had decided to close that location. She suspected that such a closing would reduce business traffic in the mall. A quick telephone call to the realty firm that operated the mall resulted in the reassuring news that a new large tenant would soon be found to replace the supermarket.

Unfortunately, the trend was swiftly in the opposite direction. A W. T. Grant store in the mall (the second largest tenant) was soon shut down. Five out of the remaining ten stores followed suit. Traffic—and Vivian's business—slowed down to a virtual standstill. For two months Vivian paid her rent and miscellaneous costs out of her own pocket. By the end of another month, Vivian had exhausted all the inheritance. As she began to dip into savings, Vivian tried frantically to sell the business. With no takers, Vivian was forced to walk away from her business venture except for the selling off of her inventory at a drastic reduction.

What Vivian Should Have Done. Vivian was well qualified to determine if the present customer situation made the plant store an honest buy. However, she was not qualified to forecast the business future of the mall. What she did not realize was that the fate of individual stores in a mall is tied to the fate of the largest customers. Few people enter a mall just to shop at a small store. As a series of stores leave a mall, they drag down the remaining stores. An isolated store in a mall can rarely survive.

Vivian should have asked an independent business consultant his or her advice about purchasing this *type* of business. A careful student of the business pages of any newspaper could have told Vivian that the mall's two biggest customers were on the brink of failure nationally. Vivian needed advice, but she did not even know what type of advice she needed. Unaccustomed to business forecasting, she focused on the plant store's past and present—not upon its future.

DON'T SWITCH CAREERS FOR THE WRONG REASON

An unfortunate aspect of career switching is that some people make this dramatic change for the wrong reason. Many a case of career switching was motivated by illogical reasons. Instead of improving or modifying the present situation to meet certain emotional problems, the person makes an entire career change. A clearer analysis of the situation would have led to an action less drastic than finding a new career.

Fritz Is Lonely. Working as a statistician in a research laboratory, Fritz underwent long and complicated divorce proceedings. Upon being granted his divorce, Fritz decided it was time to improve his social life radically. As he explained his predicament to a friend: "Now that I'm single again, I want to start having fun. But how can you have fun as a statistician in a research laboratory? I want to be out meeting people, especially women. There are very few single women in the lab, and they are hardly the fun-loving, carefree type. Besides it gets very lonely sitting down at a desk all day working on statistical problems. My mind is on my need to improve my social life."

Fritz Becomes a Member of One of the Oldest Professions.

Reading the Sunday paper, Fritz noticed a classified ad calling for mature men and women who wanted to earn a high income and be in contact with people. Asked by the life insurance agency responsible for this ad why he thought he would be successful selling life insurance, Fritz replied: "As your ad says, you want mature individuals who want to meet people. That's me. I want to meet more people. One advantage for your company is that, as a statistician, I would be very good at explaining facts and figures to people who want to buy insurance."

Although skeptical, the life insurance agency did hire Fritz, hoping that he could sell insurance to professional-level individuals. Fritz tried but failed. He soon found that he was unsuited to selling life insurance. His days were now preoccupied with worry about his social and occupational life. He wondered if he might be able to get his old job back or if he should start looking for a new job.

A Better Solution for Fritz. This lonely statistician was correct in his observations that the way to cure his loneliness was to meet other people (especially women). He was also correct in his observation that a job situation is a natural place to meet people. Fritz was incorrect, however, in his belief that he had to switch fields in order to meet women on the job.

Fritz would have been well advised to search for a job as a statistician in the home office of an insurance company. In almost all insurance companies, females outnumber males two to one. Even if Fritz could not find an insurance company looking for a statistician, he might have found another position as a statistician in any large office with an ample supply of unattached women. It was his particular research laboratory that made meeting women difficult—not his occupation.

Fritz finally understood the nature of his mistake: "As a statistician, I find that part of my work is to be able to draw the right conclusion when confronted with a large amount of information. My real problem was that I was not meeting enough women. Placed in the right work environment, I'm sure I will meet enough people. I thought I needed a new career when all I really needed was a new job setting."

How to Avoid
Going out of Style

18 "Why bother asking Herman anything anymore?" said one lab technician to another. "He'll only tell us that, as manager of the photolab, he's not supposed to be up on technical details. I think poor old Herman stopped learning anything new about the time color processing became popular."

"Don't ever tell Lucille that you spent a weekend in Montreal with your boyfriend," said one keypunch operator to another, "She'll get uptight and make some comments about the decline in morality and how somebody working for her should lead a clean life."

Herman and Lucille exhibit a behavior pattern that seems to afflict about 10 percent of all people in technical, professional, or managerial jobs. For a variety of reasons, they have lost some of their former effectiveness and are, therefore, classified as suffering from obsolescence.

What Makes Herman Obsolete? Herman is obsolete as a manager because he has lost his ability to deal with technical problems in his department. His technological obsolescence is the best-known and best-understood variety of obsolescence. If Herman were up to date technologically, he would be as effective as he was in the days prior to new technical developments in his field.

What Makes Lucille Obsolete? Lucille suffers from a more subtle form of obsolescence. Her *cultural obsolescence* stems from the fact that she cannot understand (and, therefore, cannot accept) the life-style led by some young women in her department. Even if Lucille did not travel with men in her premarital days, it does not mean that modes of behavior have not changed. Furthermore, Lucille's personal values are interfering with her ability to supervise. It is an obsolete behavior pattern for a supervisor to monitor the personal lives of subordinates —unless their personal lives interferes with job effectiveness.

A number of successful people prevent their own obsolescence in an automatic, intuitive fashion. The majority of people would do well to develop a specific program or embark upon certain courses of action to avoid the obsolescence trap. It could have a big impact upon your career.

WHAT ELSE COULD YOU DO FOR A LIVING BESIDES YOUR PRESENT JOB?

Finding a good answer to this question is an effective way of preventing obsolescence (and reducing worries about job security). In recent years an increasing number of people have answered that question by developing a secondary occupational speciality (S.O.S.). An ideal S.O.S. should be one that represents a logical transition from what you are doing now to another type of job for which there might be equal or greater demand. Sometimes an S.O.S. can be a different type of work or the expansion of a hobby into a full-time paid job.

Greg Carries a Tray. An aerospace engineer from California, Greg became tired of being laid off whenever his employer was caught between contracts. Beginning as a waiter, he worked himself up to the position of headwaiter. For a period of ten years, Greg alternated between working as a waiter and an aerospace engineer.

Asked if he found life difficult jumping back and forth between two occupations, Greg replied: "Yes, there are some stresses and strains involved, but my life is much more peaceful than it used to be. I have much less to worry about. In the past,

I found it frustrating trying to convince companies that my skills as an aerospace engineer were just what they needed when they weren't even in the aerospace business. Besides, as a headwaiter, I'm practicing my management skills, which I might be able to use if I return to aerospace."

Colonel Hutch Sells Life Insurance. Lt. Colonel William Hutch could see plainly that he would never become a full colonel in the army. His fitness ratings were only average, and there were already too many full colonels in his military occupational speciality. He told his adviser, "I wouldn't be surprised if I were asked to retire after 20 years of service even though I would like to work the entire 30 years. The army is developing a surplus of people in my category."

As an antidote to his problem, the colonel embarked upon a sideline of life insurance (and related investments such as mutual funds and annuities) sales. His adviser was pessimistic about Bill's plan: "Ugh, Bill. There are thousands of people trying to sell life insurance. That's no way to make a living. Every insurance hustler in the area will have been there before you when you try to make a sale."

Not easily dissuaded by his adviser, Bill decided to continue with his plans of becoming a modern, professional financial planner (the new term for a person who sells life insurance and related services).

The Colonel Cashes In on His Military Bearing. Although he chose a competitive field as a secondary occupational speciality, Lt. Colonel Bill made the right choice. His military bearing, emotional maturity, and ability to relate to well-educated people helped him achieve immediate success as a life insurance representative and estate planner. As Bill candidly described his situation:

> As I entered my twentieth year of service, I was happy to tell the army I no longer needed them before they told me they no longer needed me. My military pension combined with my insurance commissions was enough to provide a good living for myself and my

family. By the time I left my post for good, I was able to step into full-time selling without a hitch.

As I look back upon my military career, I have a lot of pleasant memories. I shifted into insurance just in time to prevent the gnawing feeling that I was unwanted. Many of my colleagues were not so fortunate.

ASK FOR A DEMOTION

Like thousands of other people in our society, Jean fell victim to the Peter Principle. Working away happily as a bookkeeper in a large automobile dealership, Jean was encouraged to take on the position of office supervisor. As hard as she tried, Jean was an ineffective supervisor. When a clerk in her department was having difficulty completing an assignment, Jean would jump in to do the task for the troubled clerk. She was usually too permissive with employees. In an effort to compensate, Jean would periodically become arbitrary and overdemanding, further limiting her effectiveness as a supervisor.

Jean Gets an Assistant Supervisor. One day Jean and Jim (her boss) discussed her problem. Jim offered this suggestion: "Jean, maybe we've overloaded you with work. Our business has grown faster than we predicted. What you need is an assistant. Why not ask Alma to be the assistant manager? She should be able to take some of the burden away from you."

The combination of Jean and Alma was worse than Jean alone. Jean and Alma were soon in frequent dispute over who should be doing what. Often they would both perform the same task while leaving another task undone. Jean disliked handling personnel problems; so she asked Alma to handle them. When Alma could not successfully handle such a problem, she would tell the employee to schedule a conference with Jean. Jean would, in turn, tell the employee to go back to Alma.

A More Sensible Strategy for Jean. Jean might have taken a course in human relations or supervision or else attended a similar course designed to improve supervisory effectiveness. If the learning experience did not help her (a probable outcome considering Jean's basic ineptitude and dislike for supervision), Jean should have asked to be demoted. There is no disgrace in returning to a job in which you were previously successful. Although Jean might have felt self-conscious at first, these feelings would have rapidly dissipated.

Management was probably hesitant to demote Jean for fear of hurting her feelings or disgracing her. What they did not realize is that a person's reputation in any work organization is enhanced when that person performs his or her job well. It is much better to function as an able bookkeeper than to be an obsolete office manager.

LEAVE ONCE PLACED ON A SHELF

A simultaneously cruel and considerate policy of many organizations is to place unwanted, highly paid people in trivial jobs. The shelf-sitter is well compensated for making a neutral or negative contribution to the organization. It is cruel of the company to deem you of so little value that you are placed on the shelf; yet it is considerate of them to keep you on the payroll when you are surplus. To avoid becoming permanently obsolete (while on the shelf you are at least *temporarily* obsolete), quickly find another job.

Mitch Receives an Exalted Title.   Mitch had spent a number of productive years with a company in the communications equipment field. As the company grew to a position of dominance in its industry, it became the victim of *accumulating management resources*—the new buzz word for an excess of managers. To make way for younger managers, Mitch was removed from his division head position and given the exalted title of staff manufacturing executive. His assignment was to travel around the country and overseas, advising division level managers about manufacturing problems.

Within three months it became apparent to Mitch that his high-paying, impressive-sounding job was a sham. Manufacturing heads at the divisions he visited were not particularly interested in receiving his advice. Soon he yearned for the action found in his previous managerial assignments.

Mitch Joins an Upstart. Rather than stay perched on a company shelf, Mitch sought new employment. The executive search firm Mitch registered with soon uncovered a small computer equipment company that was looking for a senior executive with big company experience to run its manufacturing operation. Byron, the search consultant, explained the situation to Mitch in an almost apologetic manner: "Mitch, I've uncovered a company that would want you, but I'm afraid they are too small potatoes for you. The company is one-twentieth the size you're accustomed to, and you would have to take about a 50 percent reduction in pay. To top that, they are located in a small, semirural area."

Mitch replied, "Byron, you're projecting your own money hang-ups onto my value system. I would rather have a real job at $25,000 than a phony job at $65,000. At age 51, I hardly want to join the legion of the dead men stuck on a shelf. Lead me to the action. I'll worry about money and location later. My wife says I'm going insane in my present job. No amount of money or choice geographic location is worth that."

Kent Loses His Dignity. A former highly placed executive, Kent was placed on the shelf with the title of vice-president, Special Projects. Unfortunately for 55-year-old Kent, the special projects were essentially high-level errands run for the president and the chairman of the board. Kent tried to maintain the appearance and behavior of an important person, but gradually he succumbed to depression over his loss of authentic responsibilities.

Kent began to drink heavily, first at night and then during lunch hours. His mysterious disappearance and his dazed look finally led the president to insist upon a medical examination by the company physician. Now the company had a tangible excuse to squeeze Kent out the door. He was given a medical discharge and a partial pension. Had Kent taken decisive action about finding himself a new job or career as soon as he was shelved, he might have prevented his counterproductive behavior pattern from developing.

ENGAGE IN PERSONAL LONG-RANGE FORECASTING

An eminently effective way of preventing becoming obsolete is to figure out what kinds of knowledge and skills you will need to handle your job in the future. In essence, the person who wards off obsolescence does so by developing a leading edge orientation in his or her field.

How Do You Develop a Leading Edge Orientation?   Unless you are a seer, it is difficult. Nevertheless, there are ways of determining what kinds of skills and knowledges are in the forefront of your field before too many others make the discovery. Check carefully into trade journals, *The Wall Street Journal,* and possibly *The New York Times* for want ads relating to jobs in your field. You should be able to notice a trend of skills and knowledge that are coming into demand.

Maria Becomes a Word-Processing Specialist.   Several years ago, Maria tried to determine where the field of secretarial science was headed. As a college graduate with a degree in secretarial science, she did not want to remain in conventional secretarial work. To figure out what knowledge would qualify her for an excellent position in secretarial work, Maria read want ads, spoke to employment agencies, and attended meetings of the National Association of Secretaries.

Maria's diagnosis was that word processing was coming into vogue—not too dramatically different in idea from secretarial pools. Maria suggested this idea to the vice-president of administration at her company. Consultation with IBM and Xerox verified that equipment was available for such a conversion from normal stenographic and typing procedures. Maria became an instant expert in this new secretarial development and was appointed as the company's first manager of word processing.

As manager of word processing, Maria was the antithesis of an obsolete person. (Nor was she obsolete as an executive secretary.) Her ability to shift into a new aspect of her field served as a deterrent against *future* obsolescence. Had Maria not become knowledgeable about word processing, another woman (or man) might have arrived there first.

Maria warded off another potential danger, for, when word processing takes hold in a company, many executive secretaries automatically become obsolete. They are not replaced by machines, but many executive secretaries become surplus. Under a word-processing system, few managers retain the privilege of having an executive secretary assigned to them. Therefore, the first secretarial workers to acquire word-processing skills get the best jobs—often of a supervisory capacity. Many former executive secretaries are demoted to ordinary jobs in the word-processing department.

Acquiring additional education or training or attending trade and professional meetings never guarantees that you won't become obsolete, but it makes a contribution. Thousands of managers and staff people have taken courses in computer technology to prevent themselves from becoming technologically obsolete owing to computerization of their field. Formal approaches to prevent obsolescence sometimes pay less straightforward dividends than the computer example just cited.

Marsha Gets into Sex Therapy.   Marriage Counselor Marsha had a penchant for attending regional conferences related to marriage and family relations. In 1972 she noted that much of the conversation at one of these conferences centered around sex (professionally, of course). Word was out that the hot new item for the upcoming decade would be male-female teams offering sex therapy to married couples in difficulty. Marsha quickly registered for two sex therapy workshops open to marriage counselors. Possessing a working vocabulary and some eyewitness experience of these techniques in operation, Marsha was ready to ward off possible professional obsolescence.

Marsha Joins Forces with a Male Psychiatrist.   Armed with her trend-setting knowledge, Marsha telephoned the three male psychiatrists in town she knew the best professionally. Burt, an age mate and a with-it psychiatrist, agreed the two of them should discuss the implications of sex therapy in their separate types of work. Starting small, Burt and Marsha teamed together for some couples counseling in the sexual realm.

In their first foursome (Burt, Marsha, and the sexually hurting husband and wife), everybody felt awkward. After working with a few more husband-wife patient teams, Burt and Marsha felt they had a useful professional service to offer the public. Within four months they had established themselves as the leading sex therapist team in their city. Marsha felt with-it instead of out-of-it, as she was beginning to feel in her usual approach to marriage counseling.

SQUEEZE SOME DEVELOPMENT OUT OF EVERY WORK SITUATION

By far the most effective method of preventing going out of style is to develop a lifelong positive attitude toward self-development. The inveterate self-developer recognizes that personal growth and knowledge acquisition are possible in almost every experience. With a positive attitude toward development, you can acquire valuable insight in situations that at first seem hopeless. You stand an excellent chance of becoming obsolete if you fail to profit from comfortable and/or frustrating work situations.

Nick Works for a Difficult Boss.   Industrial Engineer Nick was assigned to Graham, an engineering manager with a legendary reputation for poor management practices. After working for this autocratic, defensive, highly suspicious manager for six months, Nick was asked by a personnel development specialist how he liked his new assignment. Nick thought for a moment and then replied:

> I assume what I say will go no further than this room. To tell you the truth, I'm learning quite a bit from Graham. He is considered to be a basket case as a manager by many people. A lot of it isn't his fault. Management made the error a long time ago of making him a manager when he just wasn't management material.
>
> I want to be a manager someday. Graham serves as a model of what a manager should not do. You could almost make up a check

list of how not to manage people by following Graham around for a week. I wouldn't want to work under Graham for more than a year, but, in the interim, he's an excellent negative model.

What about You? It's your choice. With an optimistic and positive attitude, you, too, will keep from going out of style. With a pessimistic and dour attitude toward all work situations that don't go your way, you may never achieve growth or survival in the office.

Index

309